W9-ASI-050

BITS &
BRIDLES
Power Tools for Thinking Riders

BETSY LYNCH
DWIGHT BENNETT, DVM

BITS & BRIDLES

Power Tools for Thinking Riders

BETSY LYNCH
DWIGHT BENNETT, DVM

EquiMedia
Austin, Texas

EquiMedia
President Kanjiro Tokita
Creative Director Rob Feinberg

BITS & BRIDLES
Power Tools for Thinking Riders

Authors Betsy Lynch
Dwight Bennett, DVM

Photographers Betsy Lynch
Dwight Bennett, DVM
Gemma Giannini
Charlie Kerlee
Glory Ann Kurtz
Jenger Smith
Rick and Kathy Swan
Matthew Von Riesen

Graphic Designers Victoria J. Allen
Rob Feinberg

Library of Congress Cataloging-in-Publication Data

Bennett, Dwight, 1935-
Bits & Bridles : power tools for thinking riders / Dwight Bennett, Betsy Lynch.
p. cm.
ISBN 0-9625898-6-1
1. Bits (Bridles) 2. Horses--Training. I. Title: Bits and bridles. II. Lynch, Betsy, 1957-
III. Title.

SF309.9 .B46 2000
636.1'0837--dc21 00-026336

Published by
EquiMedia Corporation
P.O. Box 90519
Austin, TX 78709
Tel: 512-288-1676

Printed in China by Sun Fung Offset Binding Co., Ltd.
10 9 8 7 6 5 4 3 2 1
04 03 02 01 00

To all the horsemen and women who strive to ride with understanding and a light touch. —Betsy Lynch

To Jacquie —Dwight Bennett

Acknowledgments

This book has been over 25 years in the making, and nearly every horseman and horse woman we have ever known — and, lord knows, there have been hundreds — have contributed to this book in some way. Although we're sure to miss some deserving folks, we'll risk mentioning a few people by name. Our apologies to those who were equally invaluable in sharing their insights about the way bits are designed to work — in theory and in practice — but whom we haven't the presence of mind to formally acknowledge at this time. We also appreciate everyone who allowed us to intrude on them long enough to photograph their horses, their persons and their tack.

A few who have been of special help include: Greg Darnall, Al Dunning, Tony Amaral, Don Dodge, Dale Myler, Steve Schwartzenberger, Tee Crenshaw, Mario Boisjoli, Doug Krause, Judy Leister, Dennis Moreland, Dale Chavez, Terry Thompson, Dave Moore, Joel Gleason, Sharon Saare, Vicki Donoho, Mark Bernhardt, Rhoda Rein, Darren Miller, Dr. Robert Shideler, Dr. Jerry Vetter, Jack and Carol Throckmorton, Dr. Richard Park, Mike Allen, Becky Carson, Charlie Kerlee, Jenger Smith, Dr. Chris Morrow, Carla Wenberg, Troy Pruitt, Rebecca Merchant, and Heather Schoning.

Contents

Introduction 8

1. The Language of the Bridle 10
2. Anatomy and Bit Selection 18
3. Dentistry and Mouth Care 28
4. An Introduction to Bits and Bridles 36
5. Fundamental Principles of Bitting 46
6. Snaffle Bits — The Horseman's Most Versatile Tool 56
7. Mouthpieces 66
8. Leverage Bits — Putting Power in the Pull 80
9. Trade Offs — Interplay Among Bridle Parts 90
10. Gag Bits 98
11. Going Bitless 106
12. The Traditional Hackamore 112
13. The Spade Bit and Its Relatives 126
14. Bit Accessories and Training Aids 134
15. Bit Progressions and Soft Mouths 144
16. Developing Soft Hands 154
17. Problems, Solutions and Safety 164
18. Bitting and Competition 172

Glossary 182
Index 189

Introduction

When Dr. Dwight Bennett and I teamed up to work on Bits & Bridles: Power Tools for Thinking Riders we had a common goal. We wanted to write a book that would help people think in practical terms about what they put in their horses' mouths and why. We've heard it said too many times that there are no bad bits, only bad hands. Yet we personally believe this statement to be untrue. There are as many poorly designed bits as there are unskilled riders. (In Dr. Bennett 's personal collection which includes more than 300 bits, there are quite a number that we could happily pick apart due to design or construction flaws). I, too, have bits hanging in my tack room that I no longer care to use.

What we know is that when you put poorly designed bits into anyone's hands — either master or novice — the results will be less than satisfactory. At the least, a poorly made bit hinders the flow of communication; at worst, it can inflict pain or cause permanent injury. While a great horseman may be able to overcome the limitations of an inferior bit, he would not willingly choose a poor tool. Neither should you.

On the upside, there are many excellent bits that, when used with consideration and care, will help you have a meaningful dialog with your horse. Although this book is not intended as a training guide, we hope it will help you look at, think about, and use bits in a more logical way.

While some of the information contained within these pages may be new to you, in actuality what we've done is borrow the wisdom and ideas of some of the world's most respected horsemen and women. We researched our subject utilizing more than 100 different books, articles, brochures and catalogs. We interviewed bit makers. We attended clinics presented by some of the most respected authorities in the industry. We worked with scores of horse trainers from many different disciplines, and discussed some of the basic mechanics with a physics professor to make sure we were on track.

During our research, we found a tremendous amount of consensus among horsemen. We also uncovered some interesting disparities. We found ourselves asking repeatedly whether certain bits make mechanical sense, and whether their design was practical from a physical and mental perspective. We went so far as to put some of the bitting theories to the test. (You might just find the X-rays included in the chapters as revealing as we did.)

Certainly, a lot of myth and misinformation is circulated about bits and bridles. But just because you read it, or someone says it, doesn't make it so. We're probably guilty of passing along some unsubstantiated information ourselves — not intentionally, mind you — but because someone, somewhere explained something that made sense to us and we thought it was worth sharing.

So please, don't take everything you read within these pages as gospel. From time to time, Dwight and I still find ourselves debating certain points, and searching for more satisfactory answers to some of our questions. As a responsible horse owner, it is your charge to examine individual bits and make your own judgement about whether to use them or not — no matter what someone recommends.

Dr. Bennett, as a professor of equine veterinary medicine with Colorado State University, has been practicing and teaching veterinary science for more than 40 years. During this time he has seen a distressing number of mouth injuries caused by improperly used bits. Clients, too, have sought his advice on countless occasions about bitting and behavioral problems — many of which don't have easy or obvious "cures."

Dr. Bennett's interest in bits and bridles grew out of a natural concern for his clients. He undertook to study bitting from a scientific standpoint in an effort to gain insights that would help people make better choices for their horses' sakes. It's so much simpler to prevent a bad habit than to resolve one. Over the past 25 years, as his knowledge and interest in bits has grown, so has his bit collection.

As a horse enthusiast, I, too, share Dr. Bennett's concerns. As an owner, rider, exhibitor and equine journalist, I have been watching other horse people all my life. I have seen abuses that have made my blood boil. I have also been inspired by riders whose finesse is well worth emulating.

For more than 20 years I have made my living by observing and putting into words why and how certain people are successful with horses. While I know unequivocally that a bit doesn't make a horseman, almost every rider I have come to respect and admire has definite reasons why they use the equipment they use — be it a simple rope halter or a particular type of bridle.

I have always been curious about the role bits and bridles play in the education of outstanding equine athletes. Like many of you, I have bought bits, bosals, sidepulls and martingales — optimistically and enthusiastically — hoping, believing, wanting to improve my ability to communicate with my horses. I have experimented with techniques and equipment trying to discern what works best for me and my horses. It's an ongoing process.

What I've found is that bridling choices do make a difference to certain horses. I own a gelding, for instance, who simply isn't content in a bit, any bit. Believe me, we've tried an assortment. Yet put a hackamore on him and he relaxes and steers like a dream. His choice, not mine. I have other horses who are relatively content regardless of what goes into their mouths. Any smooth-mouthed bit is fine as long as it is artfully handled.

Understanding those choices is, in essence, what this book is all about.

— Betsy Lynch

"BRIDLES AND BITS ARE SIMPLY THE TOOLS WE USE TO SPEAK TO OUR HORSES."

1

The Language of the Bridle

Think of the signals that you provide to the horse through the bit and reins as a type of language. How well do you communicate in that language? Is it the same one that your horse understands?

If someone says to you, "Comment allez-vous?", it will be difficult for you to respond if you don't speak French. The person can say it louder and more forcefully, but unless he or she provides some clue as to what the words mean (and also teaches you how to reply), you'll probably become frustrated and confused. There's a total lack of communication. The problem, of course, isn't your ability to hear, it's your ability to understand.

Unfortunately, this is what many horses experience. Too often, when riders don't get the responses they want, they change bits. While the new bit may provide more pulling power, the rider may simply be shouting the same message that the horse didn't understand in the first place.

This book is dedicated to the study of bits and bridles, but the heart of our subject is really one of communication, horsemanship and training. These will be the real keys to your success. Bridles and bits are simply the tools we use to speak to our horses.

Importantly, some bits allow us to convey our messages softly and subtly. Others let us shout. That's where the science of bits comes into play. There may be times when we choose to turn up the volume to get the horse's attention, and other times when we prefer to talk in quiet whispers. But in either case, the only effective way to get our message across is for both horse and rider to know the special language of the bridle.

While virtually every bitting discussion we've ever heard points out that there are no bad bits, only bad hands, we

(above) Resistance is often a lack of education.

believe this isn't necessarily true. While the ultimate effect of a bridle lies with the rider, bits are hardware. They employ mechanical principles. They're engineered to act a certain way in a horse's mouth when a rider pulls on the reins. Quite honestly, some bits are designed to be mean. Others are crafted to give riders certain mechanical advantages.

Almost all riders find it necessary to pull on the horse's face. Bridling provides a certain degree of control over the horse's head. It gives you a means for guiding, steering and teaching the animal to perform on command.

Without question, the potential for abuse exists with any bit. Horses don't choose the bridles they wear, people do. The purpose of this book is to arm you with enough information that you can walk into a tack shop and make a humane, logical choice.

For many horses and riders, simple ring snaffles serve them well their whole lives. Yet for a highly skilled reinsman with a finished bridle horse, a finely crafted spade bit might be just the tool for exhibiting the horse's incredible finesse, with the horse's mouth no worse for wear.

Of course, many of us like to say that our horses like one bit better than another. It's really more accurate to say that we like the way our horses work in one bit better

(opposite) This simple O-ring smooth snaffle may be the only bit this youngster ever needs.

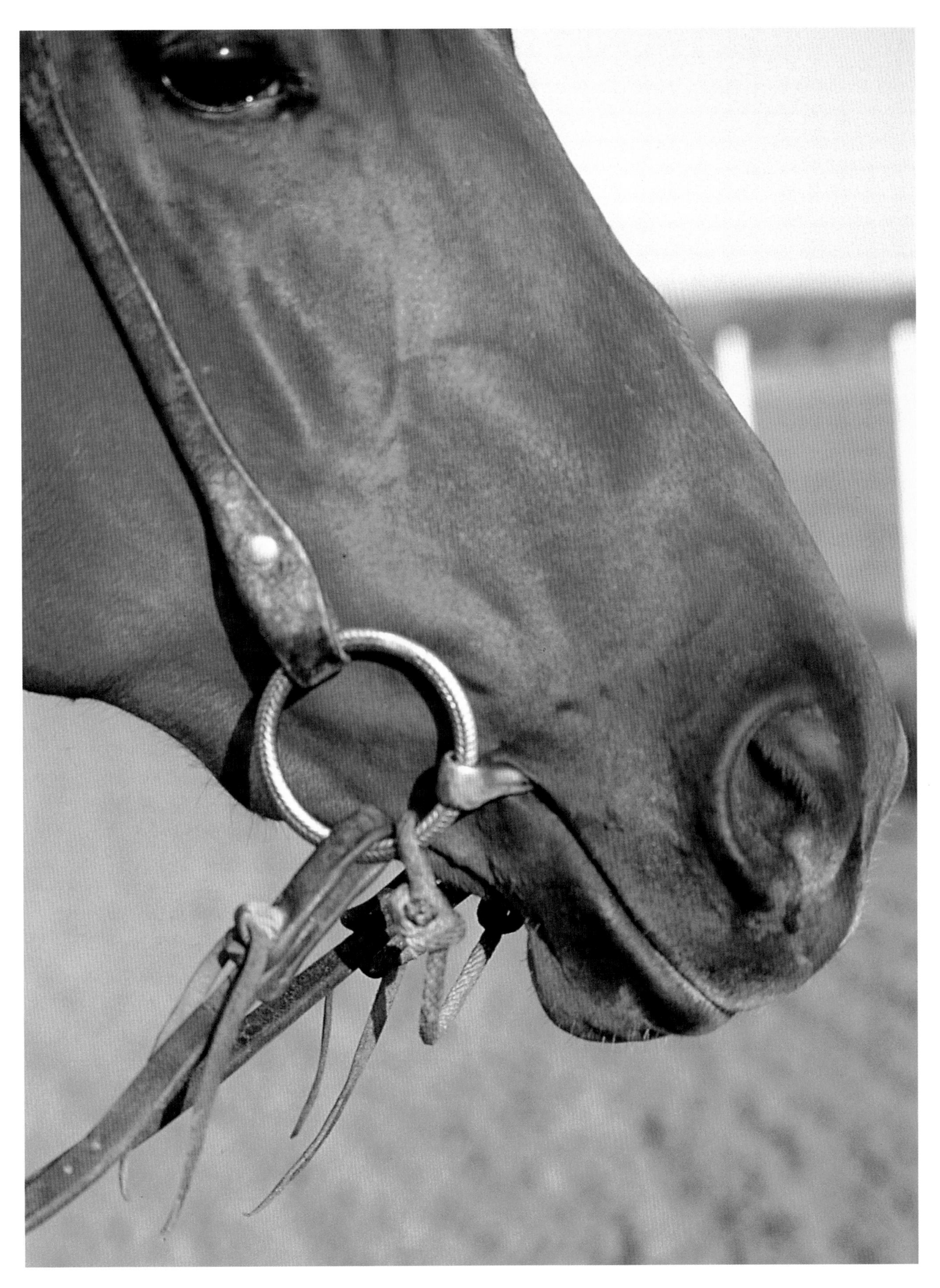

(opposite) Bridle and reins provide a physical link between horse and rider, but the mental connection is perhaps more important. Human and horse must develop a shared language.

A typical spade bit; heavy, ornate, well-balanced.

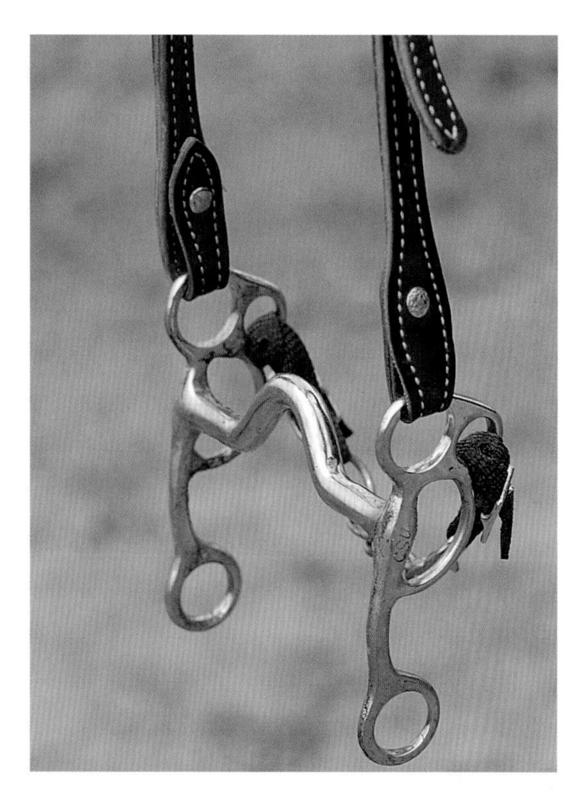

A very mild, medium port curb bit.

than another. Horses are remarkably adaptable. While it's true that horses may be more comfortable or relaxed in certain bits, ultimately the value of a bit lies in how well the animal responds to the signals you supply through it. Your own skills and comfort with using a given bit are going to have a tremendous impact on the way your horse performs.

For instance, we personally wouldn't recommend spade bits to the general public. That's a lot of hardware in a horse's mouth. Yet we've seen masterful horsemen use such bits with inspiring results. We've also seen spades handled poorly and with truly ugly consequences - gaping mouths, rolling eyes and stiff, fearful responses. But for the record, we've seen snaffle bits handled with equally bad results.

It is a combination of factors that makes one bit right and another wrong for a certain horse/rider pair. When choosing which bits you will use, it's important to evaluate your own skills with a critical eye. How much riding have you done? Do you have good balance? Do you feel comfortable and confident in the saddle? Do you rely a great deal on your hands to steer and control your horse, or do you use all your resources: legs, weight, voice and hands? What's more, do you feel you have a good sense of timing? Can you give and take with the reins instantaneously in response to the horse's actions? Or do you have to think about it?

It may be helpful to ask other riders whose opinions you respect to critique your abilities. What are their comments? If you feel your own skills are lacking, a bit that's gentle by design may provide adequate control while you work to develop a better feel for the horse's mouth. That can go a long way toward preserving your animal's desire to please.

Consider your horse's individual characteristics. His age, level of training and attitude will all have a bearing on what bits will work best. Even his physical make-up will play a role. We'll talk about that more in the next chapter. However, you're in the driver's seat. It will be important for you to interpret the horse's responses to any given bit.

For example, a young horse that is just being started under saddle may run through a smooth-mouth snaffle because the tug on his sensitive mouth as yet has no meaning. It's new and it's foreign and it scares him. With patient training, the colt learns to accept the pressure, and the bit becomes an ideal teaching tool. An older horse, on the other hand, may run through a snaffle bit because it's easy for him to ignore. The older horse may have become less sensitive to — and perhaps less respectful of — the pressure. On this horse, a medium port curb bit may work better.

Sometimes finding the right bit is a matter of simple experimentation. Yet it never hurts to give your horse the benefit of the doubt. You can always start with a relatively mild bit and step up in pulling power if you're not getting the responses you want. But once you've deadened a mouth by overbitting, it's hard to go back. So move up with care and consideration.

When selecting bits, it's also important to think about what it is that you're asking your horse to do. Are you trail riding? Running barrels? Roping? Reining? Breaking colts? Training for western pleasure or horsemanship classes? Whatever it is, what kind of responses do you want, need and expect?

While it's tempting to choose bits based on what others in your event are using on their horses, it's better to think about bit selection in terms of results. Keep in mind that whole industries go through trends. The style that's winning in the show ring will have a profound impact on what bits are popular at any given time. But as a thinking rider, you should never adopt a fad for its own sake. There are usually good reasons why top riders within specialty performance events utilize certain headgear. But it's good to find out why. Study the mechanics. Then decide for yourself whether that's what will work for you and your horse.

As trainer and veterinarian Dr. Steve Schwartzenberger points out, "The right bits make my job easier. That's why I buy them and use them." Dr. Schwartzenberger specializes in reining and pleasure horses. He owns dozens of bits, but he can count on two hands the ones he uses regularly in his training program. He emphasizes that bits are never a substitute for rider know-how. Many trainers utilize several different bitting systems on their way to producing

Mario Boisjoli and Carma Corona complete the reining pattern after the bridle has come off.

finished horses. It's not uncommon for a professional to school a horse in one bit and step into the show ring with something entirely different. There are times when bits and bridling accessories can give riders a competitive edge. We'll look at that in later chapters as well.

And while the theories you'll find in this book apply to both western and English bridles, the emphasis is on western headgear. The ultimate goal in most western disciplines is to guide a horse with a featherlight touch and a single hand on the reins. The sport of reining is perhaps the ultimate expression of this.

Yet reining is not the only event in which you will see extraordinary communication between horse and rider. Great roping horses learn to respond instantaneously to the rein signals to turn and stop, making world records possible. High performance barrel horses learn to rate and guide around the drums with the slightest of hand movements. World caliber western pleasure horses learn to carry themselves with balance, collection and style on a loose rein. Great cutting horses learn to rely more on the rider's legs and weight cues to help them get through a run than on the reins, because the rider drops his rein hand and gives the horse the freedom of its head once the cow is cut.

In fact, at the highest levels of horsemanship and training, bits and bridles become secondary — sometimes even unnecessary. A good example of this is when trainer Mario Boisjoli's entry lost its bit during a reining class. Carma Corona's headstall came unbuckled at the very beginning of the pattern in the first set of spins. In the second set of spins, the bit dropped from the horse's mouth. Mario settled himself and considered his options. With the bridle draped around his horse's neck, Boisjoli decided to forge on and his horse was with him.

"I think he was as dumbstruck as I was," Mario remembers with a chuckle. The crowd was enthralled. Through each successful maneuver — circles and lead changes, sliding stops and rollbacks — the audience cheered louder and louder. "I felt like I was in the ninth inning of the World Series with all the bases loaded," Boisjoli recalls with a laugh. Not only did he and Carma Corona finish the pattern, they won the class!

"In the truly great runs, how much does a rider really pull on his reins anyway? They're there more for security," Mario pointed out. Even so, for observers, such demonstrations of unity between horse and rider are no less remarkable.

Bridleless reining, cutting and western pleasure are possible because riders have refined their ability to communicate with their horses to an artform. But no one gets to that level without the wise, skillful and judicious selection and use of bridles, bits and reins. We'll study these things more in the chapters to come.

"MOUTH FEATURES VARY FROM INDIVIDUAL TO INDIVIDUAL, FAMILY TO FAMILY."

2

Anatomy and Bit Selection

The horse feels the signals you send via the reins directly through the nerves of its mouth, nose, jaw, poll and neck. By developing an appreciation for the horse's anatomy, physiology and chemistry, you will understand how to communicate better with the horse and select bits that are both useful and humane.

The bitting system you choose will impact almost every part of your horse, from head to hip. However, the eight areas that the bridle and reins most directly affect are the tongue, the roof of the mouth (hard palate), the bars of the mouth, the lips, the nose, the chin groove or jawline, the poll and the neck. The bit may also have some contact with the teeth, but we will look at that in the next chapter.

THE BARS OF THE MOUTH

When man domesticated the horse, it didn't take long for him to look in the horse's mouth and discover a useful adaptation of nature — the interdental spaces. These gaps between the front and back teeth are what we commonly call the bars of the mouth. The bar space divides the nippers from the grinders, with the tongue shuttling the forage from front to back. Because of their construction, the bars provide an ideal place for installing a bit.

The bar space is little more than gum tissue overlaying the horse's jawbone. Excessive bit pressure can bruise the gums, and, in extreme cases, crush the underlying bone. If the bars of the bit are sharp and narrow, they can slice through the tissue like a cheese cutter — with the tongue likely being cut as well. Prolonged bit pressure can also leave lasting indentations or ridges. The damage can be felt by running a thumb or finger along the bar surface.

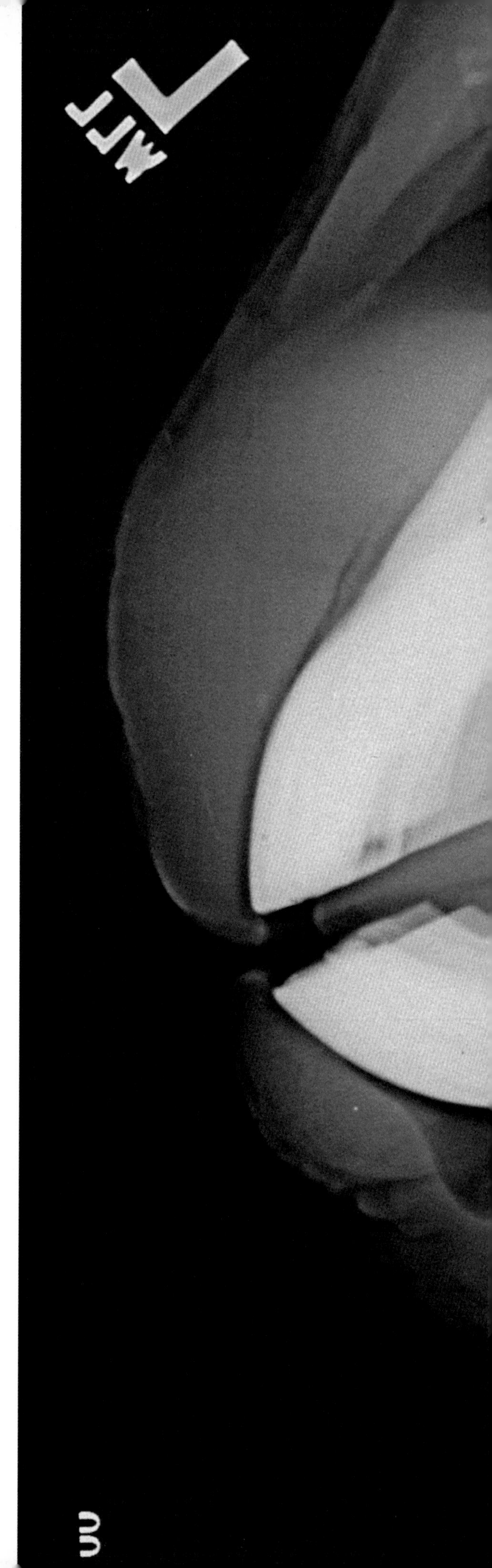

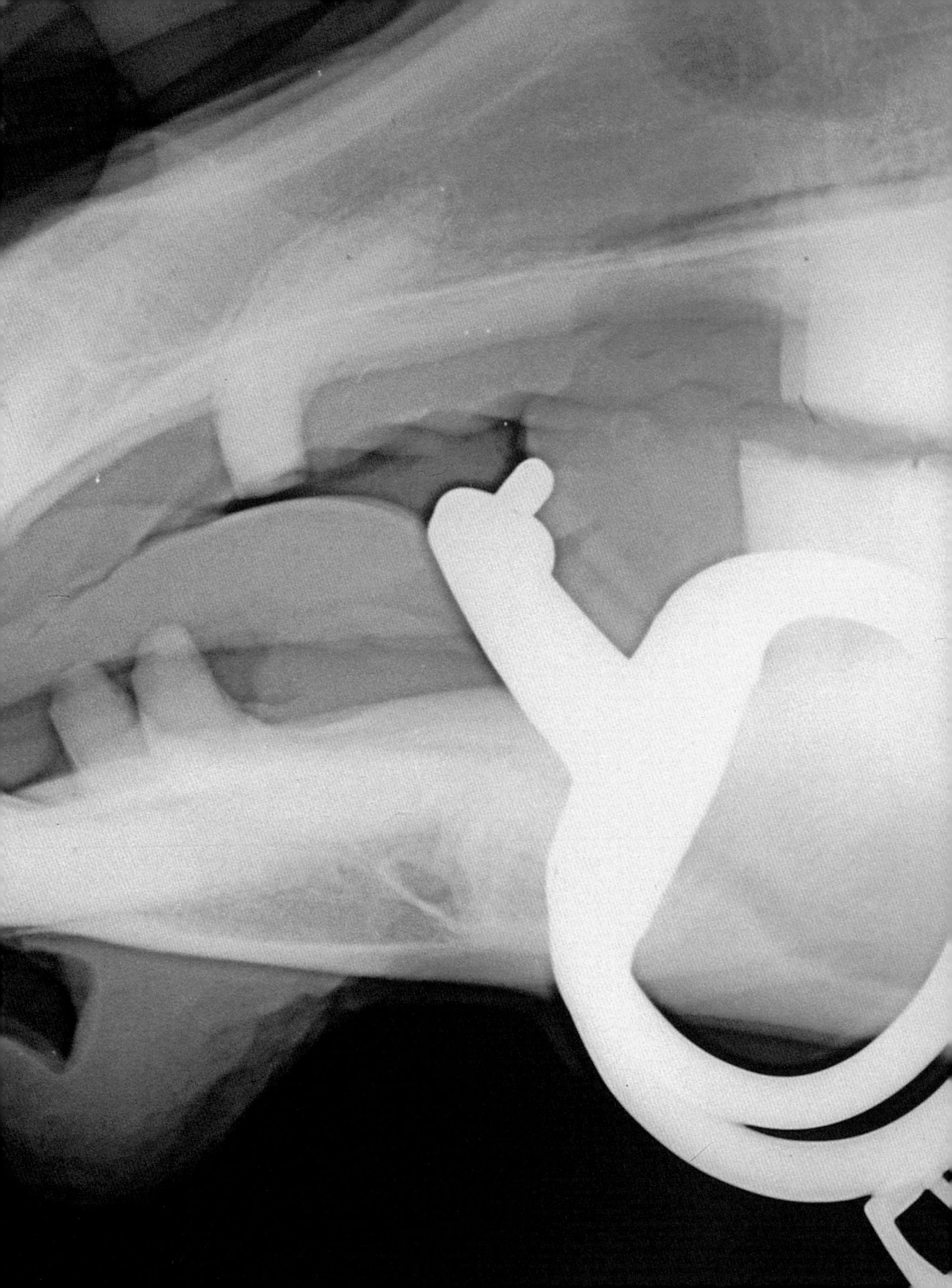

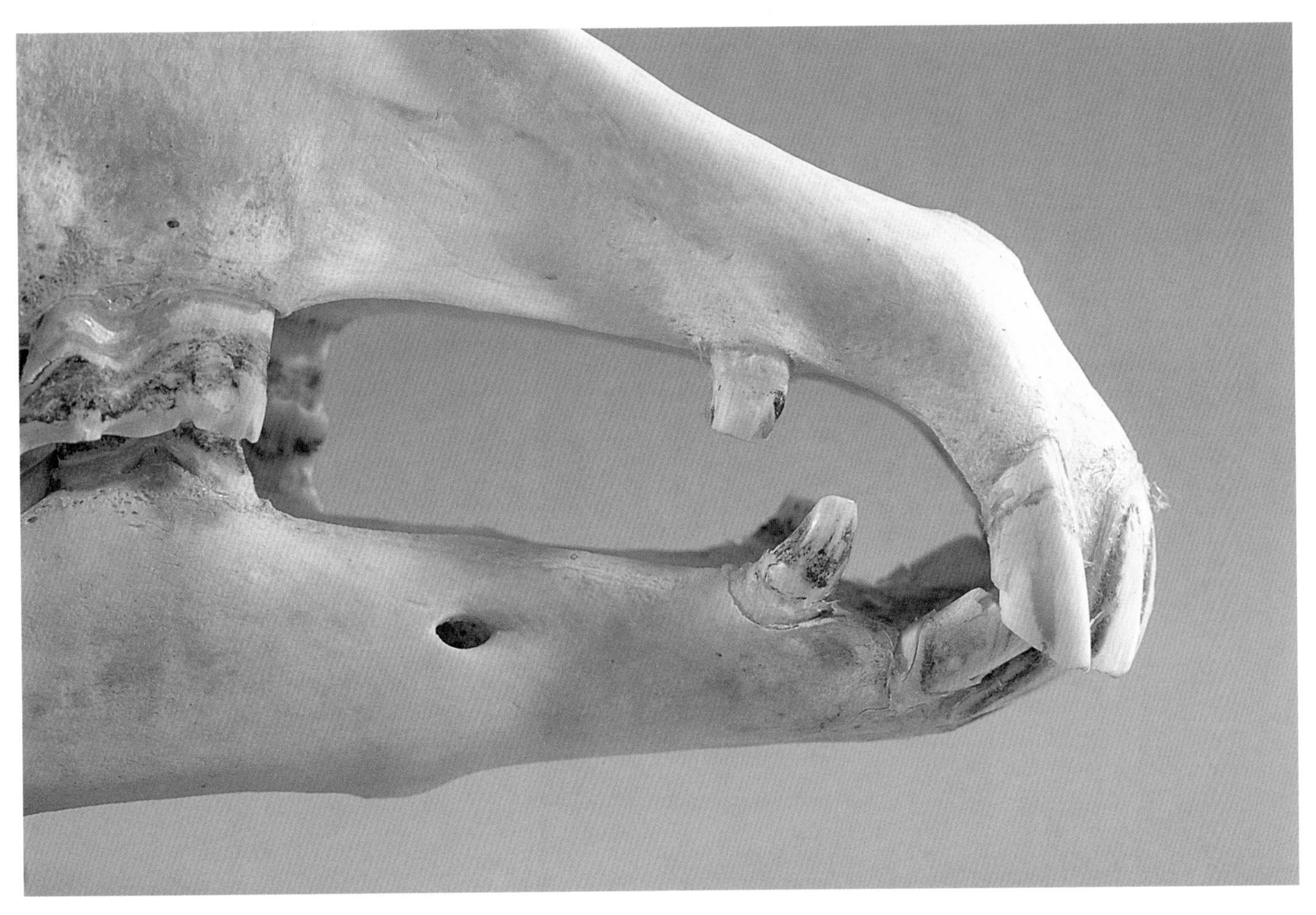

The bit fits in the interdental space between the canine teeth and the cheek teeth. The lower interdental space is called the bars.

(overleaf) There's more to selecting a bridling system than meets the eye. Riders should think about how a bit contacts the internal, as well as external, features of the horse's mouth. The most sensitive parts, the tongue and palate, aren't visible from the outside.

Having said this, it may sound contradictory to note that the bars of the horse's mouth aren't nearly as delicate as you might think. They are, in fact, relatively sturdy and resilient in comparison to the tongue and hard palate. As long as you aren't abusive, using a bit that distributes more pressure to the bars and less to the tongue and roof allows you to guide and control the horse without causing pain or fear.

Mouth features vary from individual to individual, family to family. That includes the length and width of the bar space, and the distance between the tongue and the palate. While you can make an educated guess as to how long the bar space is by observing how deep or shallow the mouth is from the outside (meaning the distance from the front of the lips to the corners of the mouth), the exterior dimensions do not always correlate to the interior bar space. Open the mouth and find out just how much room there is in there.

This knowledge can be useful in both fitting and positioning the bit. For instance, a horse with a long bar space and ample room between the tongue and the palate might readily accommodate a spade bit with a long spoon and long spacer bars. A short-barred mouth, on the other hand, may not readily accommodate a spade bit, and might do better with any number of half-breed bits. If a horse's mouth has little space between the tongue and the roof, a simple half-breed center piece might be a better choice than a bit with a thick, hooded port. The simple half-breed would minimize the potential damage to a small mouth without losing the communication provided by contact with the tongue and palate.

Significant, too, is the width from side to side between the mouth bars. In most light horses, the distance across the bars averages two and a half to three inches. The standard mouthpiece is five inches. The remaining two-plus inches of bit accommodates the lips.

The distance from bar to bar is especially significant so that the bit will contact the mouth structures correctly. A bit that is too wide may shift in the horse's mouth and may become ineffective or even painful as it interferes with soft tissue. A bit that's too short would pinch the corners of the horse's lips. One-quarter to one half inch of the mouthpiece should extend beyond the corners of the mouth on each side. Less and the mouthpiece is too short, more and it is too long.

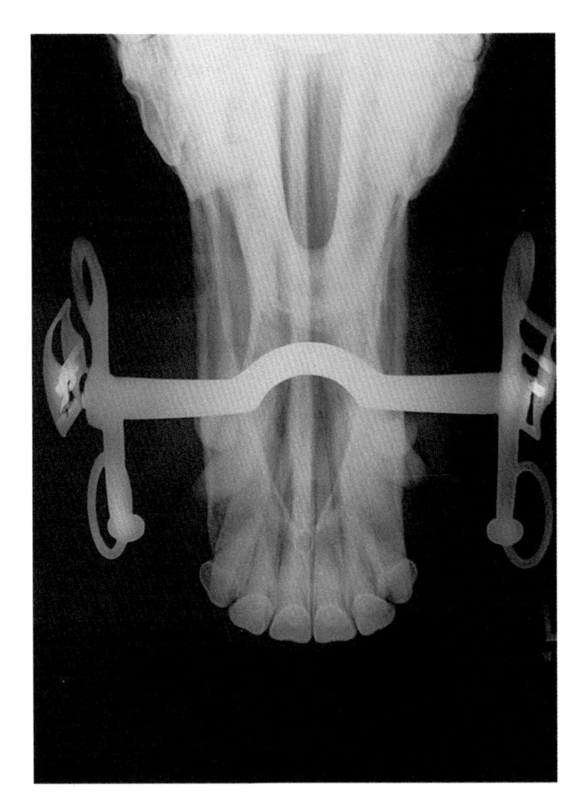

An X-ray of a curb bit in a horse's mouth. The distance across the bars is two and a half to three inches. The mouthpiece is five inches wide, to accomodate the lips.

THE LIPS

Some horses have thick lips, some have thin lips, some are tight, others are flaccid. While some people equate the thickness of a horse's lips with sensitivity, this may be more old wives tales. In all horses, the skin surrounding the mouth is thin and loaded with sensory nerves. The hair is fine and velvet-soft. The lips themselves curve inward toward the teeth and gums to protect the delicate interior.

For most horses, the corners of the mouth are a sensitive area. Snaffle bits make particularly effective contact with that area.

The muzzle contains many nerve endings and the long tactile hairs help transmit sensory data from the horse's muzzle to the brain. The muzzle's amazing sensitivity helps the animal discern the edible from the inedible, the good from the bad. Many horses can readily sort out pelleted medications and supplements "hidden" in their rations, eating the grain and leaving the offending additives.

All bits come in contact with the horse's lips at the corners of the mouth. Some bits, such as snaffles, are designed to have direct action on the lips. With others, the contact with the lips is of little consequence to actual bit function. Here, too, individual sensitivity will play a key role in how a horse responds to a bit. Some horses are naturally more responsive than others when their lips are touched. Some will immediately gape their mouths or work their lips and tongue in a mouthing fashion when a finger is gently inserted at the corners. Others take a little more prodding to elicit any type of response.

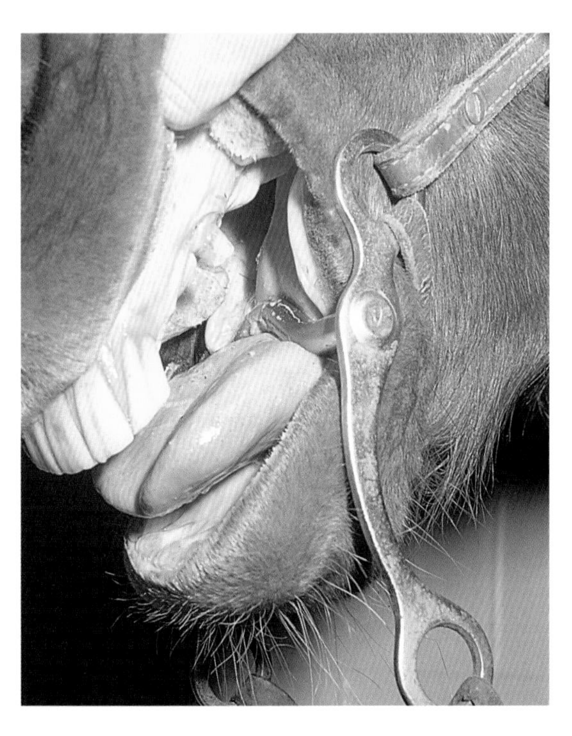

The tongue is one of the most sensitive areas of the mouth. A bit having a solid mouthpiece and a low port, or straight with no port, gives little tongue relief.

All bits should be designed, fitted and adjusted so they do not pinch or rub the lips or corners of the mouth. The thin skin immediately surrounding the mouth is especially susceptible to soring from bit friction. Sores which develop at the corners of the mouth can turn into callouses and cause a loss of feeling. It's also important to be sure that the lips are not being pressed against the upper cheek teeth by the snaffle rings or bit shanks as this can cause painful sores inside the mouth. Bit or lip guards may also be used to protect this delicate area from undesirable contact with the butt of the mouthpiece. Good mouth maintenance is also imperative, but we'll discuss equine dentistry further in the next chapter.

THE TONGUE

Without question, the tongue is one of the mouth's most sensitive features. It plays an important role in the bitting equation because virtually anything you put in a horse's mouth rests upon it.

Tongues are as individual as horses, coming in many sizes, shapes and thicknesses. Some are thin, wide and flaccid; others are thick, round and muscular. Some tongues tuck neatly into the lower jaw, while others generously fill the palate and protrude out the bar space. A rider's choice of bits should take into consideration the conformation of a horse's mouth. For example, a horse with a thick tongue may have a hard time with a bit with a thick mouthpiece or one that affords no tongue relief. A thin, active tongue may be overly sensitive to pressure from too narrow of bit bars.

Tongues can also express emotions or provide clues to a horse's temperament or level of contentment with a particular bit. A relaxed or laid back horse may keep its tongue quietly in its mouth when bitted, or may gently shift the bit in its mouth like a lazy gum chewer. A high strung horse might nervously champ at the bit. Some nervous horses show their distress by clamping their mouths shut tightly around the bit and holding their tongues rigid. A playful horse might work the bit with its tongue.

Most knowledgeable horsemen agree that some tongue movement is desirable. It shows that the horse is relaxed and accepting of the bit. Tongue movement also stimulates salivation. Keeping the mouth well lubricated is necessary if the bit is to slide properly over the tongue and bars. Excessively restless tongues can create special bitting problems. For example, horses with overactive tongues may get their tongues over the bit. This hinders communication and sets the horse up for an uncomfortable surprise when the reins are pulled. The bit could pinch or even damage the elastic attachment beneath the tongue known as the frenulum. One solution might be to use a mouthpiece with a port high enough to keep the tongue from roving. Another might be to pacify the horse with a cricket or roller mouthpiece.

If a horse's tongue is overly sensitive, the animal may never fully accept a bit — no matter how mild its design or gentle the hands controlling it. You could try a bit designed to offer "tongue relief," meaning it is constructed to alleviate pressure directly on the tongue. Such bits often have two-inch or higher ports, or specially designed cannons or bit bars. One advantage is that a well-designed bit can help position a thick tongue out of the way of the gum bars, giving the rider greater "feel" or more harmonious contact with the horse's mouth.

The tongue is not as fragile in construction as a human's. If it were, the horse would have a hard time eating the grasses, legumes, hays and grains that are a normal part of its diet. From a bitting standpoint, however, the tongue is still the most vulnerable component of the mouth. If other structures of the mouth show abuse, then it's likely the tongue has suffered its share as well.

Cut tongues are among the most frequent, serious mouth injuries riders cause. The damage can be permanent. If a cut is deep, the tongue may heal with a defect. In the worst cases, the organ can be completely severed. Fortunately, nature has provided a rapid repair system for most mouth injuries. They tend to heal quickly due to the tremendous blood supply to the head. Natural biological defenses also help ward off infection. But bitting and riding with consideration are unquestionably the way to avoid such problems.

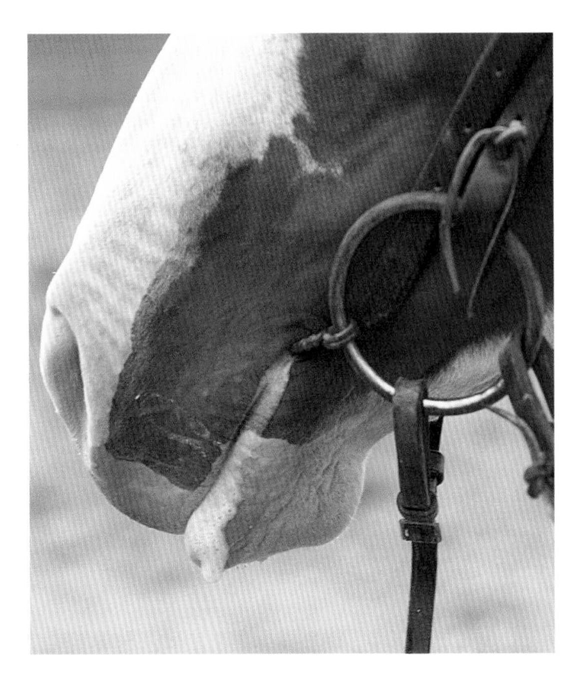

A nice wet mouth indicates that this horse is probably working the bit with his tongue and jaw. Saliva provides the lubrication needed to keep the bit comfortable.

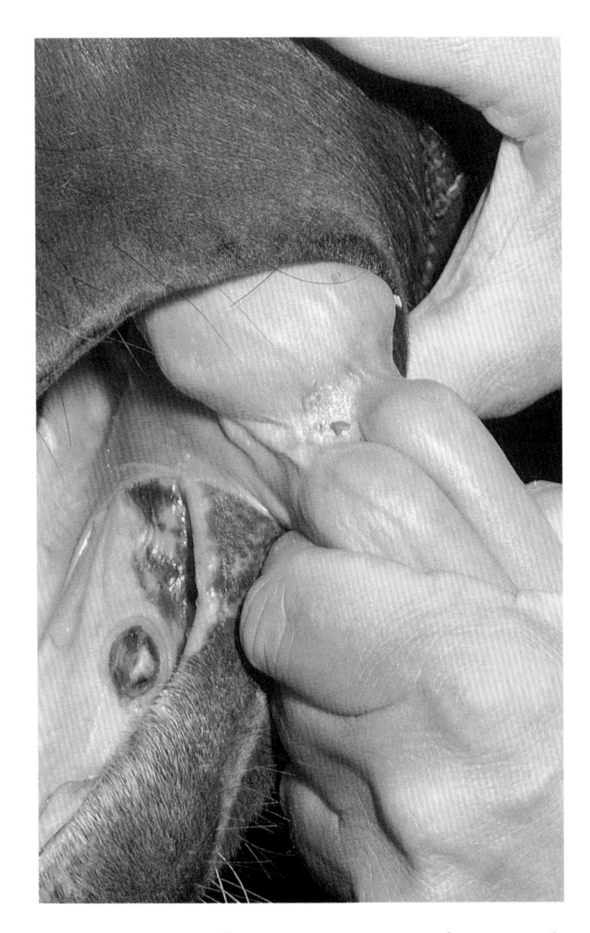

Cut tongues are the most common, serious mouth injuries caused by bits.

THE ROOF OF THE MOUTH

The roof of the mouth, or palate, is covered by tissue very similar to the gum tissue which covers the bars. The hard palate extends from the upper incisor teeth back as far as the last upper molars and fills all the space between them. Bone lies beneath this area. The soft palate, which covers the remainder of the mouth, is soft tissue and has no underlying bone.

In bitting we are concerned only with the hard palate. Relatively few bits on the market today are engineered to employ palate pressure. Because the hard palate is considered the mouth's most sensitive feature, many people consider palate pressure to be taboo. To get some idea of just how sensitive tha palate is, compare it with your own. Lightly stroke the roof of your mouth with your tongue or forefinger. Notice the tickling sensation you get with just a feather-light touch. What does it feel like when you press lightly on that area with a metal spoon? You probably won't wait long to find out. You'll automatically shift the spoon in your mouth and change position to avoid any uncomfortable contact. Bits that employ palate pressure operate on much the same principle. Light contact signals a request. In considerate, educated hands, palate type bits such as cathedrals, half-breeds and spades can give riders a way to communicate with incredible finesse and subtlety. In the wrong hands, however, such bits can be tools of torture.

Port height, design and the angle of the mouthpiece play a tremendous role in what, if any, impact a bit will have on the palate. Most mature light horses have enough room in their mouths to accommodate a 2 to 2½-inch port (measured from the bottom of the bit bars to the peak of the port), without coming into contact with the palate. In fact, the width and rise of the port may actually allow that bit to sit lower in the mouth by providing space for the tongue, keeping the port away from the roof of the mouth.

The structure and dimensions of a horse's mouth do change over time. As the horse grows, then ages, the size, shape, number and position of the teeth change. The bite plane also changes. These changes affect how much room

The hard palate and the tongue are the two most sensitive areas of the mouth. Bits with high ports or spoons make contact with the palate.

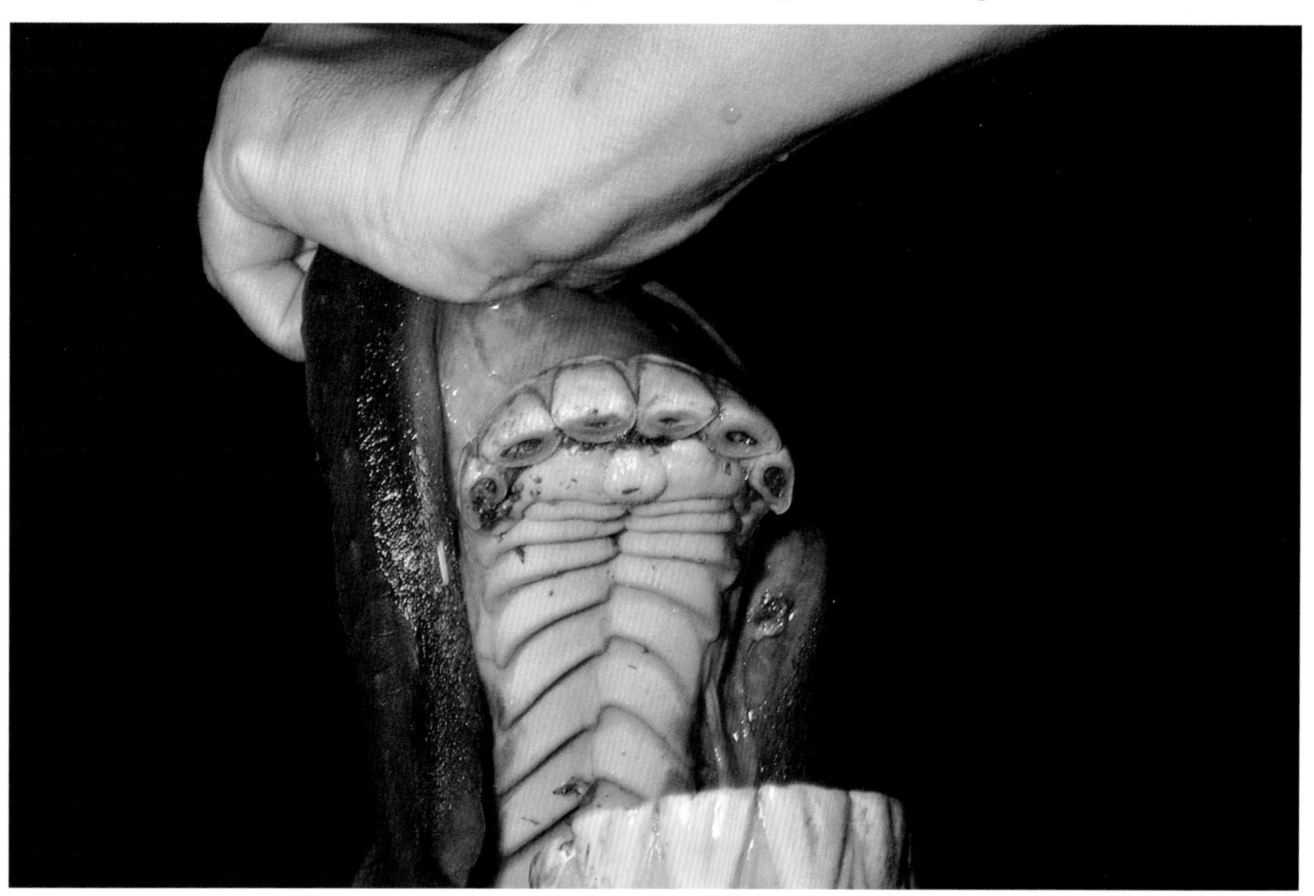

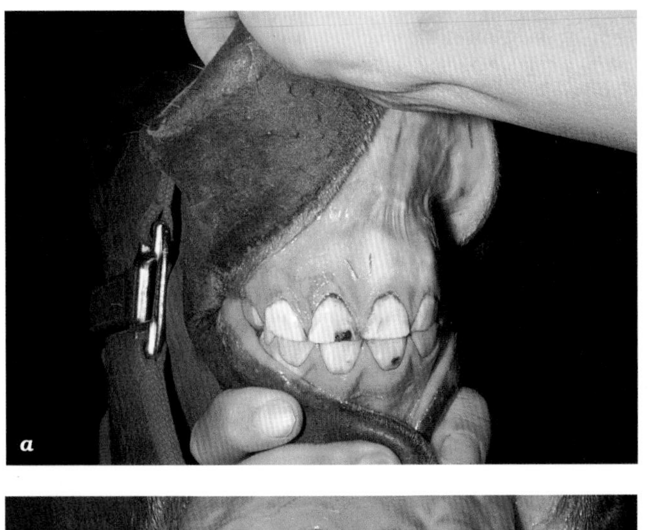

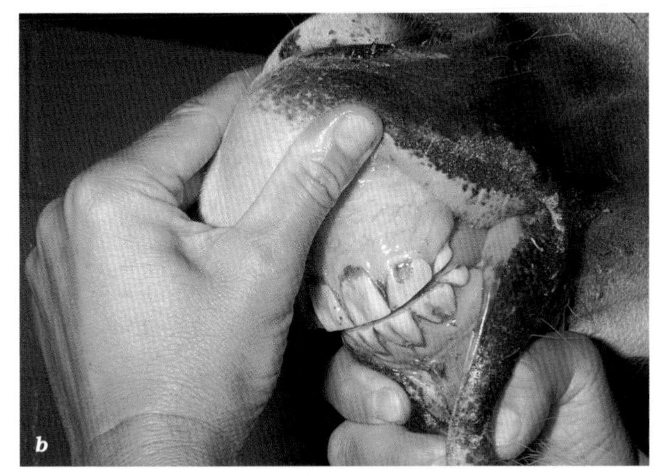

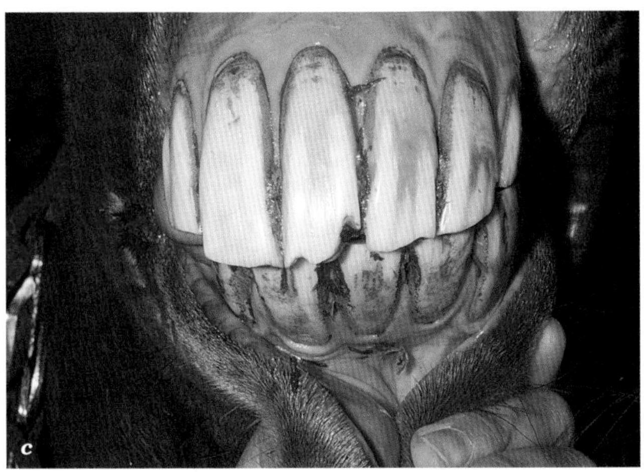

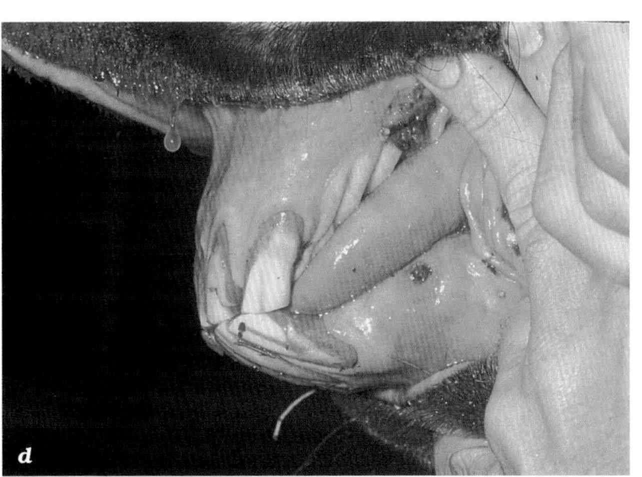

(a) The conformation of the horse's teeth change markedly as he ages. The baby incisor teeth of the two year old are much shorter than the long teeth of the 20 year old (c).
(b) The mouth of a coming four-year-old horse. The teeth of the young adult horse meet in a more vertical plane than those of the older horse.
(c) The mouth of a 20 year old horse.
(d) The mouth of a 30 year old horse. The changing shape of the horse's mouth as he ages may require corresponding changes in bits.

there is between the palate and the tongue and bars. For instance, in a young riding-aged horse, the incisors meet on a fairly upright plane, generally allowing ample room for a medium-port bit.

As the horse ages, however, the incisors begin to extend forward on the horizontal plane. Even though the horse's teeth are perpetually erupting from the gum line, they gradually wear down. There may also be some natural bone loss in the jaw, so the distance between the upper and lower arcades (rows of teeth) close. Consequently, a bit that worked beautifully for a number of years may eventually become bothersome to the horse as it comes into contact with the palate due to normal physiologic changes.

THE NOSE, CHIN AND JAW

From the moment we start handling young horses, we gain control of their heads and necks by applying pressure to key points, including the bridge of the nose, the cheeks, jaws and poll. Certain features of the head make exercising this control simple. One is the intricate system of nerves. Two is how easy these points are to access. Third, there is little padding to protect these sensitive spots so the horse is naturally eager to reduce contact.

For example, the bridge of the horse's nose is remarkably sensitive to pressure. When pressure is applied to a noseband, the horse feels it. But because there is little between the skin and nasal bone to protect the nerves of the face, it is also relatively easy to dull this area. Strong, repeated pressure can deaden the receptors.

Keep in mind the general construction of the nasal bone when fitting and using nosebands and other devices. At the bridge of the nose, the nasal bone has a relatively gentle slope from front to sides. However, the closer you get to the nostrils, the thinner and narrower the nasal bone becomes. If a noseband or hackamore is situated too low or adjusted too tight, it can damage nerves, bone and/or cartilage. It can also interfere with the horse's ability to breath.

The horse's jawline is also very sensitive. There is little padding to protect bone and soft skin from the bite of a poorly situated, harsh or tightly adjusted curb chain. The chin groove, or curb groove as it is also called, is the narrow indentation immediately behind the fleshy chin. Ideally, it is in this groove that the curb strap should hang. Farther back, behind the chin groove, the jaw branches into two sharp ridges covered by only a thin layer of skin. If the curb strap or chain sits over these ridges, the pressure on the jaw bones is localized, causing pain when the bit is engaged.

It is also important to make sure that a bit accommodates the contours of the face. For example, a horse with a narrow mouth but wide cheeks needs a bit with a short mouthpiece, but upper shanks that spread sufficiently to allow room for the cheeks. Another horse with the same narrow mouth but correspondingly narrow cheeks can be fitted with a bit with a short mouthpiece and vertical upper shanks that run parallel with one another.

The curb strap or chain fits into the horse's chin groove, where it is effective, without causing pain.

(a) The actual place where "poll flexion" occurs is the atlantoaxial joint, between the first and second vertebrae of the neck.
(b) The poll, where flexion is commonly thought to occur.
(c) Note where nasal bone stops, cartilage begins. The noseband should be placed on the nasal bone to avoid injury to the horse.

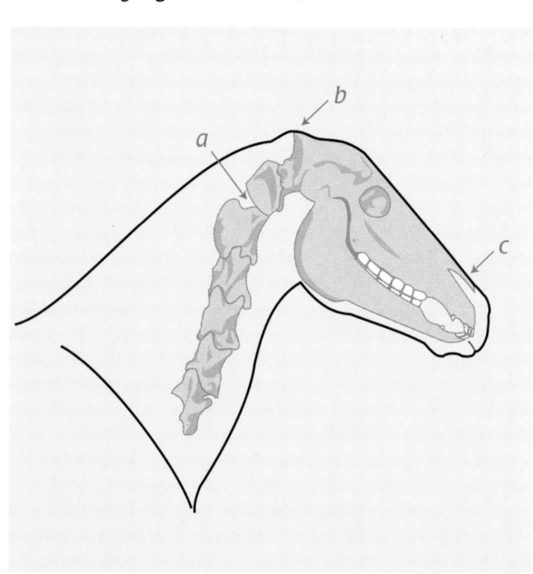

THE POLL

Virtually any bitting system transfers some degree of pressure to the poll through the headstall. But there are several bitting systems specifically designed to enhance the pressure applied to the poll. While the poll may not be especially sensitive in comparison to the mouth, nose and jaw, horses can and do learn to yield to light pressure applied to their polls. Gag bits, Gogues, draw reins and other pulley-type systems are often used to employ poll pressure in performance training. We'll explain more specifics about how these systems are designed to work in later chapters.

However, what rider and trainers are most concerned about is poll flexion — the hinge-like front to back movement of the horse's head. You'll often hear horsemen use the expression "soft in the poll" which describes the compliant, vertical yielding of horse's head, face and jaw to the pull on the reins. It's typically accompanied by a lowering of the head in western horses.

The term poll flexion is somewhat misleading. In the study of conformation, the poll is the prominent boney point on the horse's head directly between the ears. It does not flex. Instead, what we commonly refer to as "poll flexion" is really the pivoting action between the first two bones of the neck. This junction is known as the atlantoaxial joint.

It is the atlantoaxial joint in the neck which enables the horse to carry its head in front of the bit, on the bit, or behind the bit.

It is sometimes mistakenly said that a horse which has been overbitted will break farther back in the neck rather than at the poll. While there may appear to be flexion at another point along the neck, this is really just an optical illusion. An unusual bow or arch in the neck is likely due to the development of neck muscles rather than flexion at some midpoint between poll and withers, since the remaining joints between the neck bones allow very little front to back movement.

However, it is the entire complex system of muscles, bones and ligaments which allow the horse to raise and lower its head and neck, as well as to turn from side to side. This entire system also plays a major role in how your horse will respond to the bit. Basic conformation and musculature can help or hinder a horse's natural ability and inclination to bend and flex when you pull on the reins. A horse with an ewe neck (having a downward bow along the topline) or thick throatlatch, for example, will be at a decided disadvantage when asked for vertical flexion. His own muscles get in the way. Similarly, a horse with a short, heavily muscled neck may have a more difficult time bending laterally than a lean, long-necked horse. Yet conditioning these muscles to become supple and relaxed can help overcome the horse's physical shortcomings and make him more willing and able to comply with the rein signals.

When a horse bows its neck, some people mistakenly think that the horse isn't breaking "at the poll," but farther down the neck. In point of fact, the bow is caused by the neck muscles, made noticeable by his head position.

One final consideration regarding the neck is that in most western horse sports, the goal is to train the horse to guide on a light neck rein. The weight, texture or action of the reins you choose will affect the messages you convey through the nerves in the neck. Some horses are so sensitive that they flick off a house fly as soon as it lights, while others barely notice a horse fly bite. While rein styles, sizes and materials change with fads and fashions, give as much consideration to your reins and the sensitivity of your horse's neck as you do to the other elements of your bridling system.

Never underestimate the sensitivity of any horse or any specific feature of your horse's anatomy based on outward appearances. Be sure to choose equipment that fits and make accommodations for any unusual characteristics.

"THE HORSE'S MOUTH IS IN A CONSTANT STATE OF FLUX."

3

Dentistry and Mouth Care

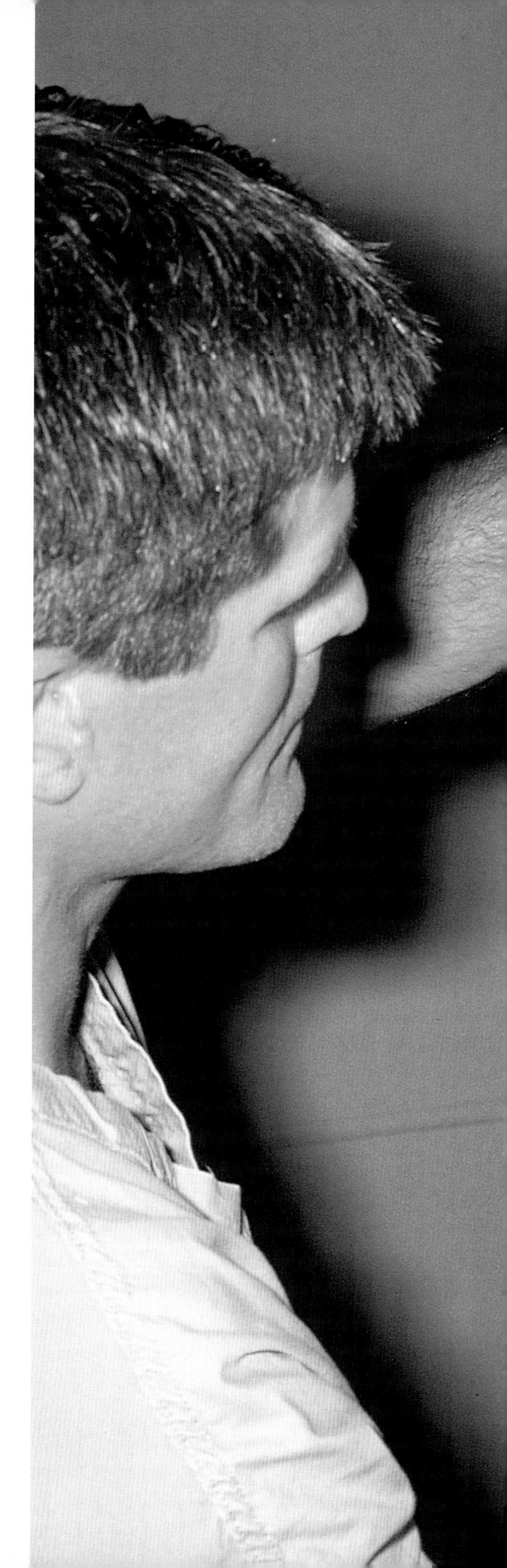

As with any high performance machine, the way to maximize performance is to check under the hood from time to time and make the necessary adjustments. A horse's performance is dependent upon having healthy teeth and a comfortable mouth. Routine dental care should be a regular part of your horse's annual physical examination.

While good mouth maintenance is important at any age, there are times in a horse's life when natural physical changes make dental care an even greater priority. One is when the horse first reaches riding age. Another is when the horse becomes a senior citizen.

The horse's mouth is in a constant state of flux. Even after a horse has lost all its baby teeth, its permanent teeth continue to erupt from the gums well into old age. This is nature's way of providing adequate nipping and grinding surfaces so the horse can continue to forage throughout its life. But this continuous dental wear and tear can also create problems that interfere with bitting and performance.

NUMBERS OF TEETH

An adult horse has a minimum of 36 teeth, and may have as many as 42. The standard complement, moving from the front to the back of the mouth, is as follows:

Incisors or Nippers	6 upper and 6 lower
Premolars	6 upper and 6 lower
Molars	6 upper and 6 lower

The premolars and molars are often collectively called the cheek teeth or grinders. The premolars and molars look just alike. The only difference is that the permanent premolars are preceded by a set of deciduous (baby) premolars. There are no deciduous molars; a horse gets

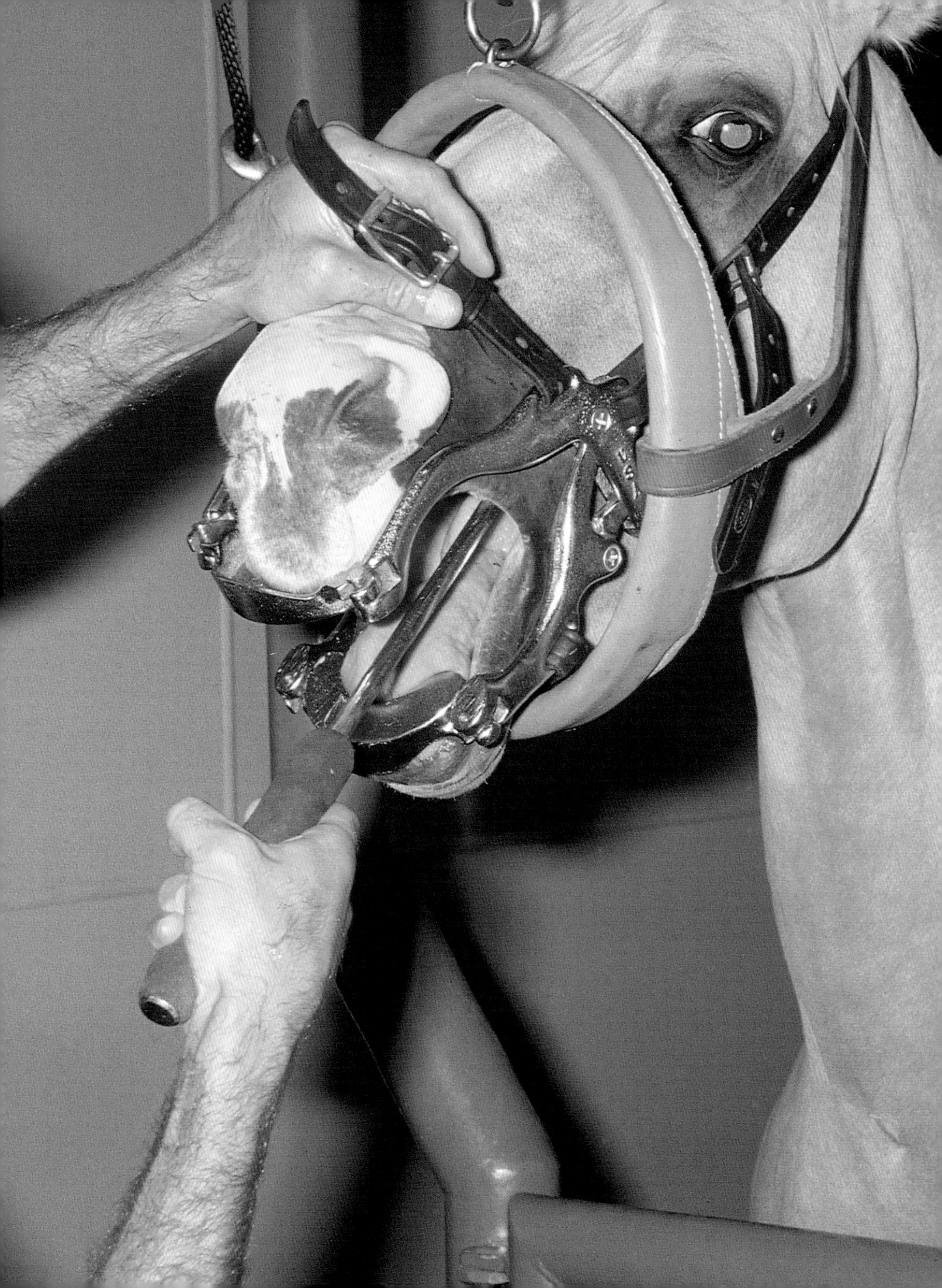

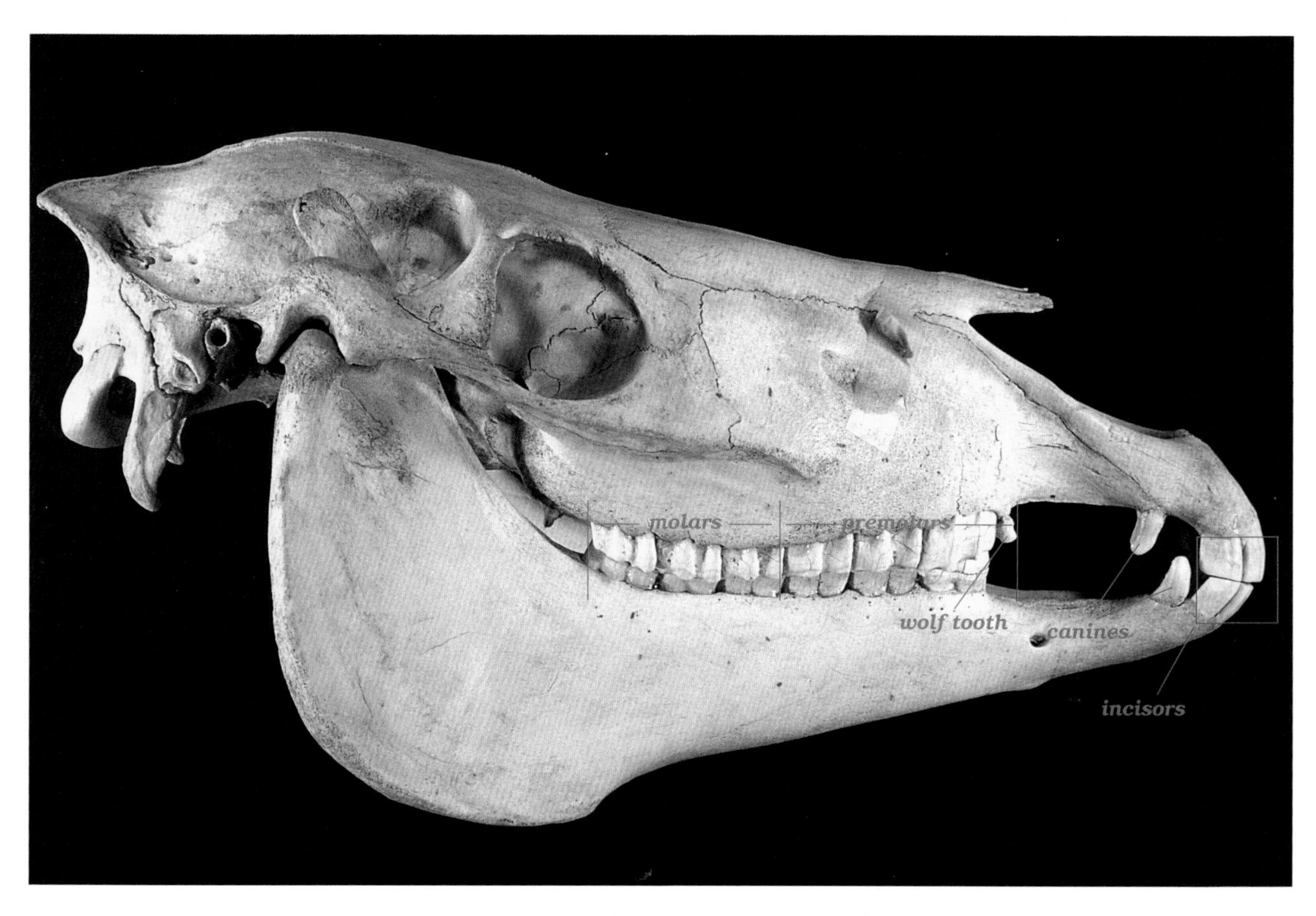

A horse with a full mouth, including canine teeth and wolf teeth, has 42 teeth. Note that the wolf tooth is also a premolar.

only a permanent set. During the first one to two years of life a horse has 12 baby incisors and 12 baby premolars. By age five, all of the horse's baby teeth have been replaced by permanent teeth and the molars have come in as well. A mature horse is said to have a "full mouth."

In addition, male horses (and occasionally females) have two upper and two lower canine teeth located between the incisors and the premolars. This makes a total of 40 teeth. Also, most males (and an occasional female) have very small upper teeth immediately in front of the premolars. These are the wolf teeth. So, a horse with canine teeth and wolf teeth has a total of 42 teeth.

AGE FACTOR

There once was a time when horses weren't considered to be of riding age until they were five years old. By then most horses have reached physical maturity and have a full complement of teeth. While bitting the mature horse is probably less troublesome than bitting a young horse, it isn't practical to delay training simply to wait for a horse to get its permanent teeth.

Like elementary school children, most young horses are losing their baby teeth at about the time they're starting their formal educations. Many show horses are started under saddle before they reach their second birthdays, then compete in major performance events as two and three-year-olds. Consequently, they're cutting teeth at the same time they're learning to carry a bit. Like any

(overleaf) Floating a horse's teeth periodically removes sharp points caused by uneven wear.

This two-year-old is just being introduced to the bit and his reaction is pretty typical. So far he doesn't think much of it. Keep in mind that a young horse's mouth may be especially tender due to teething. This is the age at which wolf teeth should be pulled.

teething baby, these youngsters are likely to have tender gums. Little wonder that they might be cross, scared or a shade rebellious when you insert a bit into their mouths and take up the reins.

There's a common misconception that a horse with a sore mouth will automatically back off a bit rather than pull on it. While this may be true for some horses, just as often, the tender-mouthed horse may actually root into the bridle or champ on the bit. This makes sense if you think of it in human terms. When a baby is teething and his gums ache, we give him a teething ring or hard cookie to chew on. The child bites down on the object and gives his gums a good workout. This not only eases the pain, it also helps the teeth to break through the tissue. For much the same reason, a horse with a sensitive mouth or erupting teeth may lean into or play excessively with the bit. Some riders may misinterpret this behavior as disrespect for the bridle and opt for a harsher mouthpiece. This can compound the problem and set up a vicious cycle: The rider steps up in severity of bits. The mouth continues to be sore. The horse continues to resist the bridle. The rider installs a harsher bit. And so on....

Before you allow yourself to get into this war, consider what's happening in the young horse's mouth. From ages two to five, the horse will continue to shed and grow teeth. A handy rule of thumb to help you remember is that the cheek teeth come in about the same year as their corresponding number. For example, the first premolars (the wolf teeth) and the first molars are in by age one, the second molars come in during the horse's second year, and so on.

Take steps during this period to make the animal as comfortable as possible. It may be wise to use a mild bit and give the horse time to learn and adapt to the rein cues rather than roll out the heavy artillery. You may even want to consider switching to a bitless bridle such as a sidepull or hackamore until the horse's mouth matures.

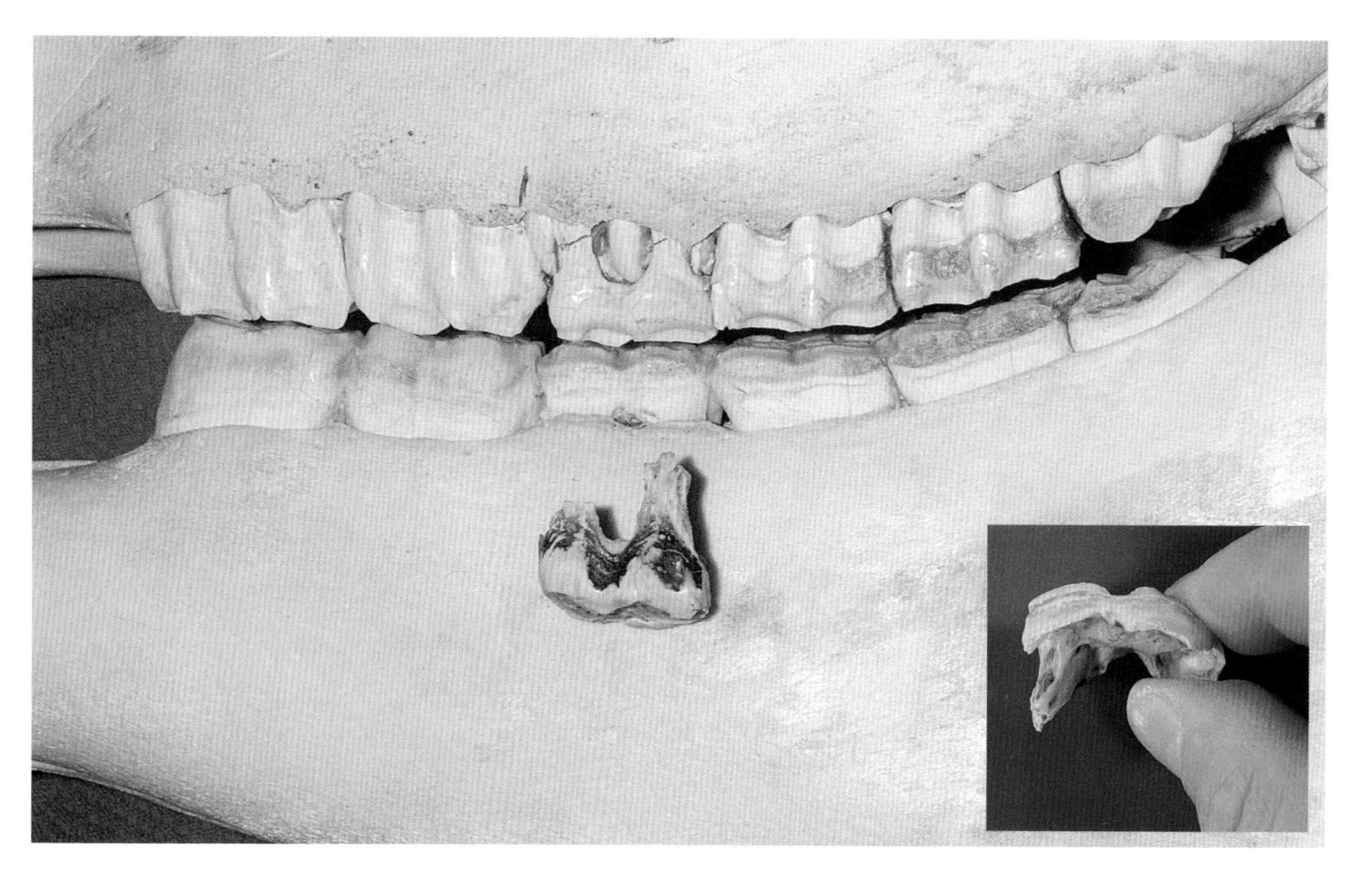

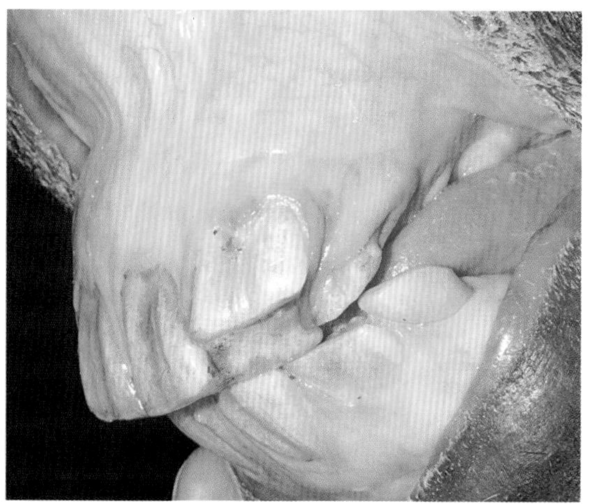

(top) A retained deciduous tooth (cap) on the third upper cheek tooth (fourth premolar), and a cap which has been removed.
(top inset) When you see the sharp edges of a cap, it becomes obvious why a partially dislodged cap can cause problems. The sharp points gouge the cheeks and gums.
(above) This retained deciduous incisor may result in a sore mouth.

RETAINED TEETH

Most horses shed their baby teeth without mishap. Occasionally, however, they fail to fall out and the new teeth come in underneath or behind them. Retained premolars are commonly called caps. Caps not only interfere with eating, they can also bother the youngster who's just learning to carry a bit. The caps should be removed, but be aware that your veterinarian will not be inclined to force them off too early. The underlying teeth need adequate time to harden and close. If not, you risk exposing an open artery which could lead to a sinus infection. Should your veterinarian determine that the caps should be taken off, they can usually be removed with the horse mildly sedated.

WOLF TEETH

Wolf teeth are the small, undeveloped teeth that erupt just in front of the cheek teeth in some horses. They can appear in both upper and lower jaws, but are more common in the top. As far as we know, they serve no practical purpose. Some horses go through life without ever having any problems with their wolf teeth. In others, wolf teeth are a nuisance, causing pain when the bit comes into contact with them, or when the lips or cheeks are pinched against them. For these reasons wolf teeth are routinely removed.

As a general rule, the more a horse must extend its nose for peak performance, the more likely it is that the bit will contact the wolf teeth, and the more important it is that they be removed. For example, speed event horses extend their noses to run their fastest, so the removal of wolf teeth is especially recommended. Wolf teeth usually come in when the horse is five to seven months old. Yet most owners wait until their horses reach riding age to have the teeth extracted. The procedure is simple because wolf teeth are small and their roots are shallow. A veterinarian can usually pull them with little difficulty.

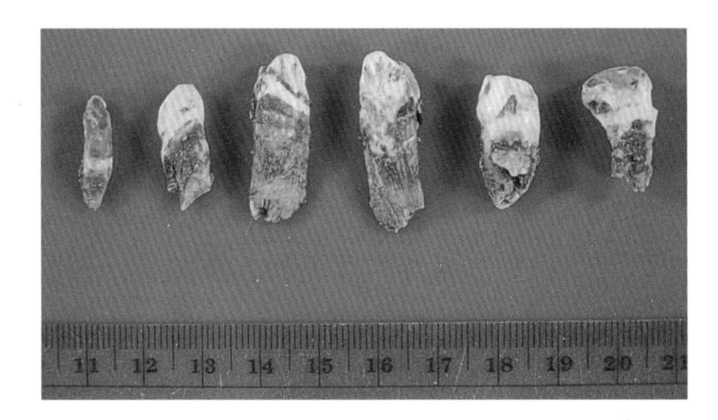

Wolf teeth which have been removed.

CANINE OR BRIDLE TEETH

The canine or "bridle" teeth are curved, tusk-like teeth that grow in the bar space. They are more common in stallions and geldings than in mares, and account for the usual difference in the numbers of teeth between the sexes. Some mares do grow canine teeth, but they are usually small and undeveloped.

The canine teeth typically emerge during the horse's fourth of fifth year of life. While these bridle teeth are coming in, young horses might become fussy and less content in a bit. Cutting teeth can be painful. The old time California cowboys, the vaqueros, traditionally rode their horses in a hackamore and didn't introduce a bridle bit until age five or older when the horse was done teething. From a developmental standpoint, it makes sense.

In most horses, there is ample room in the bar space for both the bit and the bridle teeth. However, as horses age, the canines can become unduly long and sharp, making it more difficult to insert and remove the bit. Long, sharp bridle teeth also create a hazard for both horse and human. Bridle teeth should be maintained by cutting, grinding or rasping, also called floating, to keep them low and smooth. In rare cases, if the canine teeth are especially troublesome, the teeth can be surgically removed, but it is a major undertaking.

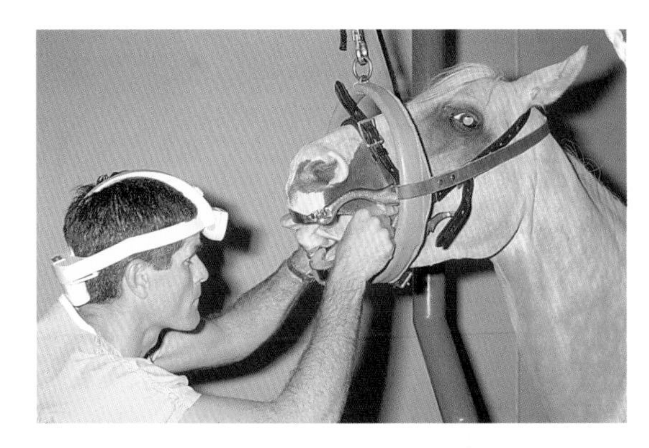

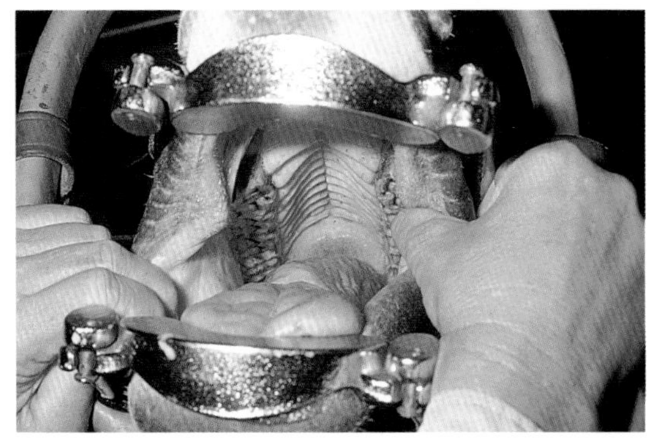

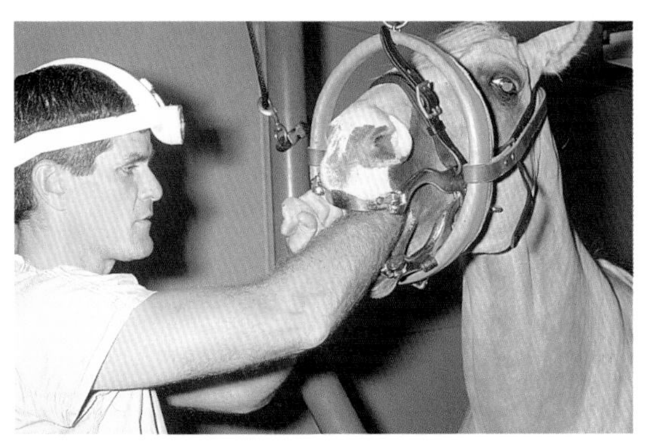

A veterinarian can detect many abnormalities of the mouth and teeth with a visual examination utilizing a head lamp and speculum, but some problems can be detected only by touch. Any hooks or points requiring filing down are safely discovered and dealt with by the veterinarian.

FLOATING

Most bits are designed so that the bars of the mouthpiece rest comfortably in the interdental spaces where there are no teeth. There is usually ample room for the bit to move forward and backward with very little direct contact with the teeth. However, this does not downplay the importance of floating the teeth to maintain smooth, properly aligned surfaces.

Because the horse's upper jaw is wider than its lower jaw, the teeth tend to wear unevenly. When the horse chews, it moves its jaws from side to side. The sharp points which form on the outer edge of the top teeth can cut the inside of the mouth when the rings, shanks or butt of the mouthpiece press cheeks and lips against hard enamel. Likewise, the inside ridges that form on the bottom teeth are apt to cut the tongue and make it painful for the horse to carry the bit. The discomfort can cause a horse to stiffen or resist the bridle.

An animal's head carriage will also play a role in which surfaces, upper or lower, play the greatest role in bitting. The more vertical the headset, the more the lower teeth come into play. The more horizontal the headset, the more the upper teeth factor in. That's why experienced

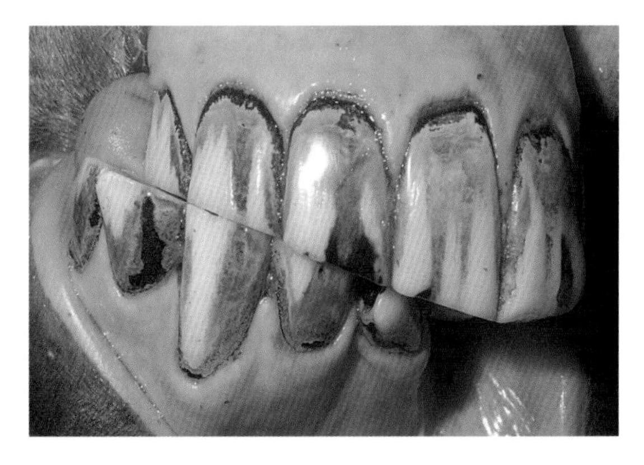

Incisors as well as cheek teeth may benefit from being leveled. An injury to the mouth has led to abnormal wear.

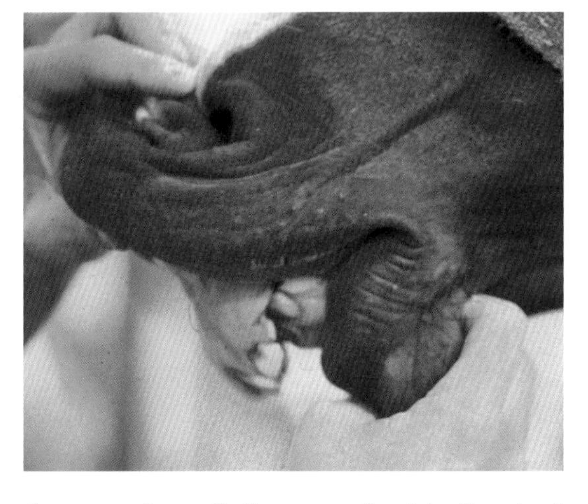

In a parrot mouth the upper front teeth extend beyond the lowers. Hooks are probably present on the first upper cheek teeth.

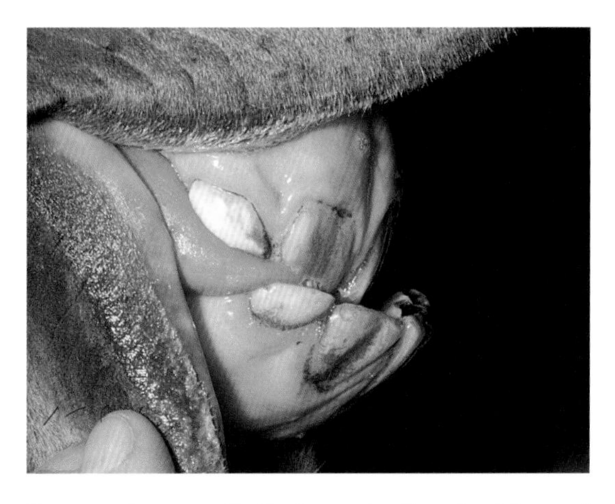

In a monkey mouth the lower teeth extend beyond the uppers.

equine practitioners often consider the horse's job and level of training when deciding how to properly float or care for its teeth.

Incisors, canines, and cheek teeth benefit from being smoothed and leveled. As a horse ages, its bite plane changes. Natural bone loss and tooth wear cause the teeth to extend forward. They meet at an angle rather than upright as in young horses. A horse's teeth continue to grow throughout most of its life. Ideally, the upper and lower teeth continue to wear each other off so they don't get too long. However, if the alignment gets skewed or a horse loses a tooth, the unopposed tooth will grow up or down into the space left by the missing tooth. This may result in the jaws locking up. It is essential that any unopposed teeth be filed regularly. In order for a horse to respond well to the bit, it must be comfortable and have full mobility of its mouth.

In advanced age, tooth growth eventually stops and the teeth may need special attention in order to keep the surfaces meeting properly. Older horses are more likely to have damaged teeth, because as teeth become worn they are more easily broken.

CREATING "BIT SEATS" OR A "SNAFFLE MOUTH"

There is approximately an inch or so between the corners of the horse's lips and the first cheek teeth. When the reins are pulled, particularly on a direct action bit such as a broken-mouth snaffle, the skin on the lips stretches backwards and frequently causes the lips to be pinched. At the same time the tongue may be pinched against the lower teeth. This happens even though the bit bars seldom come into direct contact with the first cheek teeth. For this reason, when floating teeth, some veterinarians pay special attention to rounding and filing the fronts and sides of those first cheek teeth to keep pressure points to a minimum. This technique is sometimes referred to as creating "bit seats" or putting on a "snaffle mouth." This generally includes the removal of wolf teeth as well.

ELIMINATING HOOKS

Often, at the back of the bottom jaw and the front of the top jaw, "hooks" form because the two surfaces don't align properly front to back. The unopposed portions of the teeth grow long and must be cut or rasped to maintain their ideal height. Hooks can interfere not only with chewing but also with the natural mobility of the mouth when a horse is ridden. Eliminating hooks is important for all horses, but it is essential in parrot-mouthed or monkey-mouthed horses. Parrot mouth describes an improper bite alignment in which the upper front teeth extend beyond the lower ones. Monkey mouth is when the lower incisors jut beyond the upper ones.

CLUES OF DENTAL PROBLEMS

Ideally, dental exams should be done every six months regardless of the horse's age. Regular preventative maintenance can reduce the likelihood that teeth are at the root of any bitting problems.

Between visits, stay tuned for abnormal behaviors that could be related to mouth trouble. These might include flinching, stiffening, head-tossing or mouth gaping when you put pressure on the reins; lugging on or champing at the bit; running through the bridle; head cocking; or refusing to be bridled. Another clue might be the horse that suddenly becomes one-sided or carries its head in front of or behind the bit to avoid contact. Even changes in body posture and attitude may signal mouth discomfort.

Too often, horse owners don't look for these telltale signs. Not until the horse starts dropping feed, shows difficulty chewing, or becomes thin or unthrifty, does it dawn on them that the teeth might need some attention. Yet these horses have probably lost their performance edge long before.

One simple test to see if your horse's teeth need to be floated is to press your thumb against the horse's cheeks where the premolars are situated. If the horse flinches or tries to pull away, he may need dental work. You can also ease your hand into the bar space and gently pull the tongue out the side of the mouth for a better look inside. But use extreme caution. Those teeth are sharp and even experienced practitioners have crushed or lost fingers. Better still, let your veterinarian do the exam. He has the tools to do a much more thorough job.

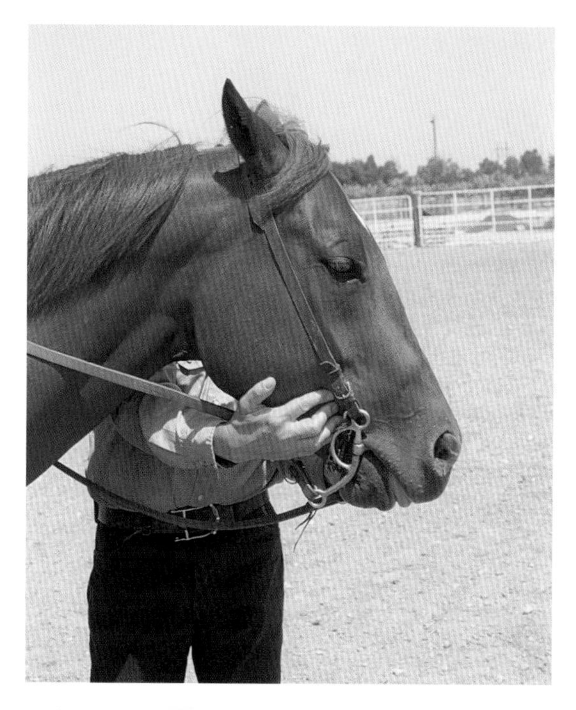

Points may sometimes be detected by pushing the cheek against the upper cheek teeth. If the horse flinches in pain, points may be present. If you are uncertain of your horse's reaction, call in a veterinarian.

"BITS SHOULD BE WELL-DESIGNED AND THE WEIGHT PROPERLY DISTRIBUTED."

4

An Introduction to Bits and Bridles

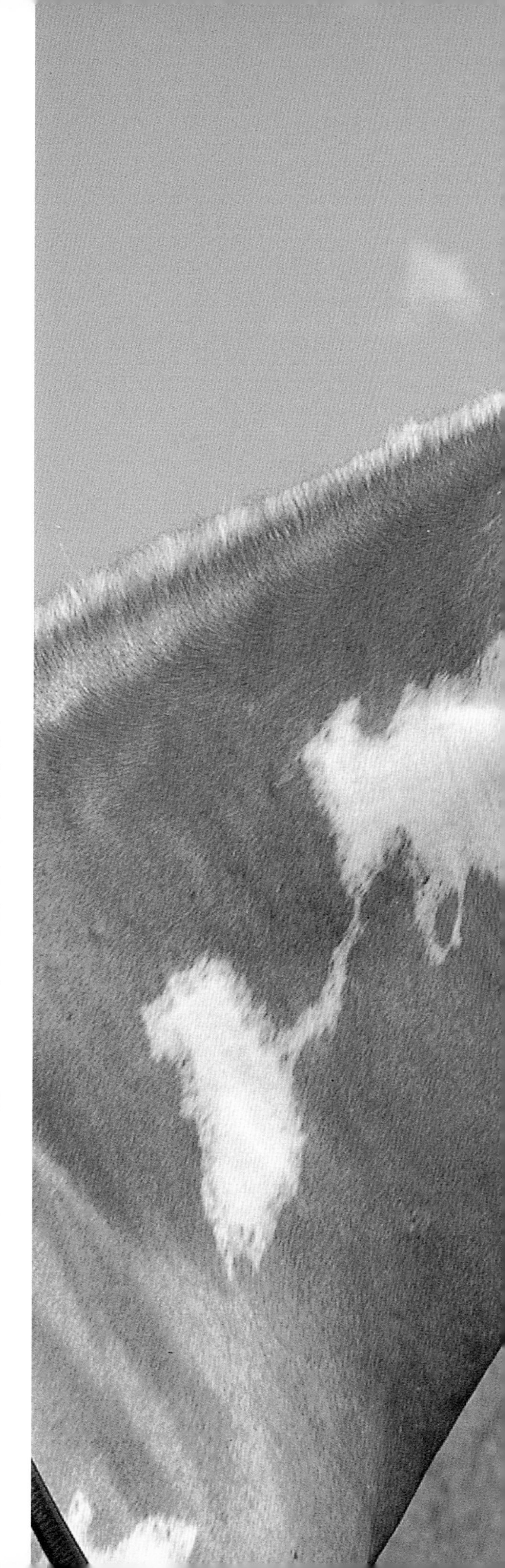

Bits have a profound influence on a horse's head carriage, balance and maneuverability, as well as attitude and responsiveness. Different performance horses may have different bitting requirements based on the types of work they do. For example, the western pleasure horse performs best with a nearly vertical headset and its weight carried largely on its hindquarters. The racehorse needs to run with its head at a 45- degree angle and its weight carried largely on its forehand for maximum speed. Reining and cutting horses are expected to run, stop and turn on a dime, so their head position, weight and center of balance are in a constant state of flux. Little wonder that these athletes probably won't be wearing the same type of head gear as the pleasure or race horse.

Whether you compete or not, your own choice of bits should allow your horse to do its job to the best of its ability. There are literally thousands of bits on the market. Selecting one may seem like a complex and time-consuming chore. Yet common sense and a basic understanding of the bridle's parts and purposes will help you quickly sort through those on display and ultimately end up with one that works.

Bits typically fall into one of two categories: snaffles or curbs. There are combination bits, but generally such bits have features dominant to one classification or the other. We'll discuss this more in a later chapter. First we'll provide an overview to help you become familiar with bits and bridles.

PARTS OF THE BIT

The basic parts of any bit are the mouthpiece and the cheeks. Mouthpieces come in many varieties; curved, straight, jointed, or even linked like a chain. They often have a rise or upward bend in the center known as the

(overleaf) This light-weight grazing bit, with its swept back lower shank, provides advanced warning to the horse.

Different performance horses have different bitting requirements. The reining horse (above) might need a bit that provides plenty of signal while the cutting horse (below) may work better with a bit that's extremely stable.

port. They may include "tongue toys" such as rollers, crickets, or keys, which encourage horses to play with the mouthpiece. This is thought to help them relax and better accept the bit.

In a broken or jointed mouthpiece, the separate halves of the mouthpiece are known as cannons. In a solid mouthpiece, the segments of the mouthpiece on either side of the port are known as the bit bars. The butt of the mouthpiece is the junction where the bit bars join the cheeks.

The cheeks connect the mouthpiece to the headstall and reins. They also have a direct impact on the action of the bit in the horse's mouth. The cheeks may be simple rings, as found in many snaffles, or shanks which extend above and below the mouthpiece. Shanks add leverage to the bitting equation. They increase the pressure which is exerted on the mouthpiece when you pull on the reins. In combination with the mouthpiece, the cheeks give a bit its own special balance, speed and function. We'll discuss these topics more in later chapters. Like mouthpieces, cheeks and shanks are designed in endless variety.

SNAFFLE BITS

In its simplest definition, a snaffle is any bit which acts by direct pressure. The rider pulls on the reins and that signal is translated pound for pound in a direct line to the horse's mouth. There is no leverage. In the classical interpretation, snaffles can have either solid or jointed mouthpieces — or any other type of mouthpiece for that

matter — because it is not the style of mouthpiece that determines the line of pull, but rather the cheeks. In true snaffles, typically the headstall and reins attach to the same or adjacent cheek rings.

Over time many horsemen have come to regard a snaffle as any bit with a broken mouthpiece. English riders will often differentiate between a bar bit (which lacks a joint) and a snaffle bit (which has at least one). In western circles, you'll often hear the euphemism "shanked snaffle." What these riders are really talking about is a broken-mouthed curb bit. Remember, if there are shanks attached to a mouthpiece — jointed or otherwise — it no longer acts as a snaffle. The direct action of the bit is changed to leveraged pull. In this book we will reserve the term "snaffle" for direct-pulling bits, including a variety of ring-cheeked bits. We'll talk about mouthpieces separately as being either solid or jointed. We'll also refer to jointed mouthpieces as being "broken."

Snaffle bits are generally designed to be used with two hands on the reins. In western riding, they are primarily reserved for training and showing young horses. In many English disciplines, however, snaffles are used for training and showing horses throughout their lives.

CURB BITS (LEVERAGE BITS)

The term curb bit applies to any number of bits which utilize leverage. Curb bits have shanks which extend both above and below the mouthpiece, with the headstall attaching to the upper shanks (cheek rings), and the reins attaching to the lower shanks (rein rings.)

Essential to a curb bit's proper function is the use of a curb strap or curb chain. The curb strap, sometimes called a chin strap, attaches to the upper shank rings and fits beneath the jaw in the chin groove. Some bits feature separate rings below the headstall rings for the curb strap to prevent pinching. The curb strap stops the rotation of the shanks and mouthpiece. When the reins are pulled and the curb strap engages, pressure is applied to the horse's mouth, chin groove and poll.

Curb bits are designed with many different mouthpieces and shanks. It is the mouthpiece in combination with the shank and curb strap that determines how much and precisely where the pressure is distributed when the reins are pulled. The placement of the mouthpiece within the shanks, as well as the length of the shanks, directly impact how much force can be applied. We will talk more about chin straps and leverage ratios in Chapter 8, "Putting Power in the Pull."

Curb bits have a broad application in horsemanship and training. They are used in many disciplines. The type of curb bit used depends largely on the given sport. Because of the sheer variety of curbs, they can be used either two- or one-handed. However, in the show ring and certainly in the true western tradition, "finished" horses are ridden with one hand on the reins using a light neck rein.

A curb bit, whether it has a solid mouthpiece or a jointed one, will have shanks extending above and below the mouthpiece. Without the curb strap, this bit would exert little leverage.

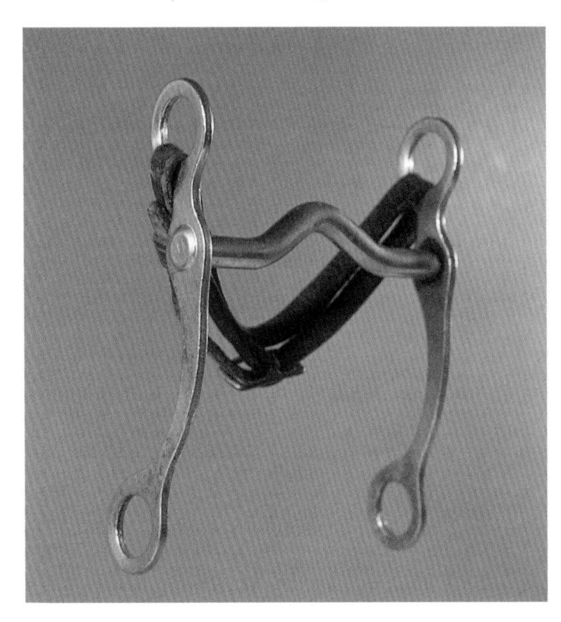

English huntseat riders (above) maintain constant contact with the horse's mouth, using a direct pulling "snaffle" bit. Western horsemen rely on the weight and balance of a bit — rather than rein tension — to achieve a high degree of finesse with slack reins.

WEIGHT, MATERIALS AND CONSTRUCTION

Tradition, old wives' tales, economics, experience and preference all play a role in what bits are made of and why. Some people prefer heavy bits, others choose light bits. The weight of a bit, however, is really only relevant in terms of balance and function. How does the weight affect the bit's action and utility?

An English hunt seat rider maintains almost continuous contact with the horse's mouth using a snaffle bit. Weight probably isn't a major consideration here. While some people might choose a hollow mouthpiece because it is lighter, the extra weight of a solid mouthpiece probably wouldn't make much difference to the horse. The weight of the bit is slight in comparison to the weight of the horse's own head.

In extreme contrast, the weight and balance of a spade bit, with its ornate shanks, high spoon, cricket and spacer bars, has a very definite impact on the way it hangs in a horse's mouth. When there is no pressure being exerted on the reins, the bit should have enough weight in the shanks to swing back to a neutral position instantaneously so the spoon no longer contacts the palate.

Grazing bits, commonly used on ranch and western performance horses, have traditionally been made with light-weight, swept-back shanks (often of aluminum.) The light shanks keep the jarring action of the bit to a minimum as the horse starts, stops and turns in rapid succession in pursuit of a cow. A bit with straighter, heavier shanks, would start to act as a hammer on the horse's mouth. Although an aluminum grazing bit's shanks are light, if it has been well made, its natural forward balance will allow

The more backward sweep in the shank the more signal the bit provides. This grazing bit, with a swept back lower shank provides advanced warning to the horse.

the bit to drop back to a neutral position as soon as the reins are released. Thus the chin strap disengages, as does the pressure on the horse's mouth.

Bits should be well-designed with the weight correctly distributed so that both the bit and the reins hang properly. When strategically engineered into the bit's design, weight can enhance the signals you communicate to the horse through the reins.

Regardless of whether a bit is hand-made or machine-manufactured, the surfaces should be smooth and free of defects. The joints should be well-tooled and fit together so as not to cut or pinch the mouth.

The most common materials used in bit-making are stainless steel, cold-rolled steel (sometimes referred to as "sweet iron,") brass, chrome-plate alloys, nickel, nickel silver, aluminum, and copper. Leather, rubber and vulcanite (a type of hardened rubber), are also sometimes used in mouthpieces to produce a softer bit. Other synthetics have also entered the picture, although, metal remains the choice among most bitmakers and horsemen.

Materials should be considered for their strength, durability, comfort, and appearance. If the materials are thin or of poor quality, the cheek rings and shanks may

(opposite) Whenever a rider slips a bridle onto a horse's head, the choice should be made with the end result in mind and the interest of the horse at heart. Colorado trainer and veterinarian Dr. Steve Schwartzenberger bits his stallion Kick Dee Bar in a slow twist snaffle for a training session.

bend, the joints can wear out prematurely, and the mouthpieces may chip and develop rough or sharp surfaces. High grade cold-rolled and stainless steel both provide many desirable properties. Stainless steel is prettier to look at and is easier to maintain because it doesn't rust. But many horsemen advocate the use of cold rolled steel precisely because it does rust, maintaining that horses prefer the taste of rusty iron, and intentionally allow the mouthpiece to do so.

For appearance, steel bits are often blued, browned, blackened or decorated with silver, brass and gold, and also gems or stones. But it's best if these techniques are confined to the shanks and cheeks as the chemicals used in these processes can be toxic. Even a small amount of residue can make the horse sick.

HEADSTALLS

The headstall holds the bit in place. In its simplest form, it is a strap or string which runs from one bit ring to the other over the top of the horse's head. To allow for adjustments, the headstall is generally divided into two or three parts -- the crownpiece which rests on the poll behind the ears and the cheekpieces which make up the sides and connect to the crownpiece.

Additional features help keep the bridle in place, such as browbands, earpieces and throatlatches. The browband rests across the horse's forehead and keeps the crown and cheekpieces from sliding back, which would put pressure on the bit. The throatlatch, which attaches to the crownpiece and encircles the throat, prevents the bridle from being pulled or rubbed off over the ears.

Some bridles have an ear piece instead of the browband, to hold the crownpiece in place. Ear bridles come in single, double and split ear types. Earpieces may be separate from the crownpiece or they may be cut from the same leather as the crownpiece. However, the all-in-one types can create problems if not properly constructed and adjusted. They may cause the bit to sit lop-sided in the horse's mouth, or press on the ear when the reins are pulled. Separate earpieces are more practical because they slide and can be adjusted to better accommodate the horse's ear placement. They are also less likely to shift when the bridle reins are pulled. With single ear bridles, the earpiece is generally situated on the right side. In the split ear bridle, the crown piece has been sliced in the middle to accomodate a single ear.

Ear bridles are attractive and functional, but not all of them include a throatlatch, which is a nice safety feature. Horses with sensitive ears may resist being bridled. A headstall with a brow band might accommodate these horses better. Also, what you want for training and schooling might be different than what you use in the show ring.

Some bridles also include a cavesson or noseband. In some cases, the cavesson is merely an adornment. Yet a well designed, placed and correctly adjusted cavesson encourages a horse to keep its mouth closed around the

On some bridles an ear piece is used instead of a browband to hold the crownpiece in place.

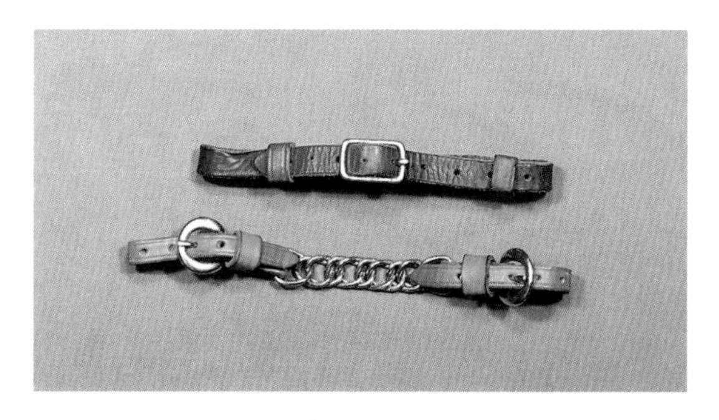

The curb strap or chain, which fits into the horse's chin groove, is essential to the function of the leverage (curb) bit.

(above) Bit guards are rubber or leather rings that fit between the mouthpiece and cheeks of the bit to protect the corners of the horse's lips.

Split reins are two separate reins, a left and a right.

bit and provides a place to attach a standing martingale or tie-down. We'll discuss cavessons, nosebands and martingales further in a later chapter.

CHIN STRAPS

In order to work effectively, leverage bitting systems should be used with a chin strap. Chin straps may be leather, chain, rope or other material, but many horse show associations specify or restrict what types of chin straps may be used. Like bits, chin straps can be inherently mild or severe depending on their materials and design. For example, a flat, smooth leather chin strap is more humane than a coarse metal chain.

The adjustment of the chin strap plays a major role in how the bit rests in the mouth and at what point leverage comes into play. We'll discuss this further in "Putting Power in the Pull."

BIT GUARDS

Bit guards or cheek protectors are rubber or leather rings that fit between the mouthpiece and the cheeks of the bit to protect the corners of the horse's lips. Bit guards help prevent chafing and also keep the bit rings from being pulled through the mouth. They either stretch over the snaffle rings or shanks, or have a lacing system which allows them to be opened or closed around the mouthpiece. Some flat or loose ring snaffles are prone to wear at the butt of the mouthpiece and may be cause for concern. Some hinged bits also have joints that can pinch the skin if not buffered. However, the vast majority of well-designed, properly fitted bits are fine without them.

REINS

Leather, rawhide, nylon, cotton, horse hair and many other strong, flexible fabrics are used to make reins. When choosing reins, your primary concerns are going to be how the reins fit and feel in your hands, how they hang, what kind of grip they provide, and how they affect the horse when you apply pressure to them. Reins are a matter of personal preference, which explains why there are so many different types: flat, round, smooth, course, braided and so on. Reins are generally 4½ to 8 feet long, but you should choose the length, width and texture that's most practical for your sport. Many barrel racers, for instance, ride with laced, plaited or rubber-covered reins because they afford an excellent grip even when the horse becomes wet with sweat. Tradition may also dictate what you use, especially in the show ring. But in some events, utility is a much higher priority.

Romal reins are closed, rounded, braided rawhide reins with an extension that has a flat leather quirt or popper at the end.

There are three basic types of reins. Split reins, roping or single reins, and romal reins. Split reins are two separate reins, a left and right. Both English and western riders use split reins. A roping or single rein is one continuous rein that attaches to each side of the bit. They're commonly used by barrel racers, ropers, endurance riders and others who want to eliminate the interference of excess rein length, and who need to eliminate the risk of a rein falling to the ground and being stepped on if accidentally dropped. English riders accomplish the same thing on hunters by buckling their split reins together.

Romal reins are the traditional closed, round, braided rawhide reins which connect to a romal, a braided extension that has a flat leather quirt or popper at the end. Romal reins grew out of the vaquero style of riding. When working cattle at speed, where a dropped rein could result in a serious or fatal injury, the closed romal reins provide another measure of safety. Romal reins are often used in the show ring, particularly on the West Coast and in reined cowhorse events. When used properly, they encourage the rider to keep the horse centered between the reins and flexed at the poll. To work well in romal reins, a horse must be extremely responsive to a neck rein. The forward portion of the reins are held in one hand to guide the horse, while the romal end is held in the other hand and is used to encourage speed or obedience.

"BITS ARE NO SUBSTITUTE FOR TRAINING."

5

Fundamental Principles of Bitting

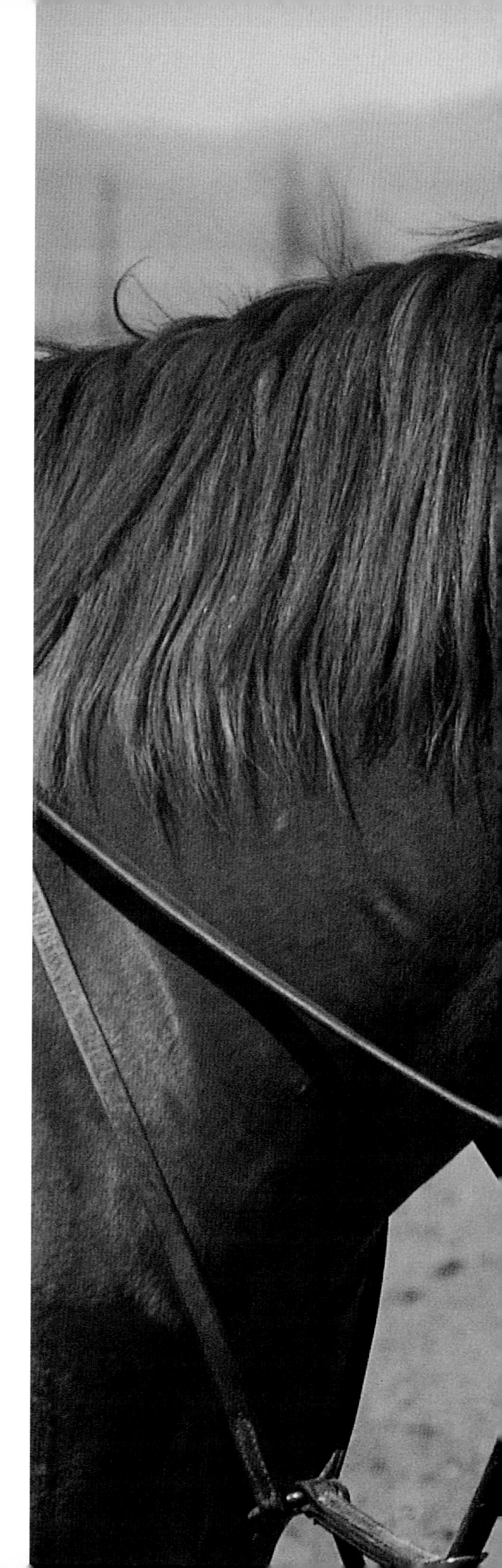

An oft repeated quote from a bitmaker goes something like this: "For every bit that I make for the mouth of a horse, I make 100 for the head of a man."

Horses are extremely adaptable. If they weren't so accepting of human whims, there wouldn't be nearly as many bits on the market today. The power of any bit lies in your understanding and ability to use it. Horsemanship always takes precedence over hardware. Many of the innovations bitmakers and horsemen come up with are practical. They make sense from a mechanical and horsemanship standpoint. Others are simply gimmicks. By understanding what you need to accomplish, and learning the basic principles of bitting, you will be able to recognize the difference between design changes done for marketing purposes and those that truly enhance horsemanship.

Further, if you do your job as a trainer and rider, the specific bit you choose may not be nearly as important as the way in which you use it. Winning horses are often sold to new owners who use different bits than the ones the horses were used to — and the horses keep right on winning. It's not because of — or in spite of — the new bit, but because the horses are well-trained and adaptable and have capable riders.

THE GOLDEN RULE

To the horse, good communication is simple communication. The first step is to allow the horse to accept the bit without fear. The second is to teach the horse to give to pressure without resistance. The third is to translate that pressure into a signal or language the horse understands.

A horse's natural instinct is to resist or escape from strange or scary things: fight or flight. Accepting a bit is

(overleaf) Kick Dee Bar is relaxed and happy with his bit.

not an inborn trait. Some horses are terrified the first time their heads are restrained by bridle and bit. They may run or buck or fight or freeze up. So the rider's first bitting task is to eliminate any fear.

For this reason many trainers choose large, smooth-mouth snaffles when first introducing horses to the bit. The mild design gives horses less reason to worry and more incentive to pick up the bit, hold it, and play with it. This experimentation is important. The horse becomes relaxed and accepting of the bridle. During this get-acquainted period, some trainers will leave the horse bridled for extended periods with a reinless bit, allowing the horse to eat, drink, and relax with it in his mouth, until the bit is largely ignored.

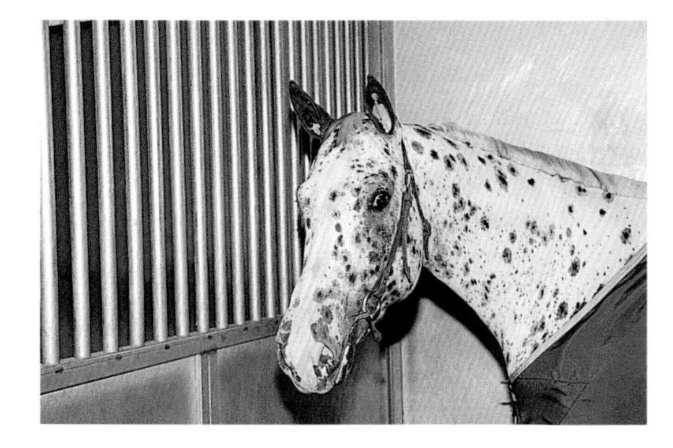

Getting used to his first bit in the familiar surroundings of his stall, this colt learns to accept the bit as a normal addition to his daily life.

Imagine the problems you could create, however, if that first bitting experience were with a severe mouthpiece. A first encounter with a harsh bit could instill fear and distrust, sabotaging the horse's training from the very beginning. Everything you do in the initial stages of bitting should work toward establishing a clear and comfortable way to communicate with your horse. That's why the horse should learn to flex at the poll and yield its head to rein pressure before you get into the saddle.

PRESSURE AND RELEASE

Many people think that horses are naturally inclined to stop or yield to pressure when the reins are pulled. This simply isn't true. Ask anyone who has ridden a runaway! Despite centuries of domestication, horses don't intuitively know what riders want when the reins are pulled. Horses have to be taught that the reins and bit provide signals that show them what to do. Through training, the signals are refined and habits are established.

With direct reining, the leading rein tips the nose in the direction of turn.

It all begins with a basic concept: teaching the horse through pressure and release. Starting with direct rein pressure, the horse's head is pulled in the direction we want it to go. When the horse responds correctly, the rein pressure is released. Through repetition, the horse learns to seek a position of relief. It is the reward for complying to the pull. We like to think of this process in terms of asking and thanking the horse for its response. To be successful, timing is everything. The promptness of the release is more important than the strength of the pull. Only when you stop pulling does the horse know that it is right. Most horses quickly learn to seek that zone of freedom.

If we are slow to release the pressure for a correct response, we effectively teach the horse that the signal has no meaning. Not only is it confusing, in a sense you punish the horse for doing what you requested. Excessive or prolonged pressure dulls the horse's responses to the bit. No matter what the horse does, your reaction is unchanged. The horse has no way of associating that what it did was right. There is no incentive to give to the rein pressure because there is no reward for doing so. Soon the horse begins to ignore the rein signals. No bit in the world can make up for a rider's bad hands.

(left) The colt must learn to yield to rein pressure. As soon as he yields, the pressure is released to reward him for the proper response.

(right) Because the horse has been taught to give to pressure, the rider can pick up the reins and direct the horse's movement in reverse.

Poor timing creates an unresponsive horse. Such a rider may think the horse is simply dull-mouthed. Pulling harder on the reins or stepping up in the severity of bits will only escalate the bitting war. The relationship is simple: You must improve the timing of your own responses in order for your horse to improve its responses.

UNDERSTANDING REIN AIDS

There are several rein aids you should be familiar with. In two-handed reining, the leading or opening rein is an exaggerated (not necessarily hard) sideways pull out to the side away from the neck. It's like opening a door with little or no backward pull. It guides the nose in the direction you want the horse to turn. It is sometimes called plow reining.

A direct rein is similar, but the rider's hand remains closer to the horse's neck and incorporates some backward pull. The pressure establishes the direction of turn and also helps shift the horse's weight rearward. It also establishes a degree of poll flexion.

Many trainers use the term direct rein for any type of left/right rein signals. In other words, a pull on the left rein signals the horse to turn left; right rein pressure signals the horse to turn right. They don't differentiate between opening or direct reins.

An indirect rein is a supporting or stabilizing rein. Pressure is applied to the rein opposite the direction of turn. For example, in a left turn, pressure is applied to the right rein; in a right turn, pressure is applied to the left rein. An indirect rein helps control the arc or degree of the turn, and, depending on how the rider positions his hands, influences poll flexion and the distribution of the horse's weight.

The neck rein is actually a cue rather than a guiding force. The horse learns to interpret a rein laid against his neck as a signal to move in the opposite direction. Applied too strongly, or on an untrained horse, a neck rein can have the unwanted effect of tipping and tilting the horse's face away from the desired direction of turn. A horse learns to respond to the neck rein through skillfully timed indirect and direct rein aids. The transitional phase between direct reining and indirect reining, where the two reins are used together in an exaggerated manner, is sometimes called "squaw reining."

PROPER BRIDLING

Horses learn to accept and carry bits by wearing them. To instill good habits, it's important to make the first and every bridling experience pleasant. Be considerate in the way you handle the horse's head and ears. Take special care when inserting and removing the bit not to bump or injure the teeth or mouth.

Tradition says that we should bridle the horse from the left side, also called the near side. However, it's probably a good idea to teach the horse to be bridled from both sides. That way, if you're ever in tight quarters, you can still get the job done.

GROUND WORK

By riding age, most horses are used to having their faces and ears touched. They've worn halters and been led and longed. From ground work, horses usually associate the command "whoa" with stopping, and having their heads pulled with changes in direction. All these things build a foundation for training under saddle. Many trainers take ground work a step farther. They teach the horse about pressure and release, gaining control of the horse's steering before the animal is ever ridden.

BITTING UP

One technique, known as "bitting up," involves restraining the horse's head by attaching the reins from the bit to a surcingle or saddle — or even to the horse's own tail. Bitting up teaches the horse that it has the power to relieve the pressure on its mouth by giving to the bit. The horse finds a comfortable position by bending its neck to the side or by flexing at the poll. It learns to respect the action of the bridle without a fight or the interference of a human. An advantage of tying the horse's head to its tail is that the animal is less inclined to yank on itself and will generally not pull hard enough to cause any neck injuries.

When bitting up, the reins can be shortened on one side then the other to get the animal to yield left and right. The reins can then be taken up equally on both sides to encourage the horse to tuck its nose in toward its chest. Considerate horsemen gradually increase the time and tension on the reins so the horse's muscles have a chance to strengthen and adapt. That way the horse can maintain the position required to keep the pressure off its mouth.

a) Balance the bit on the first two fingers of your left hand and hold it directly in front of the horse's mouth. Hold the headstall crown in your right hand, positioning it just in front of, or slightly to the right of the horse's face.

b) Insert your left thumb into the interdental space to encourage the horse to open its mouth. Gently guide the bit into the horse' mouth using your left hand while pulling the headstall smoothly over the ears with your right hand. Take care to keep your fingers out of harm's way, and don't let the bit bump the horse's teeth. Use your little finger to guide the chin strap beneath the lower lip into the chin groove. Take care not to crumple or bend the ears as you put on the headstall. Associating ear discomfort with bridling could make the horse difficult to bridle in the future. Finally, adjust the headstall so that the bit and all the parts fit comfortably.

(opposite) In neck reining the horse learns to interprest a rein laid against his neck as a signal to move in the opposite direction.

Tying a rein to one side teaches the horse to yield in that direction.

Never leave the horse unsupervised with the reins tied back — not even for a minute. Occasionally, horses will panic when they find themselves restrained. Keep a pocket knife handy, in case your horse gets into a bind and you need to cut the reins. Some trainers use bailing twine for these early bitting sessions to spare the reins in case of trouble.

Many trainers routinely longe horses or work them at liberty in a round pen while bitted up. Motion can break down resistance to the bridle and soften a horse's responses. If a longe line is attached directly to the snaffle, connect the line to both bit rings rather than just the inside ring. This will distribute pressure to both sides of the bit, much as there would be if the horse was being ridden. It will also keep the bit from being pulled through the mouth. Another option is to attach the longe line to a halter or cavesson and use side reins to position the head.

There are several advantages to using side reins attached to the saddle or a bitting harness: 1) they prevent the horse from throwing its head; 2) accustom the horse to the restraint of the reins; 3) keep the bit from moving too much in the mouth; 4) encourage the horse to find comfortable, light contact with the bit; and 5) provide the trainer with a means for adjusting the horse's head to the desired position.

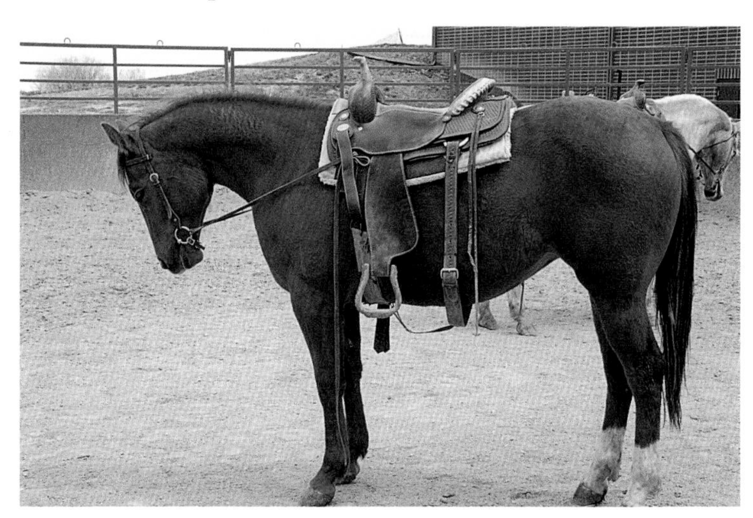

Tying the reins to the D-rings of the saddle and leaving the horse at liberty teaches him to yield to the bit by flexing at the poll. Remember to never leave a bitted-up horse unattended.

Motion can help break down resistance to the bridle and soften a horse's responses.

The horse may be longed with driving lines attached to the bit or with a single longe line attached directly to the bit.

GROUND DRIVING

Ground driving gives the handler an opportunity to teach the horse to turn, stop and back up through direct contact with the mouth. The horse learns to respond to the bit without the distraction of the rider's weight and legs. The handler develops a feel for the horse's sensitivity. The horse gains a sense of the person's touch on the reins.

There are several different ground driving techniques. Some trainers drive their horses from a center position as an extension of their longeing or round-pen work. Others drive their horses directly from behind (or just slightly off to one side) as though the horse were pulling a cart.

Driving techniques are best learned from experts. Safety considerations are paramount. The sheer length of the driving lines provides the risk of entanglement for both horse and handler. The driver must stay close enough to the horse to maintain good bit and voice contact, yet far enough back from the hindquarters to avoid being kicked. Passing the lines from the bit through rings on a surcingle or the stirrups of a saddle will help keep them off the ground, and may help prevent them from getting crossed or stepped on. It's also important to maintain adequate tension on the lines to keep them from sagging.

For ground driving, snaffle bits are recommended. They provide better independent directional control than most leverage bits and are also more forgiving. Before you attempt ground driving, be sure the horse is thoroughly familiar with the bit, understands and responds to the command "whoa,"

Ground driving gives the handler an opportunity to teach the horse to turn, stop and back up through direct contact with the mouth.

and has been thoroughly desensitized to ropes and things flopping or bumping against its body, legs, feet and tail. The desensitization process is sometimes called "sacking out". It's a vital stage prior to ground driving. Because, no matter how careful you are, there may be a time when a driving line drops down a leg or slips beneath a tail. You'll need your wits — and your horse's too — to prevent a wreck.

WEIGHT, LEG CUES AND MOVEMENT

Inexperienced riders often make the mistake of relying almost exclusively on the reins for direction and control. But the bridle provides only a fraction of your steering and control. Until you develop good control of your seat and legs, you will probably be less than satisfied with your horse's response to the bit. By recognizing that this is not a bitting problem, you'll be far ahead of the game. Learning to use your weight, body position and legs to direct the horse along the path you establish with your reins takes practice. However, your seat, legs and hands are inseparable when it comes to promoting lightness or "feel" in the bridle. We'll talk about this more in the chapter on developing soft hands.

The three elements which the rider must learn to control are: 1) the speed or pace of the horse, 2) the direction in which it travels, and 3) the frame in which the horse carries itself. Speed and frame will depend upon the the horse's job. Consider the two extremes: A racehorse runs with its weight on its forehand and leans into the bit. The western pleasure horse moves with balance and collection and yields to the bit. The racehorse's center of gravity is far forward. The western pleasure horse's center of gravity is to the rear.

In many western disciplines, the horse needs to be collected and psychologically (if not physically) "on the bit." Even though the reins are slack, the horse is ready to respond to changes in direction and speed with the lightest of cues.

In yielding to the rider's hand, the horse should not merely arch its neck, but rather should flex at the poll. The basis of poll flexion is a relaxed lower jaw. The head should give to rein pressure like it's attached to the neck on a loose spring. When the reins are pulled, the horse responds by bringing its nose in toward its chest. If the horse's lower jaw is not relaxed, there will almost always be resistance to the bit.

Constant equal pressure on both reins can give the horse something to brace against. The problem isn't the bit, but how the rider uses it. Intermittent pressure on the reins will almost always produce better results than a hard, steady tug — regardless of whether the horse is being asked to stop, back or turn.

Collection is a term that will come up time and again in riding, training and bitting theory. Collection is a state of balance and readiness, whereby the bulk of the horse's weight is shifted off the forehand. The hindquarters are the driving force. From the rider's seat, it's like trying to move both ends toward the middle. Typically the horse flexes at the poll, rounds its back and engages its hindquarters. The horse is said to be light in the forehand, which usually means light in the bridle as well.

A FINAL POINT

No matter what the discipline, the goal in bitting is to use the least amount of pressure necessary to achieve the best result possible. Bits are no substitute for training. The use of severe or gimmicky bits might be thought of as an attempt to shift the responsibility from the rider to the horse. The rider expects the horse to react to the mechanism of the bit rather than teaching it to respond in an educated way to reasonable requests made by the hands on the reins.

"TRUE SNAFFLES DON'T MULTIPLY THE FORCE OF THE RIDER'S PULL."

6

Snaffle Bits — The Horseman's Most Versatile Tool

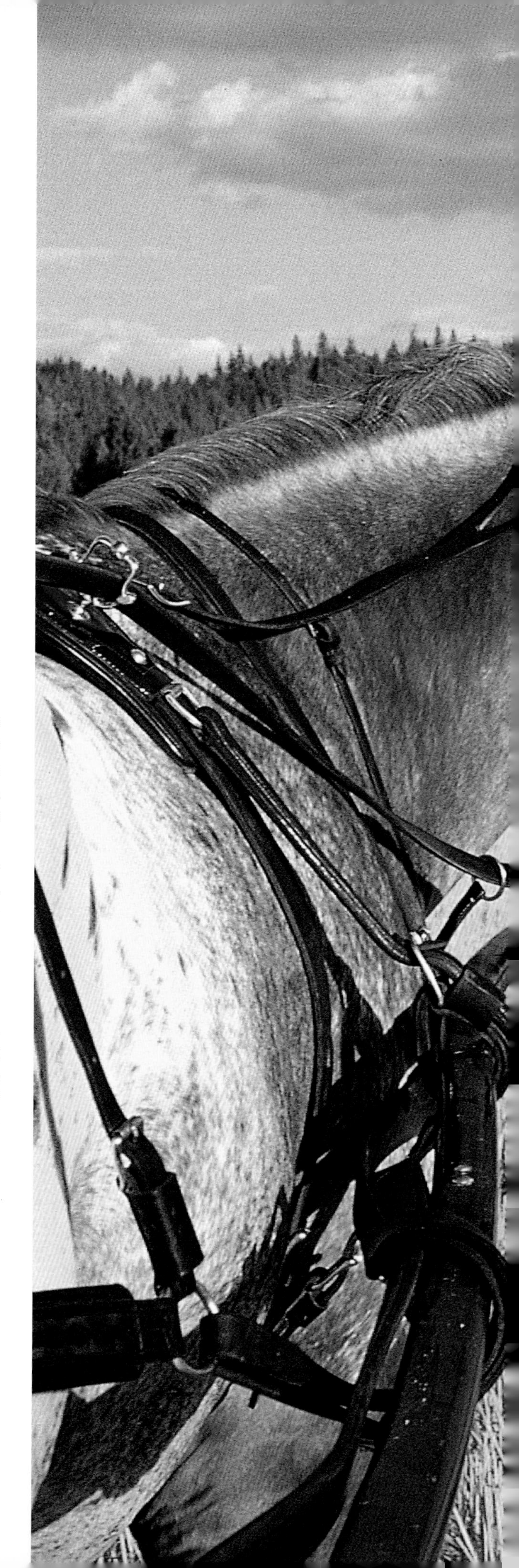

The snaffle bit is the most universal tool in the horseman's handybox. English and western riders across all disciplines utilize snaffle bits for training, competition and pleasure riding. Almost all horses will be ridden in a snaffle bit at some time in their lives — even if it's not the bit in which they're destined to remain.

The beauty of the snaffle bit lies in its simplicity and versatility. There's little technology to get in the way. It's a direct contact bit: it's like having a conversation with someone in the same room. You need the listener's attention, but your voice isn't amplified in any way.

RECOGNIZING A "TRUE" SNAFFLE

Some trainers refer to snaffles as any bit with a broken mouthpiece. However, we define a "true snaffle" as a bit that provides a direct signal from the rider's hand to the horse's mouth. There are no shanks, so neither the line of pull nor the force of that pull is altered or amplified. Snaffle bits actually come in a variety of mouthpieces: smooth, solid, twisted wire, rubber, jointed, double and triple linked, and so on. What really determines whether a bit is a true snaffle is the type and attachment of the cheekpieces to the mouthpiece. When all the slack is taken from the reins, you should see a straight line, or nearly so, from the corner of the horse's mouth to the rider's hand. That's a snaffle.

Typically, the cheekpieces in true snaffles will be rings of some sort. They may be flat or round, oval or circular, fixed or loose. Some snaffle bits are identified by the shape of their rings, such as O-ring or D-ring. You'll also hear horsemen identify the bit by its mouthpiece, such as smooth-mouthed or twisted-wire, or by a specific design feature it incorporates, such as egg-butt. The bit may also

(overleaf) ***For driving horses, whether for competition or pleasure, the direct pull action of a snaffle bit is desired. Either a single-jointed or double-jointed mouthpiece may be employed, though many driving competitors prefer two joints, such as a half-cheek Dr. Bristol.***

When the slack is taken up the reins should form a straight line from the snaffle bit rings to the rider's hands.

be identified by how it attaches to the cheeks: loose-ring or fixed ring. However, as with other bits, you can get virtually any mouthpiece in combination with any cheekpiece. Perhaps the most common snaffle bit features a mouthpiece with smooth bars (or cannons) with a single joint in the middle which is attached to O-shaped rings that run through the butt of the mouthpiece: the simple O-ring snaffle.

HOW SNAFFLES WORK

Snaffle bits are most commonly used with two hands on the reins. Imagine steering a bicycle. You pull on the left handlebar when you want to turn left, and keep a light hold on the right handlebar to steady the turn. That light pressure on the opposite side keeps you from over-steering. Operating the reins with a snaffle bit is a lot like that. The side you pull on hardest is known as the direct rein, while the opposite side is the supporting or indirect rein.

The snaffle is so widely accepted as a two-handed training bit that even in major western performance events, such as National Snaffle Bit Association western pleasure futurities and the National Reined Cow Horse Association Snaffle Bit Futurity, riders are expected to show with both hands on the reins.

With the snaffle, this rider can easily school his horse in a counterarc. His right rein moves the horse in a circle to the right while he keeps the horse's nose tipped to the left with the left rein.

However, by utilizing the snaffle bit effectively, western trainers refine their signals to such a degree that their horses learn to respond to a neck rein. This is done through directional cues, in combination with reinforcing leg and rein signals. As the horses advance, trainers make the transition to one-handed riding while continuing to ride in a snaffle bit. To help in this transition, the reins may be crossed and held across the span of the hands, or laced through the fingers, so the rider is still able to guide with each rein independently when necessary. This preserves the utility of a snaffle bit.

For most purposes, snaffles work best when used with unequal, intermittent pressure. A light tugging action on one rein prompts the horse to yield its face in the direction of the pull, while a see-saw, bumping action encourages vertical flexion.

Snaffle bits tend to be least effective when a rider pulls with hard, equal, steady pressure on both reins. That even, constant pressure makes it easier for horses to brace against the mouthpiece, especially when the bit is smooth and mild. In the case of a broken mouthpiece, extremely strong, equal pressure on both reins can collapse the cannons of the bit, causing the joint to peak in the mouth, contacting the palate.

Even when the reins are used independently, a snaffle bit acts on both sides of the horse's face. That's part of its beauty. There is direct pressure on the corner of the mouth on the side that's being pulled. There is additional pressure on the opposite cheek as the outside ring comes into contact with the face. In effect, the ring pushes the horse's face in the direction of the turn. This is sometimes called the "pull-through" effect.

RINGS

The pull-through effect is just one reason why rings can have a profound bearing on a snaffle bit's utility. The size, shape and design of the rings will either concentrate or disperse pressure in a given area.

Standard snaffle rings are 3½ to 4 inches in diameter. Although you can also find them larger and smaller, the standard dimensions seem to meet most training and show needs. They are large enough to prevent the rings from being pulled through the horse's mouth, but not so large as to make the bit heavy, cumbersome or cause them to get in the way of sensitive facial features.

The diameter and quality of the ring stock will affect the bit's weight and strength. On cheaply constructed snaffles it's not unusual to see bent rings — in fairness, it's not necessarily a result of poor horsemanship, or inadequate training of the horse, but rather the poor workmanship of the bit.

As a general rule, the larger the rings, the greater the area over which the pressure (caused by the pull-through effect) will be distributed. Also, an increase in the size of the cheek rings increases the signal you provide to the horse. Think of the ring as a ferris wheel. The rein starts at the

The diameter of the rings have a great effect on the function of the bit. The larger the rings, the greater the pull-through effect and the greater the signal to the horse.

The bent rings on this egg-butt snaffle indicate that cheap materials were used in its construction.

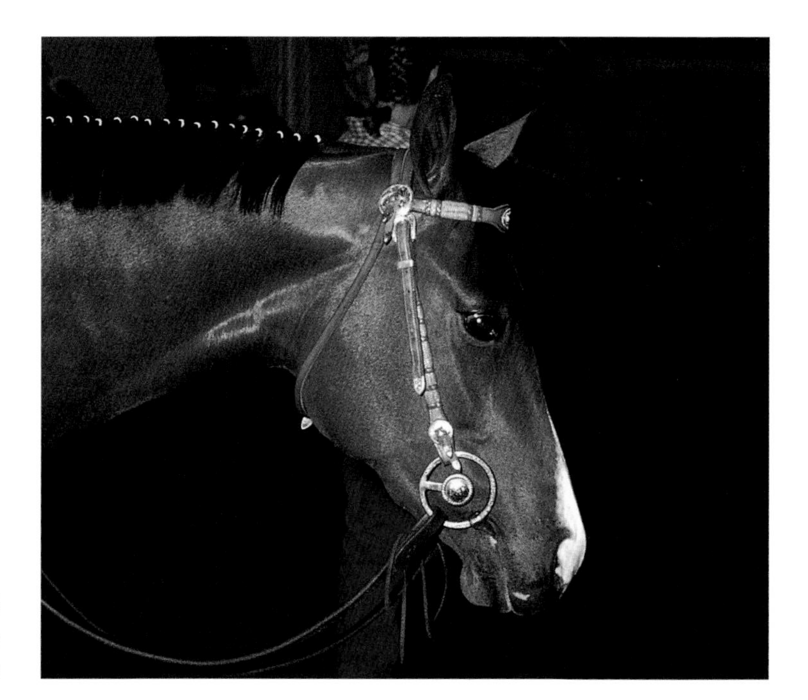

The conchos on this bit are attached by metal arms which, due to their position, limit the rotation of the rein around the ring. The result is a decreasing of the bit's signal.

bottom and moves up into a position of contact when the rider pulls the rein. The larger the ring, the more distance the rein must travel before the mouthpiece is engaged. As the rein moves up the ring, the horse gets a subtle cue that the rider is about to take a hold of its mouth.

The shape of the ring has an influence on the signal for the same reason. Oval rings, such as used with many egg-butt snaffles, or D-shaped rings reduce the distance between a neutral rein position and contact. Thus there is less signal. The same theory holds true when decorative conchos are added to show snaffles. If the conchos are suspended in the ring by metal arms in such a way as to limit the rein rotation around its perimeter, that minor modification can give the showman a subtle advantage. When he takes hold of his snaffle bit entry, he gets more immediate contact.

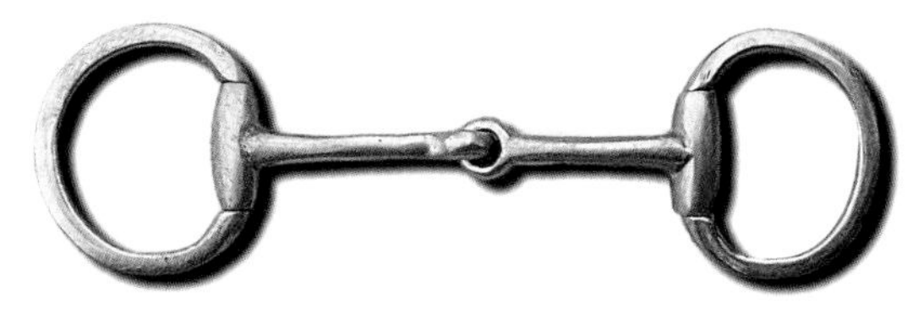

The cylinders at each end of the mouthpiece of this egg-butt snaffle reduce the chances of pinching the lips.

The amount of signal in a snaffle also depends on the way the cheeks are constructed and how they attach to the mouthpiece. The egg-butt, Don Dodge and D-ring snaffles all have cylinder butts. A metal tube connects the mouthpiece to the cheek rings. Some fit together with smooth, closely coupled hinges at the corners of the mouthpiece. Others are welded so the butt of the mouthpiece and the cylinder form a single, fixed unit and the rings connect to the cylinder at the top and bottom.

The D-ring applies added pressure to the side of the horse's face and reduces the chances that the bit will be pulled through the mouth. D-ring snaffles are popular for use on race horses.

In an egg-butt snaffle, the end of the mouthpiece enlarges into a tall, wide oval or egg-shaped cylinder (hence its name) through which the rings are inserted. This design is popular because it eliminates joints directly at the corners of the mouth which could pinch the lips.

The D-ring snaffle, with its straight cylinders, affords another advantage. Its well-defined corners (the straight line of the D) make it less likely to be pulled through the horse's mouth. That's why D-rings are so popular for racing and colt breaking. Cylinders also tend to allow less play between the mouthpiece and the rings than a loose ring snaffle. They may encourage a quiet mouth. But less play also means less signal. Cylinders will concentrate the pull in a vertical line along the sides of the mouth near the first cheek teeth, top and bottom. An O-ring snaffle tends to concentrate the pressure at the corners of the mouth.

A loose ring snaffle, in which the rings run through holes in the ends of the mouthpiece, affords the maximum signal. The rings revolve freely and tend to rotate slightly when the reins are picked up but before the bit engages. However, it's important to check loose ring snaffles for excess wear or play. If they're too loose, the horse's lips can be pinched between the ring and mouthpiece.

On bits made with flattened rings rather than from round stock, the square edges can sheer away the metal within the cylinder from the constant rotation and make the corners of the mouthpiece sharp. If you find this, dispose of the bit or use bit guards to prevent mouth injury.

The play afforded in a loose ring snaffle may also help to pacify a timid or tense horse. The natural movement encourages the horse to mouth the bit, which has the added benefit of increasing salivation and relaxing the jaw.

THE DON DODGE SNAFFLE

Among reiners and cutters, the "Don Dodge" snaffle has become a mainstay for training young horses. Yet, this AQHA Hall of Fame horseman explains that his namesake bit came about purely by accident.

Dodge's family had purchased a number of full-cheeked army surplus cavalry snaffles to use on their dude string horses. Between outings, the horses remained bridled and saddled, and were left tied to a manger. The problem was,

This Greg Darnall Don Dodge snaffle has become a mainstay among horse trainers for starting colts.

the horses were forever bending the cheeks of their bits by catching them on the feeder. To solve the problem, they simply sawed off the ends of the cheeks, leaving short stubs at the butt of the mouthpiece.

One day, Dodge happened to use one of these bits on a green colt he was starting. What he discovered was that the horse seemed to be more responsive than when Dodge was using a regular O-ring bit. He studied the bit and figured out that the butt of the modified snaffle was concentrating pressure along a more sensitive area of the horse's cheek. Because he was getting a better response, he started using the bit on all his young horses.

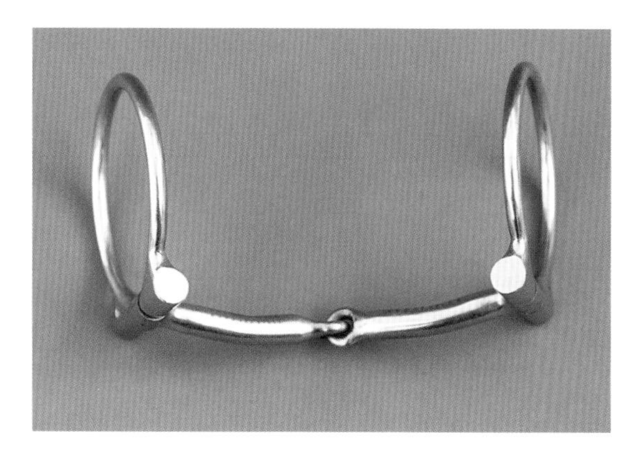

In the Don Dodge snaffle the rings are offset to the outside of the cylinder butt. The offset rings cause the pressure to be concentrated where the cylinder contacts the horse's cheeks, and tend to increase the horse's responsiveness.

As often happens with successful trainers, other riders saw the results Dodge was getting with his young horses and wanted a snaffle bit just like his. Dodge gave the tip to bitmaker Greg Darnall. Darnall started making a refined version of it and has since sold thousands upon thousands of Don Dodge snaffles. Other bit manufacturers have since jumped on the bandwagon and there are a number of copycat snaffles being marketed under different names.

The Don Dodge snaffle has several features that have made it especially popular with western performance trainers. It is technically a D-ring because the mouthpiece is joined to the rings with a straight cylinder. But the rings are actually rounder than a conventional D-ring, which preserves signal because the rein has greater circumference to travel before engaging the bit than it would on a standard racing D.

However, what really distinguishes the Don Dodge snaffle from other cylinder butt bits is that the rings are offset to the outside of the cylinder. This minor change concentrates bit pressure along the ridge where the cylinder contacts the horse's face via the pull-through effect. Hence, pressure is focused at the corners of the mouth and above and below the mouthpiece on the cheeks in line with the first cheek teeth. The Don Dodge snaffle, in effect, increases the intensity of the rein cues by isolating pressure on a more sensitive area of the horse's face and mouth. In turn, those offset rings lessen the pressure applied to the horse's cheeks by the rings.

CHEEKED SNAFFLES

Some snaffles have prongs or "cheeks" attached to the rings. "Full-cheek" snaffles have prongs both above and below the mouthpiece, while half-cheek snaffles have rings either above, or more commonly, below the mouthpiece. Like the D-ring or cylinder type snaffles, the cheeks encourage the horse to turn in the desired direction by putting pressure on the corners of the mouth and sides of the face. The cheeks also prevent the bit from being pulled through the mouth.

The upper prong on the full cheeked bit may be held in place by a strap or keeper on the headstall. This makes the bit more stable and prevents the mouthpiece from turning in the horse's mouth.

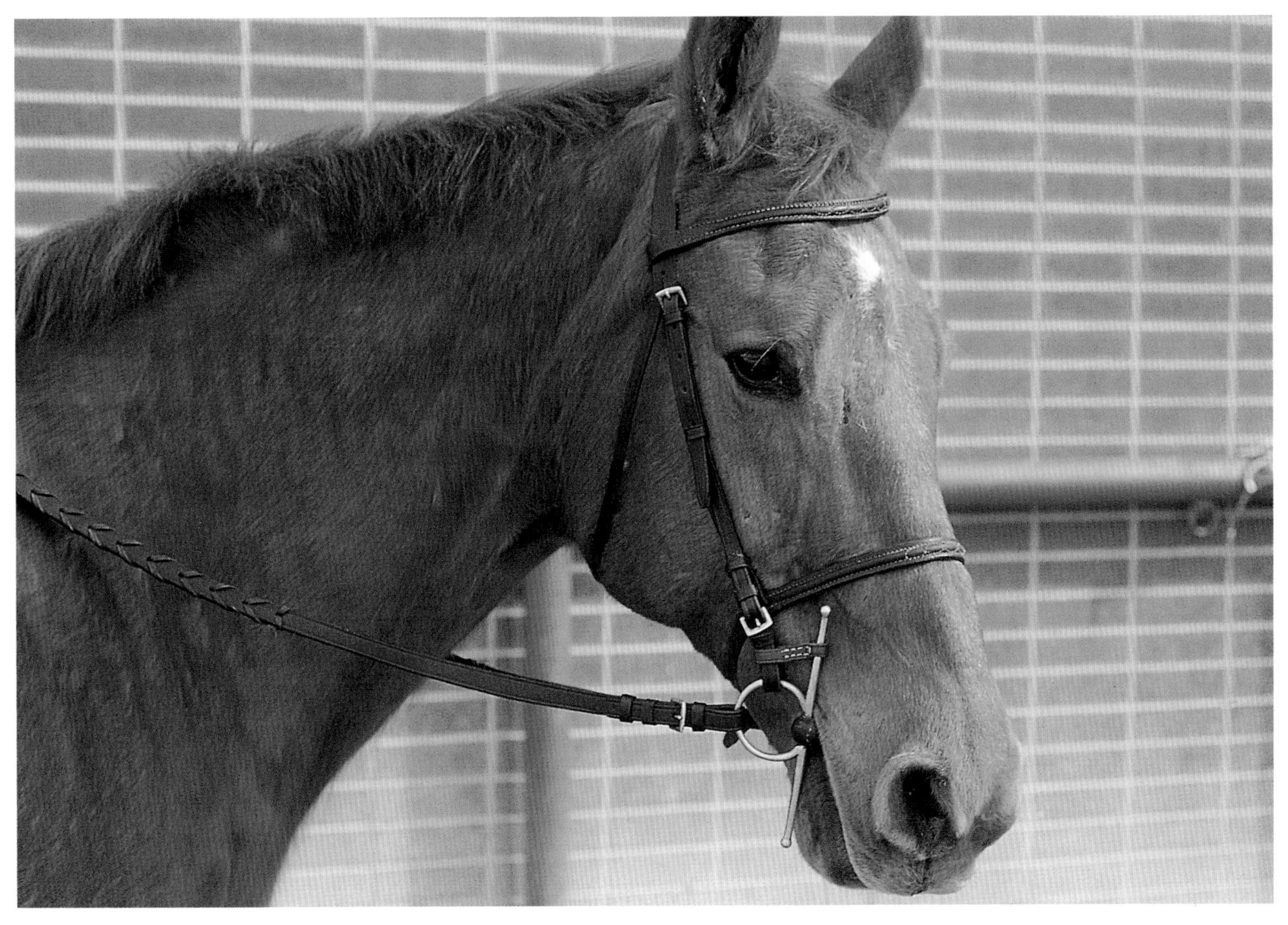

If the prongs on the full-cheeked snaffle are left free, they may rotate and injure the horse's face. A keeper which attaches the upper prong to the headstall is a useful safety feature when using the full-cheeked snaffle.

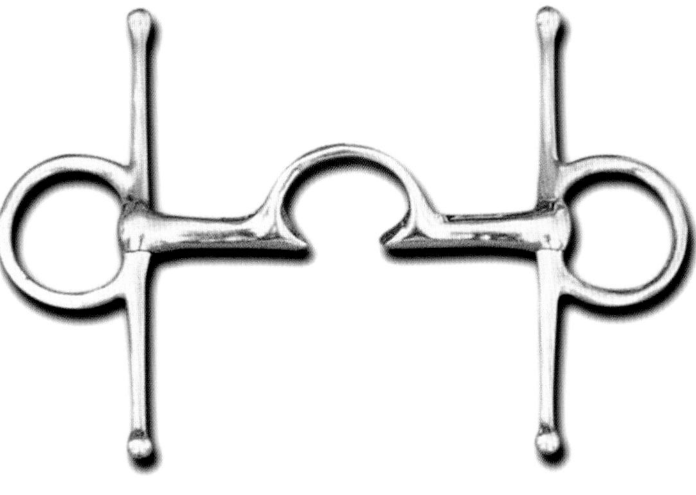

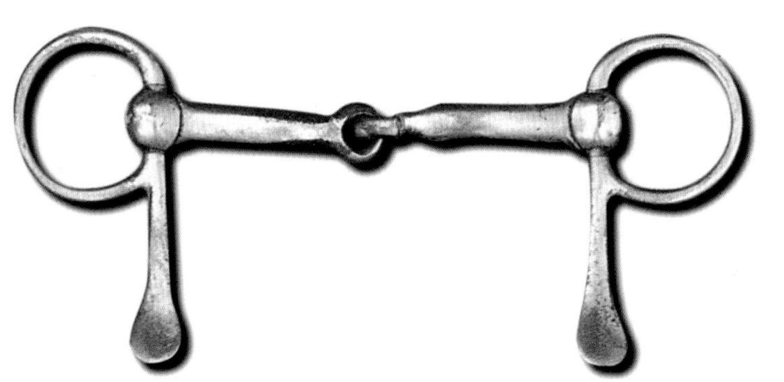

Full-cheek (upper left) and half-cheek (left) snaffle bits.

This young horse is already learning to guide on a loose neck rein, but the lack of bar contact does nothing to promote poll flexion.

PRINCIPLES OF USE

While snaffle bits are designed to be used with two hands on the reins, the way in which they are used can produce an infinite variety of responses, which is why the tool is so practical.

Both the horse's head position and the rider's hand position directly affect how the bit makes contact with the mouth. For example, when young horses are first ridden, they commonly respond to the bit by jutting out their noses, raising their heads and stiffening their necks. They often lean into the bridle. In this nose out, head-up posture, the horse is in front of the bit and the snaffle's primary contact is with the horse's tongue and the corners of its mouth. There is very little bar contact.

As the horse learns to yield to the pressure on its mouth by flexing at the poll, lowering its head and neck and assuming a more vertical face position, the action of the bit shifts. There continues to be pressure on the tongue, but less contact with the corners of the mouth. Instead more pressure is transferred to the bars.

The rider can also have a direct influence on this by where he positions his hands. The higher the hands are held, the greater the contact with lips and tongue, and the less with the bars of the mouth. The lower the hand position, the less contact with the corners of the mouth and the more with the bars.

Consider the extremes: The jockey rides with his hands placed high and forward on the horse's neck. The snaffle

has virtually no contact with the bars. Almost all the directional control comes through contact with the tongue and corners of the mouth. The western pleasure trainer, on the other hand, might lower his hands below the horse's withers to get more contact with the bars of the horse's mouth, and, subsequently, more vertical flexion.

Many performance horse trainers use snaffle bits in conjunction with running martingales. The martingale helps maintain bit contact on the bars and discourages a horse from raising its head and jutting out its nose to escape the bit's action. Adjusted too tightly though, a martingale can turn a snaffle bit's action into curb-like pressure.

True snaffles don't multiply the force of the rider's pull the way a leverage bit will. They're generally more forgiving. For this reason they are considered to be especially good tools for training young horses. Because there are no shanks, the mouthpiece plays a crucial role in the snaffle's potential severity. A snaffle with a wide, smooth mouthpiece may permit the rider to take a firm hold of a young horse's face and physically show it where to go without causing pain or fear. We'll talk about mouthpieces more in the next chapter.

As the horse learns to yield to the pressure on its mouth by flexing at the poll, lowering its head and neck and assuming a more vertical face position more pressure is transferred to the bars.

"HORSES AND PEOPLE HAVE DIFFERENT TASTES, PREFERENCES AND EXPECTATIONS."

7

Mouthpieces

The more you ride and train, the more you will come to appreciate both the subtle and dramatic differences a given mouthpiece can make in a horse's responses and performance. Horses and people have different tastes, preferences and expectations. To accomodate them, bitmakers will continue to tinker with mouthpiece design. Both snaffle and curb bits feature virtually any type of mouthpiece imaginable. However, it's important to remember that it is the cheeks, chin strap and accessories in combination with the mouthpiece that determine a bit's overall effect. We will examine how all the pieces work together in a later chapter, but the mouthpiece is a good place to begin any discussion of bit mechanics because it is the feature that comes into direct contact with the horse's most sensitive steering components.

Many trainers use a series of mouthpieces to take their horses from the breaking through the finishing stages of training. For instance, a green horse may be introduced to the bit using a soft, rubber-coated mouthpiece, then advance to a smooth, jointed metal mouthpiece to establish steering and control, and then be put into a solid, ported metal mouthpiece to promote finesse later on. Each mouthpiece plays a unique role in the horse's athletic development.

For any mouthpiece to be effective, it should have three characteristics: It should fit well and be comfortable for the horse to carry. It should promote respect and attention but not fear. It should allow the rider to communicate signals clearly.

When you consider your needs, be open-minded. Many Native Americans used little more than a rawhide thong to guide their mounts. Standard issue for U.S. Cavalry mounts was a stiff, low port, metal mouthpiece set into a

(overleaf) Mouthpieces come in an endless variety and vary greatly in their severity.

pretty hefty set of shanks. For some, less is more. For others, more is less.

While we don't condone the use of barbed, brutal or otherwise ill-designed implements, it's important to recognize that there are mouthpieces which may appear severe (and would be in the wrong hands, on the wrong horse, or adjusted or used in the wrong way) but have a practical place under the right conditions. However, if you're ever in doubt about a bit's humaneness, don't use it — and don't be afraid to ask your trainer not to use it.

There are many excellent mouthpieces that are so practical that they have gained almost universal acceptance. The smooth, single-jointed mouthpiece is just such a tool. It can be found in a wide variety of snaffle, curb, gag and combination bits.

FITTING THE MOUTHPIECE

Mouthpieces are measured two ways — the length from cheek to cheek, and the diameter of the bit bars. While the length or width of the mouthpiece is important for fit, the diameter of the stock helps determine severity as well as general comfort. The width of the mouthpiece should accommodate the width of the mouth. If it is too short, the mouthpiece will pinch the corners of the lips against the cheek teeth. Too long, and the bit can shift sideways, sawing on the lips, tongue and bars. An oversized mouth-

(below) As the diameter of the bit bars increases, the severity of the bit decreases, because the pressure is distributed over a greater area.

(right) The mouthpiece should be fitted carefully. It must not be too short, nor extend more than one-half inch beyond the corners of the lips on either side.

piece also puts the port or joint out of position and makes it ineffective and possibly painful. An excessively long, jointed mouthpiece can also contact the roof of the mouth when the reins are pulled.

Standard mouthpieces range in size from 4 to 6 inches, usually in quarter-inch increments. The average light horse uses a 4½-inch to 5½-inch mouthpiece, with a 5-inch bit being the most common size that retailers stock. Pony bits are usually 3½ to 4 inches. However, if a standard bit doesn't fit right, a custom bitmaker can make one to order for any size mouth that you're trying to accommodate.

As a rule, the mouthpiece should not project more than a half-inch beyond the corners of the lips on either side. Bit guards can fit inside the rings or shanks to protect the cheeks and give a better fit to an oversized bit. But it's best to opt for bits that fit correctly to begin with.

MOUTHPIECE DIAMETER

Generally, the larger the diameter of the bit bars, the milder the bit because pressure is transferred over a greater surface area. For example, a half-inch mouthpiece is gentler than a three-eighths inch mouthpiece (provided all other features are equal). However, if the stock has been twisted, squared or altered in some way, diameter alone is not a true test of the mouthpiece's severity.

To gauge the diameter, the bit bars or cannons are measured one inch in from the cheek pieces. Standard mouthpieces are three-eighths inch thick. Many show organizations prohibit bits that are smaller than 5/16 inch in diameter, and utilize bit gauges at the entry gates to make sure riders are using "legal" equipment.

Although larger diameter bits may be inherently milder, some horses may be uncomfortable carrying a thick mouthpiece. The position of the canine teeth, the size of the horse's tongue, and even the shape of the palate may play a role in the horse's relative ease with a given size. Some mouthpieces are designed to be thick over the bar space for gentleness, but are thinner in the center to reduce the amount of metal the horse must contend with. Thinner mouthpieces concentrate the pressure on a smaller area and may encourage trained horses to be more responsive. The message carries a little more urgency and is harder to ignore. With a young horse just learning bit signals, however, a thicker mouthpiece is probably a kinder choice because it can be used with a firm pull with less risk of causing pain or fear.

Horses with short or shallow mouths (from the front of the muzzle to the corners of the mouth) tend to carry the bit forward in the mouth. This is where the tongue rides the highest and where there is less room between tongue and palate and more space between the top of the tongue and the mouth bars. In a forward position, the bit is more likely to contact the palate. Also in a short-mouthed horse, there is typically less room between the canine (bridle) teeth and the cheek teeth.

These factors might help explain why some horsemen assert that short-mouthed horses are more sensitive than deep-mouthed ones. But it has little to do with nerve receptors and more to do with the points of contact the bit makes with the mouth. Shallow-mouthed horses will likely be more comfortable with a thinner mouthpiece and a port that provides some tongue relief. Horses with deep mouths tend to hold the bit farther back in their mouths where the tongue sits lower in the jaw space and the palate is more concave. Some horses, especially Thoroughbred types, have relatively narrow, sharp bars which are easily damaged by pressure. Such horses require thicker and/or softer mouthpieces than horses with thicker bars.

POSITIONING THE MOUTHPIECE

The position where the bit fits in the bar space is also important. However, this adjustment is going to vary from horse to horse and bit to bit. For example, a popular rule-of-thumb for adjusting snaffles has been to use the one or two-wrinkle rule. That means adjusting the bit so the lips are pulled just enough to make the horse "smile," so that one or two wrinkles can be seen just behind the butt of the mouthpiece. Yet this gives the horse no relief at the corners of his mouth.

The "two-wrinkle rule" has been in common usage, both in English and Western riding disciplines, for many years. This practice, however, doesn't give the horse the opportunity to obtain relief by giving to the bit.

Many western trainers prefer instead to hang the bit loosely at first, thus encouraging the horse to pick it up and carry it. The rider then adjusts the headstall to position the bit where the horse has determined it to be most comfortable.

When adjusting the headstall and bit, let common sense be your guide. If the bit is too loose, you're in danger of the mouthpiece contacting the canine teeth or incisors, particularly on a snaffle. You're also at risk of having the horse get its tongue over the mouthpiece. If it's too tight, it will pinch the lips and the horse may gape its mouth or show other signs of discomfort. It may be necessary for you to experiment by raising and lowering the bit until it looks and feels right to you and the horse. Also, if your horse's bars are bruised, hypersensitive or insensitive, the bit may be raised or lowered so it does not rest on the sore or numb spots.

SHAPE & DESIGN

Mouthpieces made from smooth, round stock are the gentlest on the horse's mouth because there are no sharp or rough edges to bite into sensitive tissue. Twisted metal mouthpieces, on the other hand, are often quite severe. The shape of the bar stock and the number of twists also make a difference in the severity of twisted-wire mouthpieces. Square and triangular shaped bar stock produce a series of more sharply defined ridges when the metal is turned than does round stock. Also, the slower the twist, meaning the fewer the spirals, the less surface area over which the force of the pull will be dispersed. In other words, pressure is concentrated along a smaller number of points where the ridges make contact with tongue, bars and lips. Such bits tend to be more severe. Round stock when twisted also makes a bumpy surface but without nearly the bite of square or triangular bar stock.

There's some debate as to whether single or double twisted-wire mouthpieces are more severe. On the one hand, the double wire distributes pull over a greater surface area of the mouth. On the other, it provides the potential for pinching tongue and lips between the cannons of the

The single twisted wire mouthpiece (upper bit) exerts concentrated pressure. It is considered fairly severe. The double twisted wire mouthpiece (lower bit) distributes the pull, but the offset joints effectively increase both the pressure on the tongue and the chance of pinching the tongue.

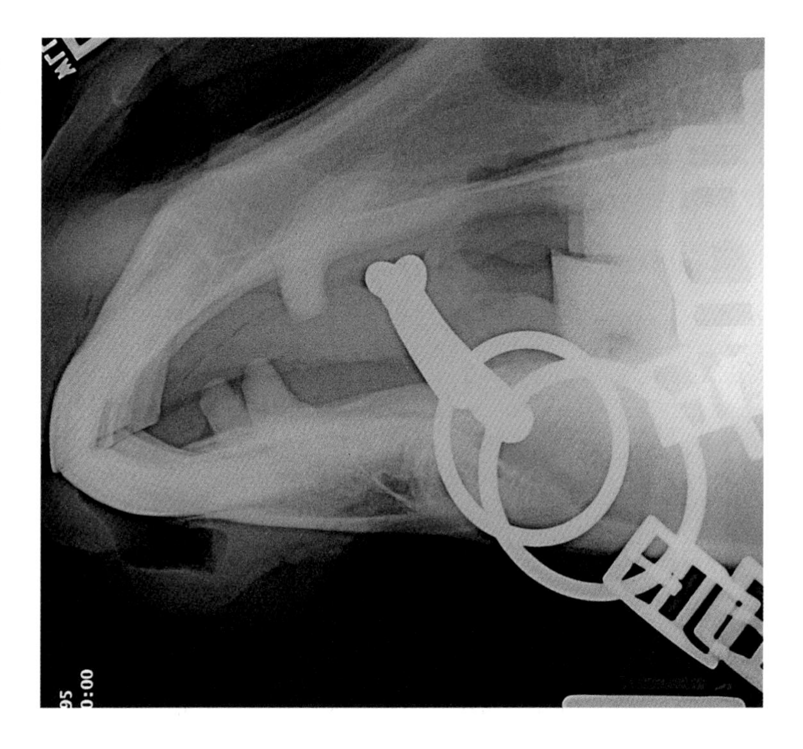

An x-ray shows how the broken mouthpiece on a snaffle bit fits between the canine and grinder teeth, and forms a roof over the tongue when the reins are pulled.

dual mouthpieces. Another word of caution: Twisted wire mouthpieces, if not handled judiciously, can saw right through the horse's mouth in pretty short order. The thinner the stock, the easier it is to slice through the tissue. The same holds true for some of the bicycle and other chain-linked mouthpieces. It doesn't take much friction to cause damage. And as with any severe bit, some hard-mouthed horses might respond to them for a little while, but with prolonged use, you may find yourself in a no-win situation. Not only do you risk doing permanent damage, you've done nothing to solve your real problem. Brute force is rarely the answer. What you need is a better way to get compliance from your horse.

"BROKEN" MOUTHPIECES

When a mouthpiece is made up of two or more pieces, we call it a jointed or broken bit. One advantage of broken mouthpieces is that they allow a skilled rider to work on each side of the horse independently. They're excellent for getting lateral (side to side) control. For training purposes, broken-mouthed bits are usually used with two hands on the reins — regardless of whether the mouthpiece attaches to snaffle rings or shanks. When a rider pulls harder on one rein, the bit bar applies more pressure to the tongue, bar, lip and chin groove on that side.

Hard, equal pressure on both reins is generally not recommended. It may cause the bit to collapse and have a nutcracker-like effect on the horse's tongue and bars. Additionally, the center of the mouthpiece may contact the sensitive palate when it peaks.

One purpose of the joint is to form a roof over the tongue, which provides some relief from the pressure of the bit. This effect is enhanced when the cannons of the bit have been curved. The joint also changes the angle of pull. As the cannons collapse, pressure is transferred from the tongue to the bars and lips.

The number of joints and the shape of the cannons will have a direct bearing on the bit's action. Mouthpieces with a single joint apply pressure to the tongue and the outside of the mouth bars. The straighter the cannons, the sharper the action. Preferably, the cannons should have a slight curve or bend. The joint between them should also be moderately loose. If the joint is too loose, though, the bit can have very sharp action and may pinch the tongue. If the joint is too tight, the cannons will have very little freedom of movement. It will take more pull to get the independent lateral response that makes the jointed bit so practical.

Secondarily, a stiff mouthpiece isn't as inviting of a play toy for the horse. A horse that mouths the bit is more likely to be relaxed and to have a soft, wet mouth. However, if the horse is overzealous in his play habits or the rider desires a quieter mouth, a stiffer bit might be in order. A Billy Allen mouthpiece provides a good compromise. It is jointed in the middle, but the joint is covered with a cylinder or barrel. The cannons still have some lateral give — certainly more than a bar bit such as the gently curved mullen mouthpiece — but not as much as the single-jointed snaffle.

Some broken mouthpieces have more than one joint. The number and shape of the links will have a pronounced effect on where and how the pressure is distributed in the mouth. In three-piece bits (with two joints), the center link may be in the shape of a ring, a flat plate or a half moon. The center link creates more room for the tongue, but changes the angle at which the pressure is applied to the tongue, bars and corners of the lips. There is more pressure on the tongue and less leverage on the bars and lips.

The Billy Allen mouthpiece offers a unique function — the barrel covering the joint causes the mouthpiece to begin functioning as if it were solid after minimal flexion.

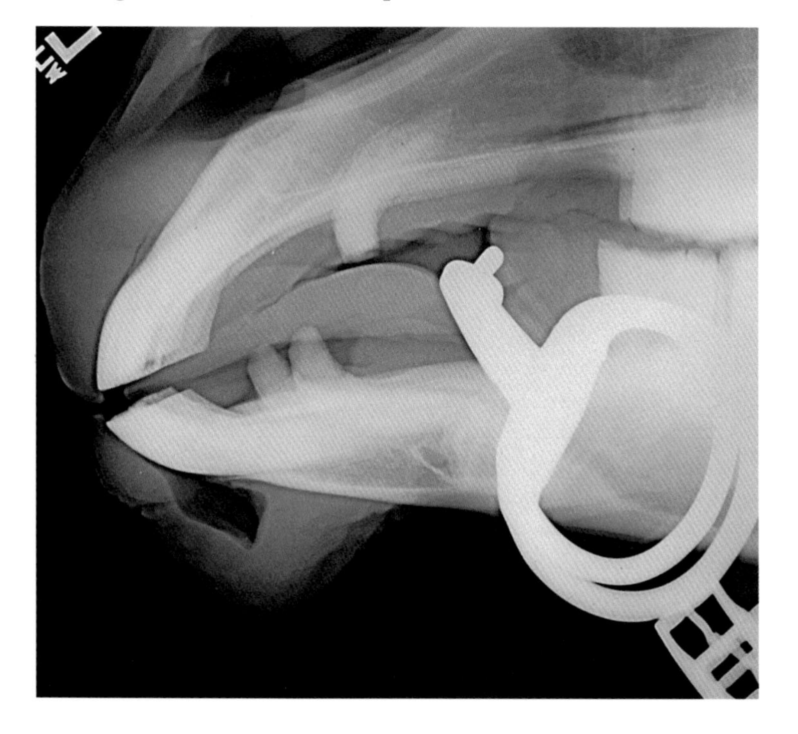

This x-ray shows a mouthpiece with a center link on a snaffle bit in a horse's mouth from a side view. Compare this with the single-jointed snaffle in the x-ray on the opposite page, to appreciate how the center link transfers pressure from the bars to the tongue.

The chain-type mouthpieces (upper bit) is less severe than the saw-tooth mouthpiece (lower bit), but both can cut tongues and bars.

The Dr. Bristol bit, for example, has a flat middle piece that presses on the horse's tongue while the cannons press mainly on the lips. When the reins are pulled, one edge of the plate presses on the tongue until the horse flexes its neck. By giving to the bit, the horse causes the plate to lie flat. In the French snaffle, the flat center link lies flat all the time, and so is inherently milder than the Dr. Bristol. A bit with a smoothly rounded crescent-shaped center link is gentler on the tongue than either the Dr. Bristol or the French snaffle.

Mouthpieces with more than two joints have little leverage action on the tongue, lips or bars, but rather exert direct pulling pressure on all three. Like a necklace, the more links in the mouthpiece, the more it conforms to the shape of the horse's mouth. Theoretically, this should make such bits mild if properly handled. The problem is that many of these chain type mouthpieces are made with extremely treacherous links. Bicycle chain or saw-teeth (sometimes called mule bits) aren't uncommon. When used two-handed in a see-saw fashion, they cut mouths. Add leverage to such a mouthpiece and you multiply the consequences. Little wonder they're prohibited in most shows.

Some jointed bits have two sets of cannons. Frequently, such as in the W-mouthed bit and the double twisted-wire bits, the two joints are off center, one to the left, the other to the right of the middle. When pressure is applied to such a bit, the space created for the tongue by the break in one mouthpiece is virtually cancelled out by the break in the other. These bits tend to be very severe because of the potential double pinching action on the tongue. They also place more pressure on the bars and lip corners than bits with a single mouthpiece. The mouthpiece that breaks to the left of center places more pressure on the right bars, and vice versa. The longer cannon has more leverage and amplifies the pressure on that side.

(below) Snaffle bits also come with a variety of solid mouthpieces. From top to bottom:
a) segunda - provides relief for the top of the tongue but presses into its sides; a severe mouthpiece.
b) low ported - provides minimal tongue relief.
c) straight bar - no tongue relief.

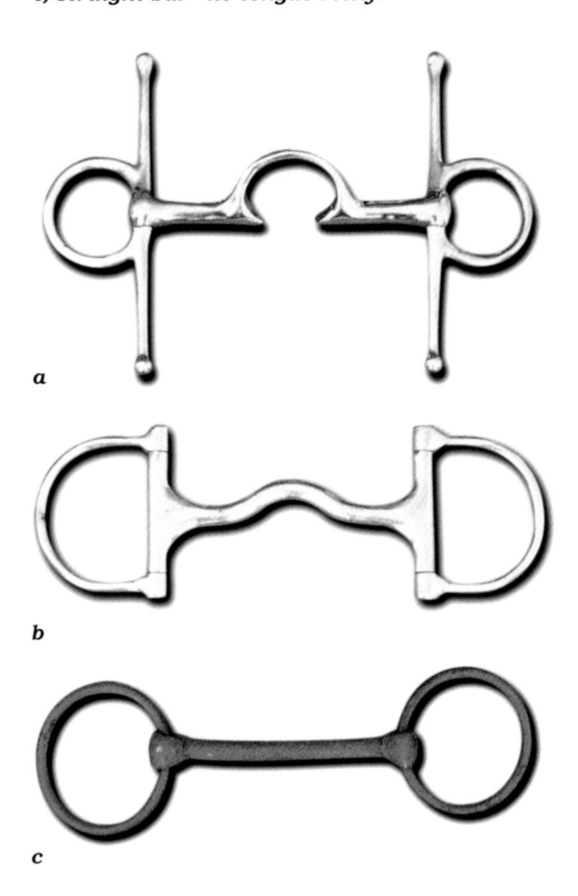

SOLID MOUTHPIECES

Solid mouthpieces come in many shapes and textures. They may be straight, curved or ported. To review from Chapter 4, the port is the upward rise (the upside down U) in the middle of the bit which provides space for the tongue and allows the bit bars to settle into place on the mouth bars.

Solid mouthpieces, by their construction, tend to act on the whole mouth (tongue, bars and lips on both sides), rather than on one side at a time as with broken mouthpieces. When used on snaffles (direct pulling bits), straight bar mouthpieces apply pressure to the tongue, bars and lips, with the tongue taking the brunt of the force. As the curve in the solid mouthpiece increases, pressure is taken off the tongue and is transferred to the lips and bars. A port in the mouthpiece, depending on the height and width, will take even more pressure off the tongue.

In leverage bits, solid mouthpieces are most practical as one-handed bits since a pull on one rein tends to have as much effect on one side as another.

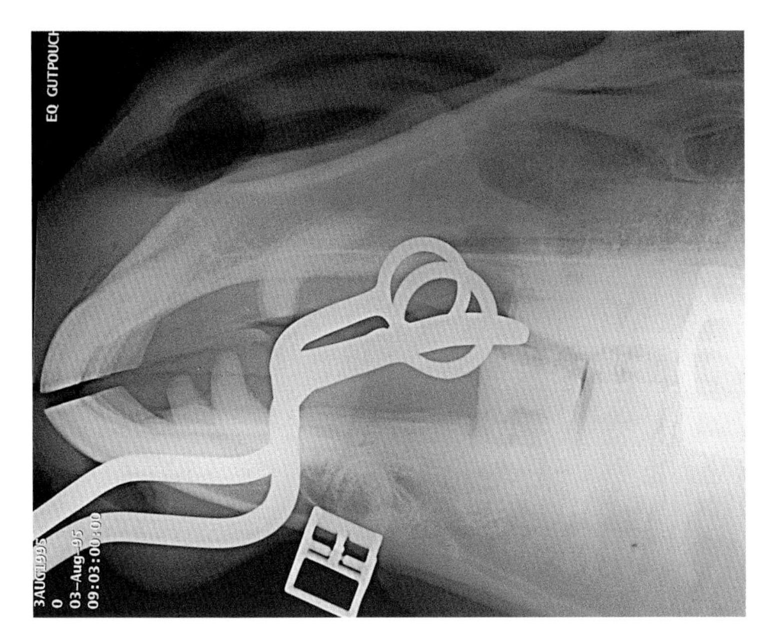

(left) This x-ray shows how a high port bit lies in a horse's mouth. There is tension on the reins, and the tip of the port is in contact with the palate.

PORT HEIGHT, SHAPE & ANGLE

When looking at mouthpiece design, consider again the features of the horse's mouth. The palate (roof) and the tongue are the most sensitive parts. While the bars and lips are less sensitive, they too provide good surfaces for contact and control. A good rule is to communicate with the horse through its tongue but place most of the pressure on its bars. But the bottom line is this: Choose the mouthpiece that will best accommodate the horse's physical features and produce the desired results.

A straight, solid mouthpiece can be severe because the tongue takes almost the full force of the pull. The mullen mouthpiece, with its gentle curve from one side to the other, still lies largely on the tongue and gives only a small margin of tongue relief. A hard jerk on the reins, especially with the multiplying effects of shanks, and a straight or mullen mouthpiece can easily cut the tongue.

In bits with ported mouthpieces, the bit bars should be sufficiently long before the rise of the port so the bit rests on the bars of the mouth. As a rule, the bars should be at least 7/8 of an inch on each side. If the port rises too soon, the bit will ride on the tongue rather than the bars.

For example, the "sweetwater" mouthpiece has short bars that rest on the gum bars with the central portion of the bit rising in a long, wide arc over the tongue. The low rise, with the mouthpiece usually angled somewhat forward in the cheeks, provides a good degree of tongue relief, but only if the bars on each corner are at least 7/8 of an inch long. Unfortunately, some bit builders fail to make this concession and begin the rise directly at the corners, which defeats the purpose of the bit. The low port mouthpiece, with a much narrower rise to the port than the sweetwater, has the potential to provide wider bar contact, but affords little tongue relief.

Many horsemen specify exactly how high they want the port to be. You'll hear the mouthpiece referred to as a 3/8 inch low port or a 1/2 inch low port. Medium port mouth-

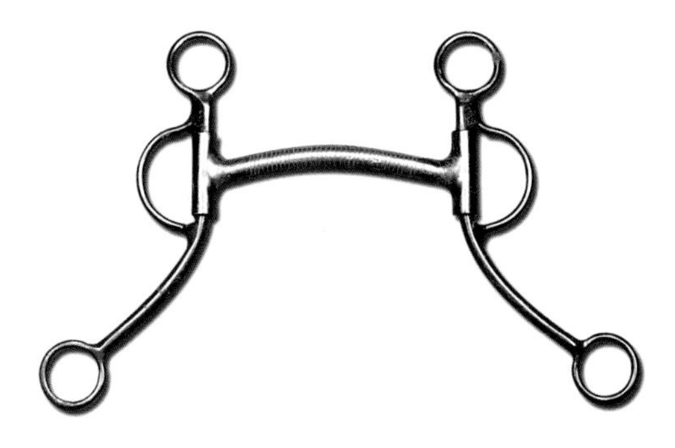

There exists a misconception that a bit with a mullen mouthpiece, such as this one, is gentle. However, such a bit affords very little tongue relief.

A sweetwater mouthpiece's design is only effective for tongue relief if the bars on either side of the port are long enough to rest on the gum bars.

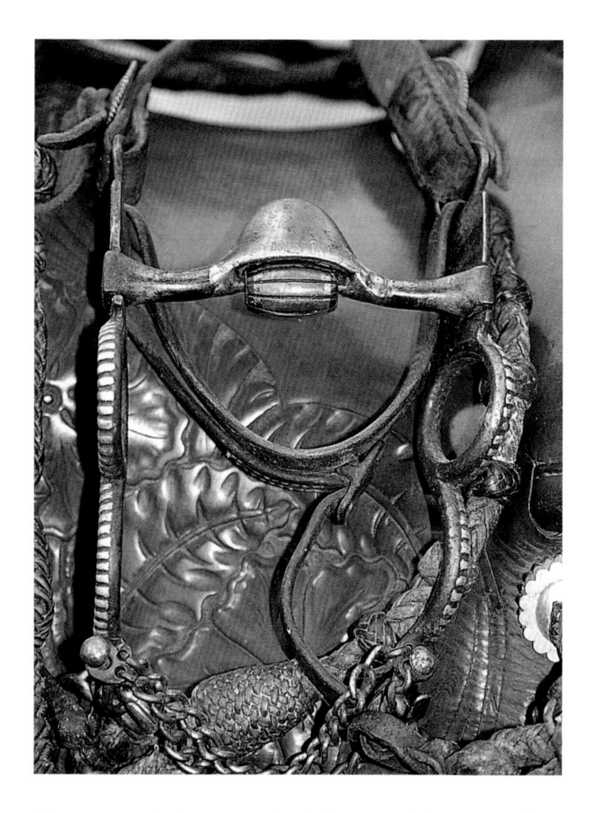

Some mouthpieces contact the palate because they have high ports or spades. Others, such as this Salinas mouthpiece (above), contact the palate because the roller and hood ride high on the tongue and fill the space between the tongue and the palate. The three spade bits (below) have spades which are designed to contact the palate. The tops of the spades are flattened and rolled back so that they do not dig into the roof of the mouth.

pieces, up to two inches in height, provide more tongue relief and are the least severe. In most horses, they're not yet high enough to make contact with the palate, but provide plenty of space for the tongue. A mouthpiece generally isn't considered to be a high port until it is two inches or above.

Port shape is also extremely important. A port which slopes gradually and smoothly upward from the bars of the mouthpiece gives gentler tongue relief than one of equal height but which joins the bars at a right angle. Sharply angled ports, and those with hard edges, points or corners, or with excessively narrow openings, may still provide relief for the central portion of the tongue but put pressure on the sides of the tongue. This is often the case with some U.S. mouthpieces and frog mouth bits. Bits with A-shaped ports (sometimes called "whoa bits") can also be severe. If the high A-shaped port is too wide at the base, it may come into contact with the cheek teeth.

If a bit's port is two inches or more in height, the apex may come into contact with the palate — depending, of course, on the shape of the horse's mouth. The higher the port, the greater the likelihood of palate pressure. Also keep in mind that there may be less space for a high port bit in the mouth of an older horse as the bite plane changes and the palate sinks closer to the tongue.

A mouthpiece designed to contact the palate is far gentler if the top of the port is flattened and rolled back. The curvature should begin where the port joins the bars of the mouthpiece. That way the port stays relatively flat against the palate even when the bit is fully engaged. A high port which is not rolled back will put severe pressure on the palate as it makes contact with the roof of the mouth. Too much rein tension on any bit which exerts palate

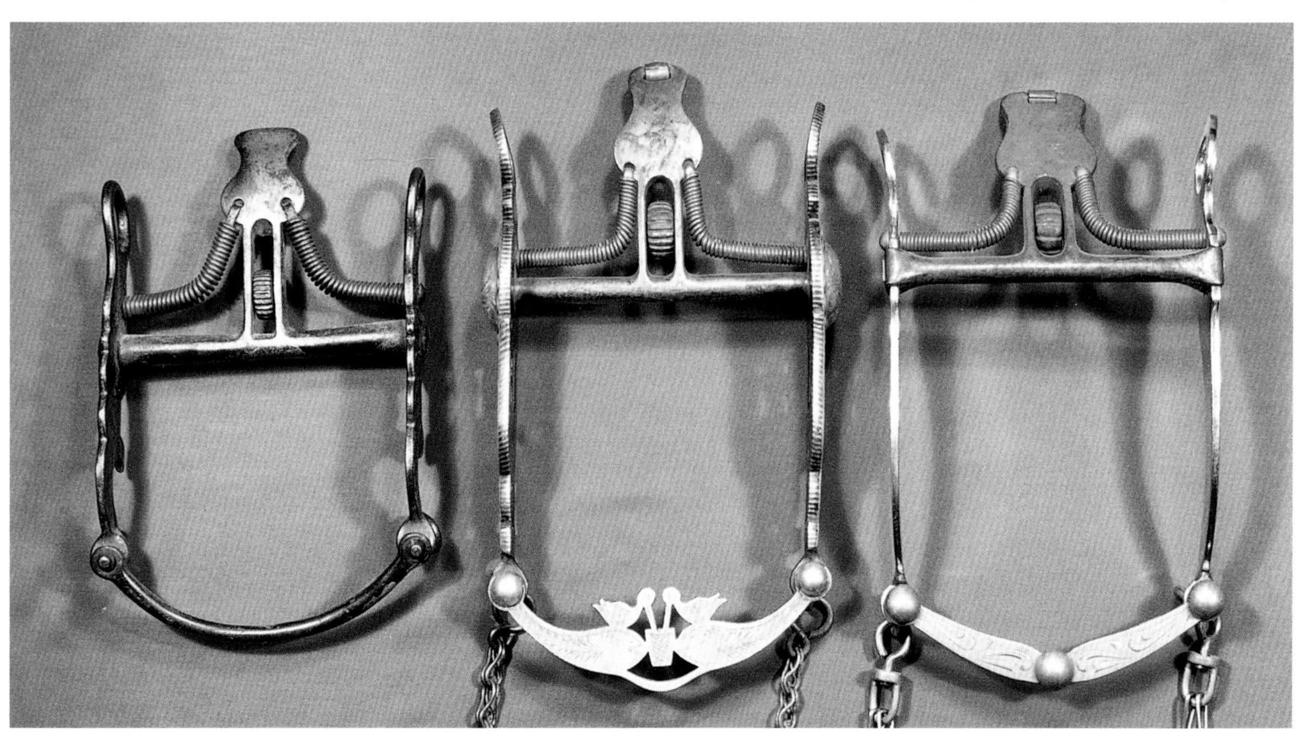

A standard correction bit. Such bits have loose cheeks as well as swivel mouthpieces, so there is a hinge at every joint in the bit.

pressure tends to pry the mouth open. When this happens, not only does the bit lose its function as a communication device, it can damage the palate. In most cathedral bits, the spoons are rolled back and, because they are so long, the apex cannot contact the palate. But these bits are capable of causing severe damage if the reins are jerked.

The way the curb strap is adjusted will have a profound influence on mouthpieces designed to exert palate pressure. If the curb strap is extremely tight, the port may not be able to contact the palate no matter how high it is because the curb strap prevents the bit from rotating in the mouth. Of course, the tight curb strap will also reduce the signal of the bit and increase the pressure on the tongue, bars and chin groove.

In swivel-ported mouthpieces, often called "correction" bits, there are joints on each side of the port where it joins the bit bars. The junction between the port and bars is usually at a right angle. Some correction bits even have additional joints within the port itself. Such mouthpieces are capable of exerting tremendous bar and tongue pressure particularly along the sides of the tongue as they collapse and capture the tongue and bars in a vise-like grip. Such mouthpieces are prohibited in most western performance classes.

This is the "polo" or Rutledge Roper mouthpiece.

Another type of mouthpiece is a wide, flat, thin-gauged bar that connects into cheek pieces that swivel. This is often referred to as a "polo" or Rutledge Roper mouthpiece. While the width disperses rein pressure over a greater area of the tongue, and the swivel cheeks are designed to keep the mouthpiece flat on the tongue's surface, the thin edges can bite into soft mouth tissue. Polo type mouthpieces are generally prohibited in western performance classes, but they are often less severe than many "legal" bits.

Most show associations restrict port height and also prohibit mouthpieces with features that protrude beneath the bit bars. Such bits are severe and have a detrimental impact on the tongue. Every organization has its own guidelines concerning mouthpieces so it's best to check the rule books. We'll discuss some of the reasons behind legal and illegal bits in a later chapter.

The bars of this frog-mouthed Santa Barbara curb bit have been wrapped in latex, to lessen the pressure on the horse's tongue and bars.

MATERIALS USED IN MOUTHPIECES

Mouthpieces are constructed of many different materials and combinations of materials. When sizing up a mouthpiece, consider whether its metal or material component will enhance the life, comfort or performance of the bit in the horse's mouth. Be forewarned. Many cheap bits are made of inexpensive alloys or are plated with metals that will chip or peel away with use. Avoid such bits.

Some riders choose to wrap their metal mouthpieces with latex in the early stages of training or for very soft-mouthed horses to protect the bars and tongues. Rubber and leather-covered mouthpieces are also available. They are gentle but should be disposed of if the material becomes cracked or worn to prevent pinched or cut tongues. Plastic and synthetic mouthpieces are also coming into greater acceptance, and may be especially useful for winter riding because they aren't as cold in the horse's mouth as metal. Despite the traditional prejudice against synthetic bits, alternate materials continue to be improved and may offer a practical bitting option in some situations.

For the bit to function comfortably, the horse's mouth should be wet rather than dry. Salivation is linked to the type of materials used in the mouthpiece as well as mouthpiece design. Aluminum, chrome-plated alloys, rubber and leather-covered mouthpieces are thought to produce dry mouths. Iron, steel and copper are said to promote wet mouths. Cold-rolled steel, sometimes called "sweet iron," is prone to rust. And while it may not be as attractive to look at as stainless steel, it is thought to stimulate salivation better than stainless steel because of its porous molecular structure.

Some horsemen assert that mouthpieces which combine two different metals are superior for saliva production and transfer signal better than those made from a single metal. In the western world, copper inlaid sweet iron or stainless steel mouthpieces are common. Copper is also incorporated into hoods (port coverings), rollers (crickets), danglers and keys. Copper, in fact, is the most popular metal incorporated into bits to promote wet mouths. It is seldom used in the rings or shanks because it is too soft. Copper mouthpieces usually have steel cores to keep the horse from wearing through them. However, there is no universal endorsement of copper. Some people feel that copper causes excessive salivation because of its nauseating (at least to some humans) taste.

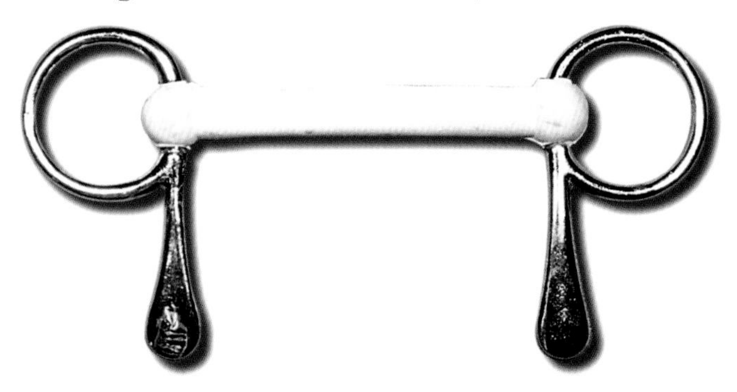

This straight-bar mouthpiece is covered with plastic, to protect the tongue and bars, but may cause a dry mouth.

The copper roller encourages the horse to play with the bit, while promoting salivation.

It's important to remember that bit chemistry is not the only thing involved in producing a wet mouth. In the horse, as in the human, a dry mouth may indicate anxiety, fear or stress. Such emotions cause adrenaline and other mediators to be released in preparation for fight or flight. Energy is diverted to the nerves and muscles for these reactions. Since saliva is not important to the fleeing horse — none is produced. So, when it comes to generating a wet mouth, the horse's mental state is probably more important than the type of metals used in the bit. A severe mouthpiece that causes the horse to worry or fret is unlikely to promote a wet mouth regardless of its chemical make-up.

It's also important to look at chemistry in terms of the processes used in the bit's construction and ornamentation. Some cosmetic techniques, such as bluing or blackening of the steel, require the use of chemicals that can be toxic to the horse if residues remain on the mouthpiece. Ornamentation is probably best left to the outer surfaces of working bits.

ROLLERS, CRICKETS AND TONGUE TOYS

Some mouthpieces incorporate rollers, commonly called "crickets." Others have danglers or keys in the center. The various types of rollers and tongue toys stimulate tongue movement and thus enhance salivation. They may also have a pacifying effect on nervous horses. While horse show judges generally prefer quiet mouths, only you can decide what makes the horse happy and more accepting of the bit.

"TO SELECT THE RIGHT CURB BIT, IT'S IMPORTANT TO UNDERSTAND LEVERAGE."

8

Leverage Bits — Putting Power in the Pull

When it comes to sheer, unbridled power, the horse clearly has an edge over man. And while thinking riders rarely rely on brute strength to get their way with horses, strategic use of pressure can be useful for getting and keeping the horse's attention. Leverage bits, also called "curb" bits, are tools which can give a rider a measurable mechanical advantage.

A curb bit operates on the same principle as a mechanic's wrench. It utilizes leverage to amplify the forces applied to it. The tool's effectiveness will depend on the skill of the user, but also in large measure on the way that it has been engineered. Handle length, weight, design, strength and composition all play a part in the suitability of a particular tool for a particular task. Hardware stores carry pipe wrenches, crescent wrenches, allen wrenches, monkey wrenches, pliers, and so on because they serve specific purposes. For the same reasons, tack manufacturers supply many different types of leverage bits.

While the analogy to the wrench may be startling, the similarities should be considered. Because while it may be true that a bit is only as severe as the hands that pull on it, design will have a tremendous impact on the bit's mechanical action on the horse's mouth, chin and poll. Some bits allow the rider to exert tremendous pressure with very little pull. Others require more muscle to produce the same effect. This is not necessarily bad. Consider that an 8-year-old girl has a lot less pulling power than her 35-year-old father. A bit with 8-inch shanks might give her just enough extra leverage to steer and stop her seasoned campaigner — with the horse's mouth no worse for the wear. Her 180-pound dad, on the other hand, might be wise to opt for a shorter-shanked bit, something that won't

(overleaf) When the action heats up, a leverage bit may provide the rider with a greater measure of control.

unduly amplify his strength — especially in his excitement to put on the brakes during the jackpot roping.

When selecting a leverage bit, it's important to ask yourself "How forgiving will this bit be?" Does it allow for errors in horsemanship without unduly punishing the animal? How sensitive or responsive is the horse to bit pressure? How far along is the horse in its training. And again, what kind of response do I want and expect?

UNDERSTANDING LEVERAGE

To select the right curb bit, it's important to understand the principles of leverage. The lever is one of the oldest and simplest machines known to man. It is an instrument that modifies or balances forces applied to two points as they turn about a third. A crowbar, a teeter-totter and a wheel barrow all use leverage principles.

Look at how a teeter-totter works. When the pivot point is directly in the center, the weight on each end must be equal for the see-saw to balance and for each child to have the same ability to move the other up and down. If one child is lighter than the other, the fulcrum can be repositioned so the smaller child sits at the long end of the teeter-totter while the heavier one sits at the short end. You must set the fulcrum at the point that balance is restored.

Now apply the concept to bits. Like the teeter-totter, there are basically only two components to the curb bit: the shanks (also called the cheeks) and the mouthpiece. The shanks are the arms of the lever and the mouthpiece acts as the fulcrum. The fulcrum is the pivot point between

Horsemen discovered ages ago that they could use leverage principles to their advantage. To understand leverage principles better consider the seesaw: When the fulcrum (pivot point) is in the middle, the weight must be equal on both sides to achieve balance. When the weights are unequal, the fulcrum can be shifted toward the heavy end, thus restoring balance. In shanked bits, the mouthpiece acts as the fulcrum. Moving the mouthpiece up toward the bridle rings and lengthening the lower shanks increases the rider's mechanical advantage. In other words, the longer the lower shanks are in relation to the upper shanke, the more pressure the rider can exert on the horse's mouth.

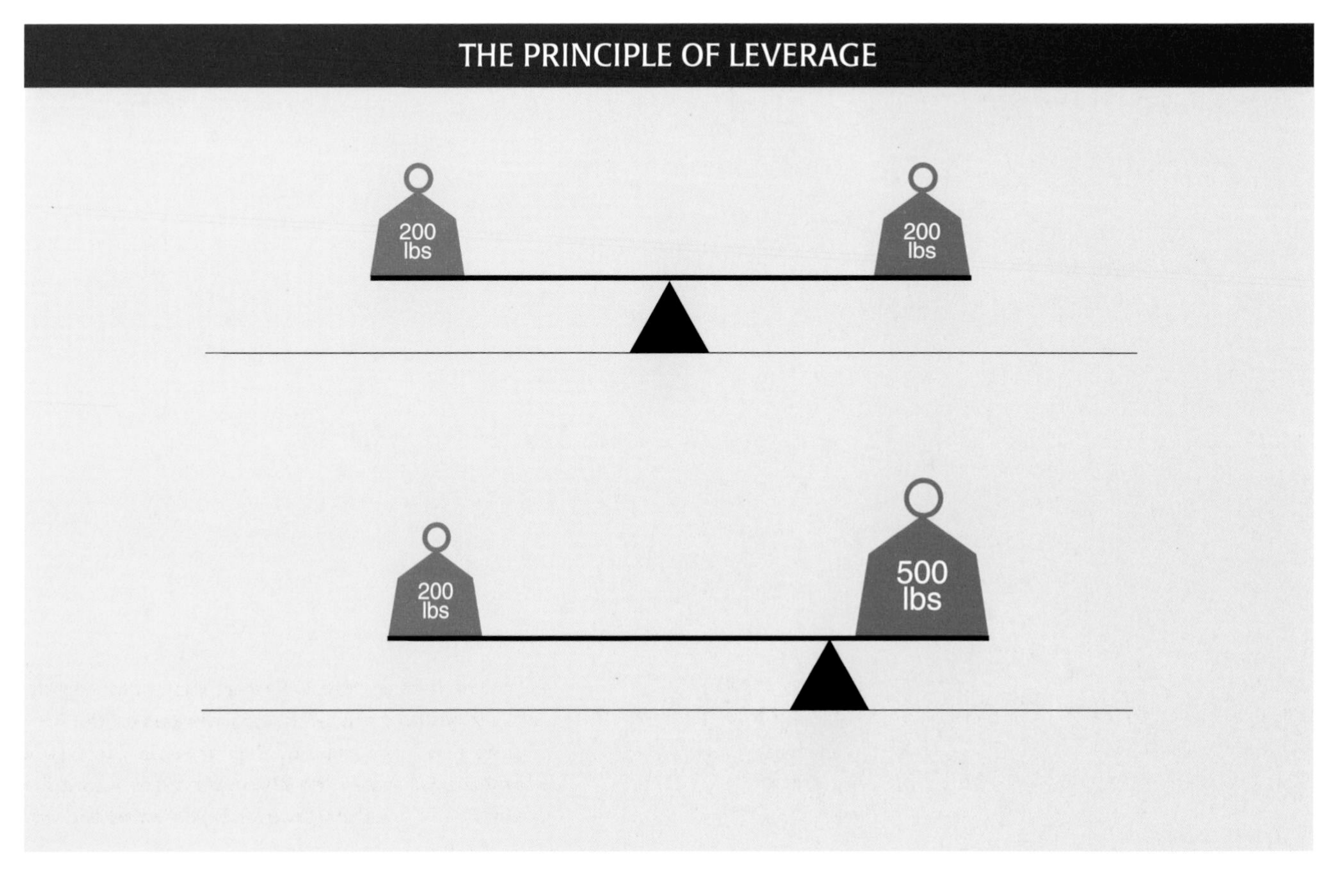

the load end and the handle or force end. In this case, the load is the horse's mouth or head. As with any simple lever, the longer the distance from the handle to the fulcrum, and the shorter the distance from the fulcrum to the load, the easier it is to shift the weight. In other words, it requires less effort to move the object because the lever multiplies the force applied.

BIT RATIOS

When evaluating bits for their relative leverage advantage (i.e. severity), we talk in terms of bit ratios. Like the see-saw, we move the fulcrum to suit our needs. Simply put, we compare the length of the cheeks (the portion of the bit from the headstall loop to the mouthpiece) to the length of the lower shanks (from rein ring to the mouthpiece). For example, in a curb bit, the upper shanks might be 1½ inches from the mouthpiece to the headstall ring, while the bottom shank might be 4½ inches from the rein ring to the mouthpiece. This bit, with a total shank length of 6 inches, would be said to have a 1:3 ratio. Similarly, a bit with 8-inch shanks, with 2 inches above the mouthpiece and 6 inches below it would have exactly the same leverage ratio, 1:3.

In the western horse industry, a bit with a 1 to 3 leverage ratio is considered a moderate bit. Shift that mouthpiece up an inch in an 8-inch shank (putting only an inch above it and 7 inches below) and you've multiplied the force substantially. It now has a 1:7 ratio. For

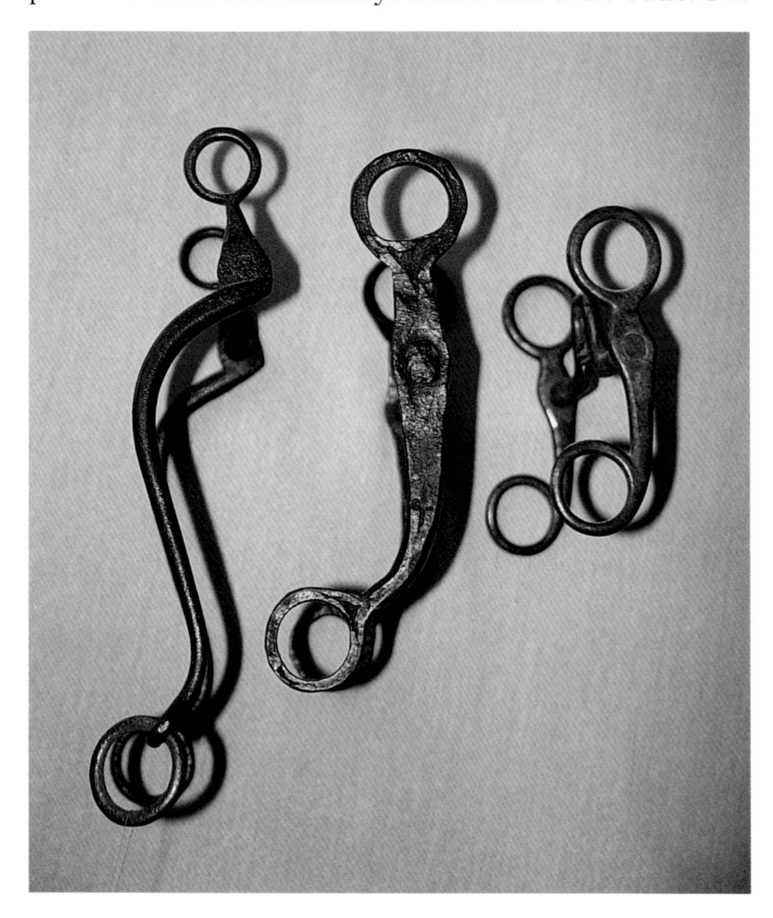

(left) The ratio of the length of the lower shanks to that of the upper shanks determines the bit's mechanical advantage. The middle bit has a standard 3:1 ratio; the bit on the right has a 2:1 ratio; the bit on the left, a walking horse bit, has a 5:1 ratio.

The ratio is determined only by the straight line distance from the mouthpiece to the cheek ring and the rein ring. A curve or S in the shank does not change the ratio.

This "elevator" bit is very mild, its 1:1 ratio giving some of the mechanical advantage back to the horse.

every one pound of pull you put into it, the horse feels seven pounds of pressure on its mouth, turning a moderate bit into a severe one.

By industry standards, bits with total cheek lengths of 4 to 6 inches are considered short-shanked bits. Eight to $8^1/_2$-inch cheeks are considered long. In fact, most horse show organizations restrict total cheek length to $8^1/_2$ inches maximum, because length is generally related to the severity of a bit. But as you now know, shank length doesn't tell the whole story. The ratio between the upper and lower cheeks, determined by where the mouthpiece is placed, is the real key. The lower the bit ratio, the less the force will be multiplied when the rider pulls on the reins.

Don't be deceived by the shape of the shank when trying to determine shank length. Six inches of steel curved into an S may actually equate to a 4-inch shank. It is the straight-line distance between the mouthpiece and the rein and headstall rings that determines shank length, not how many bends the metal takes.

One advantage of longer shanks is that the mouthpiece can be positioned to whatever leverage ratio suits the horse, yet leaves ample room for the lips when the curb strap is engaged. To prevent the corners of the mouth from being pinched between bit and curb strap when the reins are pulled, the upper shanks should be at least $1^1/_8$ to $1^1/_2$ inches long. Upper shanks which are angled slightly outward also help prevent the lips and cheeks from being pinched. A separate curb strap ring can also eliminate the problem.

Some riders intentionally return a certain degree of mechanical advantage to their horses by riding with "elevator" bits. Such bits have long upper shanks, generally equal to the lower shanks, providing a 1:1 leverage ratio. The reason, as the elevator's name suggests, is that such bits have proven useful in encouraging poll flexion from the horse without a corresponding lowering of the head. The bit influences the face without necessarily transferring a great deal of downward pressure to the poll via the headstall. Such bits can be used with or without chin straps.

THE CHIN OR CURB STRAP'S ROLE

Without a chin strap, a shanked bit will rotate in the horse's mouth a half turn or more before the headstall stops the movement and the bit engages. Only when the rotation stops can the leverage action of the bit take effect. By adding the chin strap, bit rotation is controlled, which is why it is called a "curb" strap.

To curb means to check or restrain. With a curb strap, the bit engages more rapidly, with greater consequence. In effect, the chin strap balances or positions the load onto the lever so the shanks can do their job. The chin strap also puts pressure on the chin groove and brings the mouthpiece into greater contact with the tongue and bars. The lower jaw is literally caught in the squeeze between mouthpiece and chin strap.

The adjustment of the chin strap will determine how quickly and where the bit makes contact with the mouth, the point at which it snugs up into the chin groove, and how far the mouthpiece will rotate. The tighter the setting, the less pull it requires to activate the bit. This impacts the amount of signal the horse will receive. Also, the more the bit rotates before the chin strap engages, the more the pressure is transferred to the corners of the lips and the poll, and less to the tongue, bars and chin groove. Of course, if the bit has a high port or spoon, and the curb strap is loose, the rotation may be halted by contact with the palate, which then becomes a part of the load.

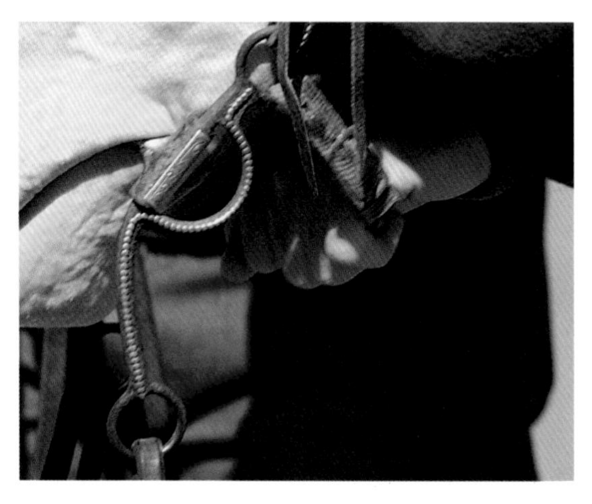

The effect of any given bit can be altered or refined by how loose or tight the curb strap is.

SIGNAL — THE FIRST CLUE BEFORE CONTACT

Signal is an important concept in bitting. Simply put, signal is the amount of warning a bit gives the horse before it actually engages and puts pressure on the mouth, chin and poll. Signal can be thought of as the clue that prepares a horse to respond to the bit.

Choosing a bit which provides adequate signal is a courtesy. It's like saying "please." It makes the horse receptive to our requests and gives the animal time to mentally and physically prepare to comply. In general, the greater a bit's signal, the more forgiving the bit will be.

Some of the factors that affect a bit's potential for signal are:

* Shank length
* Ratio of upper to lower shanks
* Shank shape and design
* Overall weight and balance
* Shank attachment to the mouthpiece (loose or fixed)
* Rein ring attachment to the shank (loose or fixed)
* Mouthpiece design (solid or jointed)
* Curb strap adjustment

LOOSE SHANKS VERSUS STIFF SHANKS

Typically, the more moving parts within a bit, the more signal it will provide to the horse. For example, a loose-jawed bit, one which attaches to the mouthpiece via hinges or swivels, will provide a certain degree of rotation before the bit engages. The horse can feel the shank movement and therefore mentally and physically prepare to respond. The greater the amount of shank rotation before contact, the greater the signal to the horse. Add a loose rein ring to the loose jaw, and the bit will provide even more signal. Install a broken mouthpiece in those shanks and you amplify the signal even more.

As anyone who rides a great deal will attest, even the most minute differences in bit signal can affect performance. Conditioning will then determine how the horse reacts. A horse whose mouth has been repeatedly abused will probably recognize bit signal as time to brace itself for the worst. It may automatically stiffen and resist the bit. A horse who has learned to trust its rider to take gentle hold of its mouth will probably relax and soften at the poll in preparation for its next maneuver.

This Weymouth bit has stiff shanks which eliminates quite a bit of the signal to the horse. The rein rings however, being loose, do provide some signal.

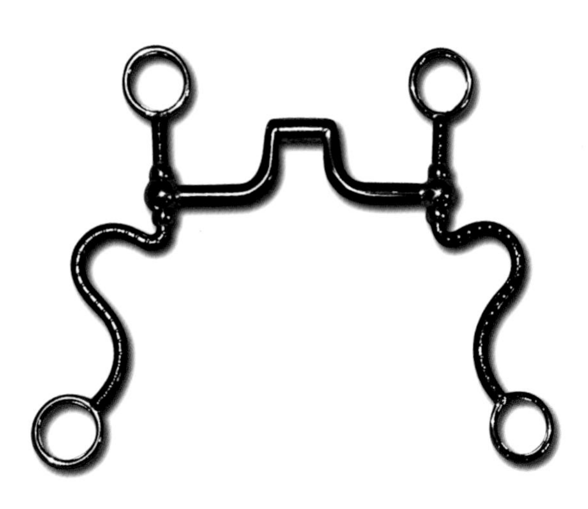

When they have broken or hinged mouthpieces, loose-shanked bits offer an advantage over fixed shank bits when used two-handed. Pressure on one rein has more effect on the side that's pulled than on the opposite side in the loose-shanked, broken-mouthed bit. The Balding ball hinge bit (above) gives the horse a great deal of signal, between the hinged mouthpiece, and shanks which swivel.

The way in which loose shanks attach to the mouthpiece also influences the bit's function. The slip-cheeked bit has shanks which rotate front to back as well as slide up and down a few millimeters when the reins are pulled. This type of attachment provides a great deal of signal, but is also more likely to cause the bit to pinch the corners of the mouth. When the mouthpiece attaches to the cheeks via cylinders, the potential for lip pinching is reduced. There are other closely coupled hinges that eliminate pinch points. For example, Wyoming bitmaker Tom Balding has patented a special ball hinge that's smooth and functional.

In addition to the signal they provide, loose shanked bits offer an advantage over fixed shanked bits when used two-handed. Pressure on one rein has more effect on the side that's pulled with a loose-shanked bit. In a fixed shank bit, a pull on one rein tends to influence both sides of the bit more equally. In so-called "roping bits," this combined affect is taken a step further. Both shanks are fused into a single rein ring centered beneath the horse's chin.

Myler Bits of Missouri has developed a cylinder shank attachment with internal bushings that allow the upper and lower shanks to swivel independently of one another. This allows the rider to isolate the bit's influence not just to one side at a time, but also to specific body parts. For example, if the rider wants to ask the horse to lift a shoulder without creating a lot of lateral arc, the bit allows him to do that. Some of Myler's hinges are also designed to lock the mouthpiece into a fixed position when the reins are released. It gives the rider the advantages of a stiff bit without losing the flexibility of loose cheeks and a broken mouthpiece.

The opposite extreme from the loose-shanked, broken mouthed bit is the roping bit in which both shanks are fused into a single rein ring beneath the horse's chin.

HOW SHANK LENGTH, RATIO AND SWEEP RELATE TO SIGNAL

We discussed shank length in relation to pulling power earlier in this chapter. But it's also important to recognize that the length and ratio of the shanks also affect a bit's signal. Think of the shank as a pendulum. The longer the shank, the greater the distance the arm will rotate before the bit engages. Therefore, a bit with long shanks typically provides more signal. But depending on the ratio of upper to lower shanks, the bit may also apply more pressure to the mouth and chin groove once it engages. Long-shanked, low ratio bits are said to be "slow" — meaning they don't react as quickly as a short-shanked bit with an equivalent ratio. For riders who don't as yet have expert timing, that slower bit might be more forgiving. The rider is able to give the horse more warning, therefore the bit allows a little more room for error. For a skilled show ring professional, the rapid-fire response of the shorter shanked bit might provide a competitive edge, eliciting split-second compliance from the horse.

The angle between the upper and lower shank also affects the speed of communication. The straighter the shank, the less signal the bit provides. Conversely, the further the headstall and rein rings are swept back from that straight line, the more signal the bit will provide. To understand this concept, study the angles of different bits. Regardless of the actual shape of the shanks, simply draw a line from the headstall ring through the butt of the mouthpiece and a second line from the rein ring through the butt of the mouthpiece.

Then look at the dimension (degree) of the angle which has been formed. The smaller the angle (remember a circle divided by a straight line is 180 degrees) the greater the amount of signal the bit will provide. In other words, when the angles becomes compressed, the farther the rider must raise his rein hand in order to engage the mouthpiece. The swept back shanks of the grazing bit are a good example of this theory in action. When the reins are raised and lowered, the mouthpiece tends to rotate less than those with straighter shanks. Also, because of its forward balance, a well-made grazing bit will be quick to release when the reins are released.

In the so-called Walking Horse bit, the line drawn through the upper shanks (which are parallel to the port and much shorter than the lower shanks) form a 45-degree angle with the lower shanks. The port lies in an exaggerated horizontal position in the mouth compared to a straighter-shanked bit. Even though the Walking Horse bits tends to have long lower shanks, which increases its leverage, it takes more tension on the reins to rotate the bit and exert pressure than one with straighter shanks.

The more backward sweep in the shank the more signal the bit provides. This grazing bit, with a swept back lower shank provides advanced warning to the horse.

MORE ABOUT SHANK DESIGN

While shank shape may not change the bit's leverage, it can affect its response time. What riders really need to know is how reactive a bit will be when they take up on the reins. Or perhaps more important, how quickly the bit will return to neutral when the rider releases the reins. A swept back shank will afford more signal than a straight-shanked bit, and it will be quicker to release pressure. The reason relates not only to the distance the shank has to swing in order make contact or disengage, but also to the overall balance of the bit.

Shank length and weight will also have an impact. Riders who compete in sports such as cutting and reining, in which split-second timing is critical, often choose light, short-shanked grazing bits. They want hair-trigger release and they're often willing to sacrifice leverage for speed. A light weight, well-balanced grazing bit is also less likely to jar the horse's mouth as the animal stops and turns with great force.

Even though differences in recovery time due to shank shape might be measured in thousandths of a second, horses respond to these differences. Importantly, the quicker a rider can release a horse for a correct response, the faster the training will progress. In fact, recovery time, meaning the time it takes for the bit to disengage, is perhaps the true measure of a bit's balance. Shanks that are too light or poorly balanced may not release the chin strap rapidly enough and may fail to settle back into a disengaged position properly.

THE BALANCE OF A BIT

The overall balance of a shanked bit is critical to its function. Bits need to be balanced in several ways. The bit should be balanced from side to side so it rests evenly and comfortably in the horse's mouth. This is a matter of making sure a bitmaker has conscientiously measured (to the gram) the materials he puts into each side, whether adding decorative silver or crafting a unique shank design.

Bits also have a natural balance from front to back. When rested lightly on your finger tips, bits will usually hang one of three ways, straight up and down, forward, or backwards. Bits that appear to be top heavy (reverse balanced) should be avoided as they provide little or no release. Unless you are in need of a correction device, bits that naturally balance so that the lower shanks fall forward and the upper shanks fall back are generally the best choice. They give more signal and reward the horse the moment the reins are loosened. Recognize, too, that the minute you pull on the reins, the natural balance of a bit becomes irrelevant. You overpower gravity's influence on the bit. Not until you release your hold does the bit's balance come back into play.

The balance of a bit may be checked by balancing it on the spread fingers on one hand. The bit on the right, in which the upper shank rocks back and the lower shank rocks forward, will provide more signal and be less severe than the bit on the left which is reverse balanced. When the slack is taken out of the reins, however, the natural balance of the bit becomes irrelevant.

The type and degree of balance that will be appropriate depend a lot on your horse's job. A western pleasure rider, for instance, might choose a bit that is designed to hang vertically. His or her goal may be to encourage the horse to travel with its head in a vertical frame without constant contact on the bridle. A reiner or cutter might be more

inclined to select a bit that has a lot of natural forward balance. This means that the lower shanks of the bit tend to fall forward away from the jawline.

The advantage of a forward-balanced bit is that it assists the rider in releasing pressure on the chin groove and allows the mouthpiece to disengage as soon as the reins are released. However, a forward balanced bit may do little to promote a vertical headset. Instead, it may actually encourage the horse to travel with its nose extended forward. A reverse-balanced bit may help encourage a horse with an excessively extended nose to bring it in. The downside is that such bits provide little relief to the mouth and chin groove, so it's hard to reward the horse when it assumes the position you want. A reverse-balanced bit may also encourage horses to overflex and get behind the bit, which also takes away the rider's control.

"THE IDEA IS TO FIND THE RIGHT COMBINATION OF ELEMENTS TO SATISFY YOUR NEEDS."

9

Trade-Offs — Interplay Among Bridle Parts

In the preceding chapters we presented a basic introduction to mouthpieces, shanks and bit balance. We also looked at the important role the chin strap plays when using leverage bits. Now it's time to consider these parts in relationship to one another. In order to fully evaluate the function of any bit, it's essential to consider how the individual pieces interact with one another to create a total effect. The idea, of course, is to find the right combination of elements to satisfy your needs.

Bit choices become more significant as you strive for greater finesse and responsiveness. A weekend trail rider may never see a compelling need to use anything other than a well constructed mechanical hackamore. The reining competitor may experiment with any number of shank, mouthpiece and curb strap combinations in pursuit of a $100,000 futurity paycheck. When you consider that major events can be won and lost by half-point differences, that world championship roping and barrel racing titles are made and measured in hundredths of a second, it becomes apparent why highly competitive horsemen and women pay careful attention to their equipment.

Individual horses tolerate pressure on some parts of their mouths and faces better than others. For example, one horse might be perfectly content with a short-shanked, low port curb bit. Such a bit is relatively mild. Yet on a horse with a sensitive tongue, it might be uncomfortable enough to cause the animal to loll its tongue or root out its nose every time the reins are pulled. While putting a sweetwater mouthpiece into the same set of shanks wouldn't change the amount of leverage, it would transfer some of the pressure off the tongue and onto the bars and perhaps make the horse a happier, more responsive mount.

COMPARING BITS

In bitting, it's important to look beyond superficial characteristics. Two bits can share similar features yet provide very different effects. For instance, when a broken mouthpiece is set into simple ring cheeks it has a far milder impact than when set into shanks. Sweep back those shanks and the bit provides a much different action than if the shanks are designed to hang straight up and down. Add a chin strap and the bit's effects are further altered. Snug up that curb strap and the bit's signal decreases as its speed of engagement increases. Change that chin strap from smooth leather to a flat metal chain and there is less give, which further concentrates pressure on the chin groove and mouth. Put a twist in that chain and the previously mild links take on a serious bite.

While this may seem like a lot to consider in one paragraph, it demonstrates why it's so important to consider the sum of a bridle's parts. When you find two bits in a tack shop that appear to have only minor differences, study them closely and give careful thought to the type of accessories you'll pair with them.

To illustrate, consider two bits that are identical in every way but one. Both have U.S. mouthpieces (a U.S. mouthpiece is a 2-inch, U-shaped port which joins the bars of the bit at a right angle) set in 7-inch, S-shaped shanks. The port of each affords enough height to contact the palate when the bit is fully engaged. Both ports are flattened through the apex. However, one port has been rolled back while the other has been set into the shanks without any rearward arc. The second bit is far more severe. When the port comes into contact with the roof of the mouth, it is at the maximum strength of pull. It is abrupt. It will likely be painful. In contrast, the rolled mouthpiece is designed to signal the horse by gently gliding along the palate as slack is taken from the reins. Even at the apex of engagement, the port rests softly against the roof of the mouth. It provides the horse more warning and is by construction more humane. Two almost identical bits; one very substantial difference.

BALANCE AND STABILITY

The balance of a bit is important because it affects the bit's speed and release as well as its signal. It also has a profound impact on the horse's head and neck carriage. In the last chapter, we discussed bit balance in relationship to the shanks.

The overall balance of a bit is influenced by a number of factors, such as: 1) the shape and angle of the shanks 2) the ratio of upper to lower shanks, 3) the angle at which the mouthpiece has been set into the shanks, 4) the relative weight of the bit and how it is distributed throughout its parts, and 5) the number of joints or moving parts that make up the bit.

A bit constructed so that its lower shanks naturally swing forward is said to be overbalanced. When the shanks rotate rearward, the bit is said to be underbalanced. You

(overleaf) This correction bit has a relatively severe mouthpiece, but its 1:1 ratio and swept back, teardrop shaped shanks decrease its leverage, increase its signal and allow higher or lower hand positions to concentrate the pressure in different locations in the mouth.

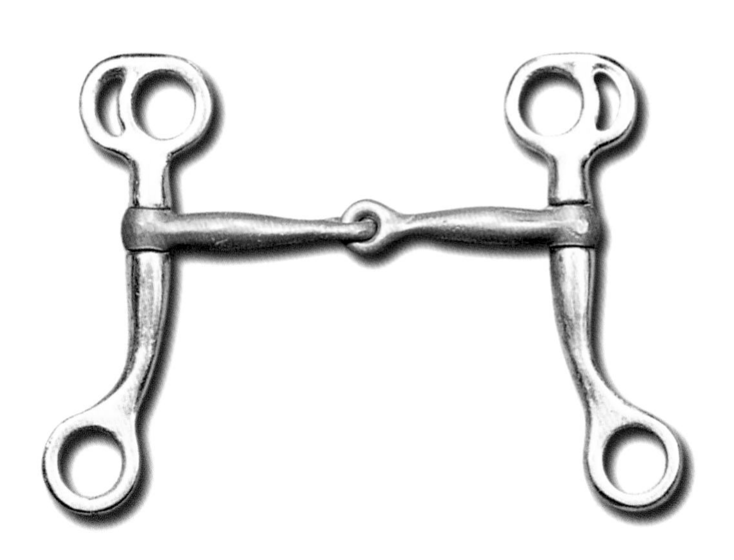

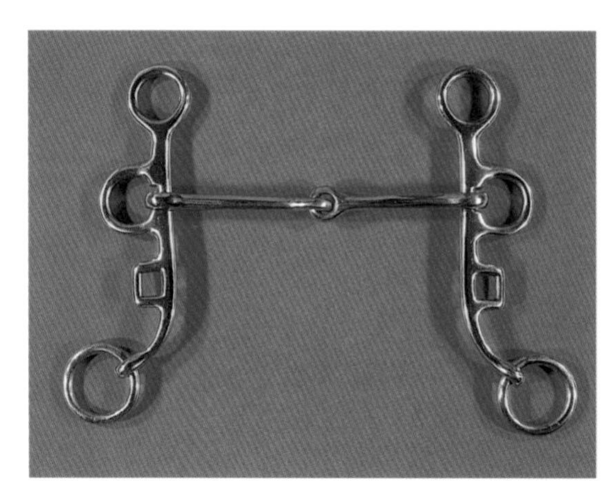

The Tom Thumb snaffle (left) and the Argentine snaffle (above) have similar mouthpieces and shank ratios, but the rearward sweep of the shank of the Argentine snaffle make it a more forgiving bit with more signal.

can get some idea of how the horse will have to position its head to keep the pressure off its mouth and chin groove by hanging the bit on your thumb and index finger.

Some bits have very little natural balance. This is especially true of bits with a lot of moving parts. A Tom Thumb bit is a good example with its jointed copper mouthpiece, swivel butts, and straight, short shanks. Dangle a Tom Thumb from your fingertips and it will wobble or fold in any number of directions. The two shanks might swing in opposite directions. In application, the Tom Thumb's balance and stability comes from the horse holding the bit in its mouth and the rider steadying it with pressure on the reins. The curb strap also helps to control the rotation of the shanks. If the rider plans to use this bit with constant rein contact, the bit's lack of balance probably isn't of major concern. But that's true of almost any bit with which a rider plans to maintain continuous contact.

A problem with the Tom Thumb is that it tends to be top heavy. The addition of a curbstrap loop on the headstall ring doesn't help. Because the Tom Thumb tends to rotate in the mouth, it is notorious for pinching and/or cutting tongues despite its low leverage ratio. Even though it continues to be popular, it should be handled with care.

In comparison, the so-called Argentine snaffle (which is really a curb bit) shares attributes of the Tom Thumb; yet if well-constructed, it has a built-in degree of overbalance. The rearward sweep to the lower shanks helps to stabilize the mouthpiece and allows the shanks to drop forward without adding leverage. This in turn helps balance the position of the upper shanks despite the low ratio and the loose-jawed attachment of the mouthpiece to the cheeks.

MOVING PARTS

Bits with moving parts are useful because they provide a greater degree of signal than solidly constructed bits. They also afford more independent lateral control. But they do have their down sides. Craftsmanship is critical

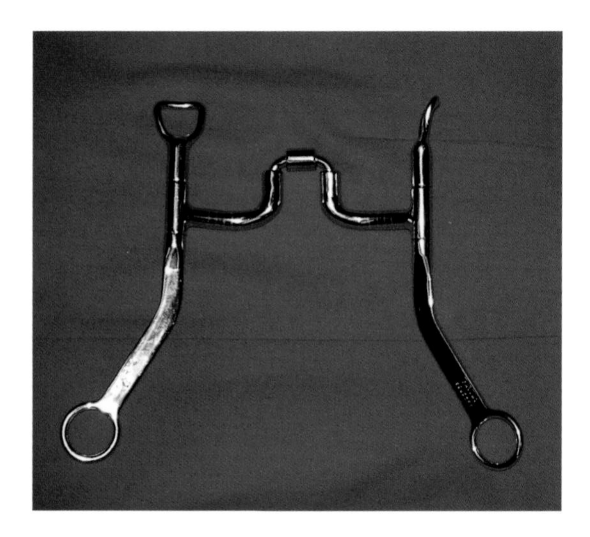

This Myler bit has a patented shank design that allows the lower shank to rotate independent of the upper cheek which reduces torsion on the headstall when the rein engages the bit.

so that delicate mouth tissue isn't pinched or serrated by poorly constructed joints. There's also the risk that the parts may come unhinged, so it's wise to inspect your bits regularly.

Also, decide what parts should move. A busy-mouthed horse might do better with a solid mouthpiece yet still benefit from the signal provided by a loose-jawed bit. There are many such bits on the market. Also consider whether the bit incorporates useful innovations. Myler Bits, for example, has patented a cheek design that allows the lower shanks to swivel independently of the upper shank. When the rider pulls on the rein, only the portion of the shank that has a direct bearing on the horse's action turns. The rider gets lateral control, without twisting the headstall loop into the side of the horse's face.

Another important consideration is how much slop (looseness), you'll accept in a bit. Keep in mind that movement begets movement. A bit that incorporates a lot of play may unduly amplify or call attention to unwanted motion in the horse.

For example, some horses will begin to chase a rein or bob their heads in rhythm to the pendulum-like swing of the shanks as they trot or lope circles. Others may worry the bit with their tongues or lips, or make a hobby of trying to grab the shanks with their lips. Stiffer bits may reduce some of this excess baggage. The trade-off might be an overall increase in the stiffness of the horse's performance. For a horse that overflexes or bends like a noodle, this can be a decided advantage. For horses that are naturally stiff, bits with joints and hinges in key places may help the rider loosen the horse up and establish greater flexion, bend and control.

Some riders choose to compromise, combining the benefits of stiff and loose-jawed bits. They do this by hobbling the shanks (connecting the lower ends) with leather, chain, wire or solid stabilizer bars to reduce the amount of motion to whatever degree is desired.

BIT WEIGHT REVISITED

Another important consideration is that loose-jawed bits with long, heavy lower shanks will amplify motion more than lighter weight ones. If your horse is an especially rough mover, opting for a stiff bit with short, light, swept-back shanks might be wise. This will keep the pendulum from rocking excessively and keep from calling attention to unattractive motion. Such a choice will also reduce the wear and tear on the horse's mouth. Heavy shanks combined with rough gaits can turn a bit into a hammer, with the tongue and bars taking a pounding.

Bit weight also plays a role in cueing. The mouthpiece, of course, has a bearing on how messages are received, but shank and rein weight also influence the horse's ability to feel and recognize the rider's signals. For instance, pleasure horse riders strive to maintain an exceptionally quiet frame. They want to give the appearance of guiding the horse without any perceptible cues. An inch or two of

This California style straight-shanked bit belonged to the late Tony Amaral. Amaral replaced the mouthpiece with this hinged, ported mouthpiece. The combination worked well.

hand movement in any direction is plenty. Straight, heavy shanks can help create this illusion because the weight of the bit amplifies the signal transmitted through the reins. In effect, the rider guides the horse off the weight of the reins, giving a soft, light appearance.

The shape and weight of the shank also combine to hold the horse's face in a more vertical position. If the upper shanks are long, two inches or more, this further encourages the horse to flex at the poll. A longer upper shank will require a looser curb strap setting to keep the strap situated in the chin groove. The rider may opt to utilize the curb pressure higher up on the bony ridges of the jawline, which, when combined with the longer shanks, provides the rider better control of the front of the horse's face.

Curb chains, as seen on the pelham bit, tend to be more severe than leather or nylon straps. The severity of this chain is increased, because it fits behind the chin groove over the relatively sharp edges of the mandible.

CURB STRAPS

The curb strap has a definite impact on how leverage headgear works. Some riders also use chin straps with snaffle bits, but the purpose, if any, is simply to prevent the rings from being pulled through the horse's mouth. On a direct pulling bit, the curb strap does not increase the bit's pulling power. However, on a leverage bit, the curb strap adjustment can profoundly change the bit's action. A very tight strap will decrease the signal, reduce or eliminate any palate pressure, and increase the pressure on the tongue, bar and chin groove.

An excessively snug setting may even move the curb strap out of the chin groove and onto the slender bony ridges beneath the jawline. In fact, a problem with many mechanical hackamores is that the curb chain rests no where near the chin groove. Bits with exceptionally long upper shanks also tend to shift the curb strap onto these sharp bones making the contact more severe. Some bits accommodate this problem by adding separate curb strap loops behind and below the headstall rings to keep the strap in its proper position. Bits with especially short upper shanks also benefit by having curb strap loops. They help prevent the lips from being pinched between the mouthpiece, shanks and chin strap when the reins are pulled and the bit rotates in the mouth.

The tightness of the curb strap has a profound effect on the bit's action. A tight strap can negate reverse balance and palate contact, even in a spade bit.

Many trainers adjust and check the curb strap by how many fingers they can slip between it and the chin groove. Two to three fingers of clearance is a common rule of thumb. But it may be more helpful to actually rotate the bits shanks to see how far they move before the curb strap makes contact with the chin groove. If you want the bit to engage more quickly, tighten it up. If you desire a lot of signal, then loosen it.

If you're utilizing a bit which employs palate pressure, make sure that the curb strap is loose enough to let the port take effect. Just as with your other bit adjustments, you may have to experiment with the curb strap setting and see how the horse responds. If your horse acts surprised every time you take hold of the reins, he's probably telling you to cut him some slack — literally.

WESTERN PELHAMS

Necessity is the mother of invention and the pelham is yet another example of this in the world of bits. The pelham combines the utility of a snaffle with that of a curb bit. The tool is meant to be used with two pairs of reins (which some critics say is at least one pair too many for most riders). A rein ring attaches to the butt of the mouthpiece while another attaches at the bottom of the shank.

Pelhams are primarily meant to be ridden off the snaffle rein, meaning the majority of the guiding force should be applied to the top rein. For this reason, the rider holds the snaffle rein to the outside of his or her hand, encircling the little finger, or is sometimes held between the little and ring fingers. The curb rein is held between the next two fingers. The curb rein is used to encourage vertical flexion and to promote collection by containing and directing the forward motion.

The western pelham was popularized by the late horseman Monte Foreman, and still has a place in the training pen. A similar bit popularized by reining horse trainer Bob Loomis is a 7½-inch shanked snaffle (in truth a pelham-like curb with a broken mouthpiece), which also has rein rings at the position of the mouthpiece. However, most western riders generally work off the leverage end of the bit. As bitmaker Greg Darnall explains, the snaffle ring remains an accepted feature of the bit primarily because it makes positioning the mouthpiece within the shanks quick and easy for the bitmaker.

Some riders choose to utilize pelhams with a single rein, bridging the upper and lower rein rings with connecting straps called pelham roundings. This tends to equalize the pressure between the two points of pull and ultimately reduces the bit's effect to that of a short-shanked curb.

Pelhams were designed to be used in place of full double bridles with separate snaffle and curb bits. For small-mouthed horses, a single mouthpiece can be a blessing, giving them less metal to contend with. While the pelham might not work with exactly the same precision as the two separate bits, it's often a useful compromise.

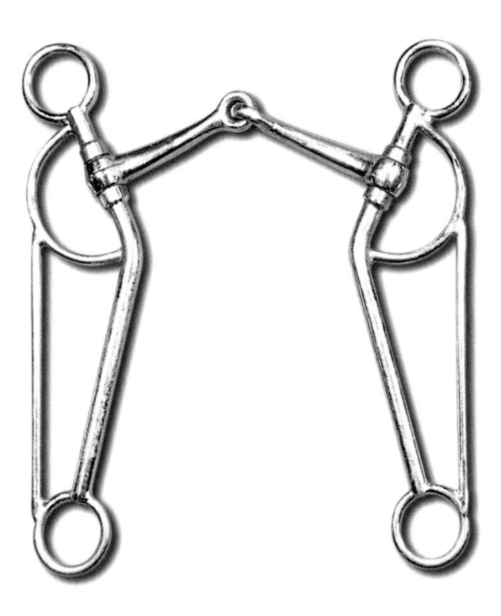

While most western riders choose to use the lower, curb rein rings only, the western pelham bit is very useful to facilitate the transition from a snaffle to a curb bit. With reins at both sets of rings, the rider can teach a young horse what the leverage bit is all about, while maintaining the control already established with the snaffle reins.

SOLUTIONS AND COMPROMISE

When it comes to selecting bits, compromise is often the name of the game. You must determine what pressure points you can use most effectively, and how much leverage is required to ride your horse to its best advantage. A bit that's too mild to elicit an appropriate response isn't a solution, nor is one that is so powerful that it inflicts pain or fear. You must look for the combination of shanks, mouthpiece and curb strap that preserves your horse's confidence, promotes a positive attitude, builds trust, provides a certain margin of error, and, as always, lets you communicate as clearly as possible.

"GAG BITS GIVE THE HORSE GREATER CONTROL OVER ITS OWN REWARD."

10

Gag Bits

The very name "gag bit" is a turn-off to some people, but these bits do have their uses. The distinctive feature of the gag is that the mouthpiece is designed to slide upward into the horse's mouth when the reins are pulled. Some people prefer to call them "draw" bits because the term doesn't conjure up the same negative images and is essentially what the bit does — it draws up into the horse's mouth when the reins are pulled.

HOW GAGS WORK

Riders in many disciplines have come to appreciate the value of well designed gag bits. The reason is simple. Gag bits give the horse greater control over its own reward. As we have noted earlier, horses learn through pressure and release. When they give to bit pressure by flexing at the poll, tipping their noses or complying with whatever is required, the pull on their mouths lessens or stops. In a standard bit, the horse relies on the horseman to relinquish the hold on its face. The rider's timing is critical. The quicker the rider reacts to a correct response, the faster the training will progress and the lighter the horse will become. However, in a gag bit, the horse isn't quite as dependent on the rider's sense of timing. As soon as the animal submits to rein pressure, the mouthpiece itself responds by sliding into a more neutral position. The bit disengages even if the rider is a little slow to react.

According to custom bitmaker Gordon Hayes, the essential feature of any gag bit is in the smoothness of manufacture. There should be nothing in the attachments between mouthpiece and cheeks, or reins and cheeks, that would allow the bit to hang up. The bit should glide easily upwards into the mouth when the reins are pulled,

(overleaf) Gag bits are versatile tools, whether for training, competition, or show. (Gemma Giannini Photo)

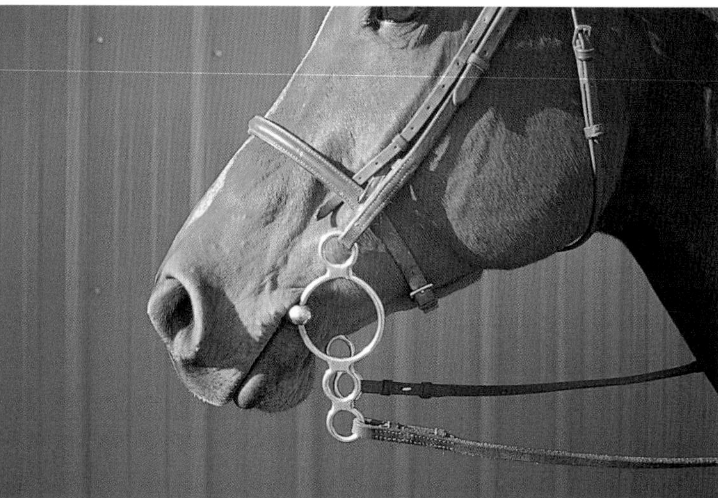

(upper right) A pull on the rein rotates the Pessoa gag bit within the mouthpiece. The cheekpiece of the bridle is pulled towards the nose, resulting in poll pressure and increasing the pressure on the corners of the lips.

(lower right) The rein tension is released, and the cheekpiece rotates back to its neutral position.

and drop away from the mouth the instant the horse gives. If not, the tool is worthless. The reward is in the release.

Gags may also be useful in athletic contests such as barrel racing and polo. In these events the rider's attention may be distracted and his seat may be less than firmly engaged in the saddle. Sudden jerks on the reins, which may inadvertently occur during strenuous horseback athletic activity, may be at least partially transferred to the poll, lips and even the teeth from more sensitive tissues of the mouth. The gag also puts an effective brake on the horse when the rider must stop and turn in a split second. The gag bit is popular with some riders because direct contact with the mouth can be maintained. It is quick-releasing and the cheeks act like a full cheeked snaffle, keeping the bit from being pulled through the mouth.

Some riders attach a pair of ordinary reins to the bit rings above the gag reins and use this set unless the gag rein is needed to position the head. The gag rein is particularly useful in getting the horse to break at the poll because there is more relief when the horse flexes and brings its face in than when it roots its nose out. The concern is that riding on the gag rein alone may lead to an artificial head carriage with the horse finding further ways to evade the bit, such as getting behind the bridle. However, in western riding, the gag rein is frequently used alone. It might be thought that the gag functions to lower the head because tension on the reins places pressure on the poll. But head carriage is more a factor of where the horse finds relief from bit pressure. If the gag is used with no auxiliary aids, its net function may be to accentuate the basic head raising action of a snaffle bit. This is because the horse's mouth is generally much more sensitive to pressure than its poll is.

Gag bits are frequently used in conjunction with standing martingales, as on barrel racing and timed event horses. In this case, the horse's ability to raise its head is limited by the martingale. The gag can be used to keep the horse from lowering its head excessively, and the martingale keeps him from raising it beyond a certain point. The combination is quite powerful. Two directly opposing forces are brought into play. There is the upward pull of the bit and the downward pull of the martingale. The horse's head is fixed between the two. Theoretically, the combination of the gag and the martingale allows the rider to control a headstrong horse with less chance of injuring its mouth. However, it is certainly possible to injure the mouth with this system. In effect, you've trapped the horse's face, and the animal has no way to escape the pull. Harsh use of the gag snaffle can still cut the tongue or lips.

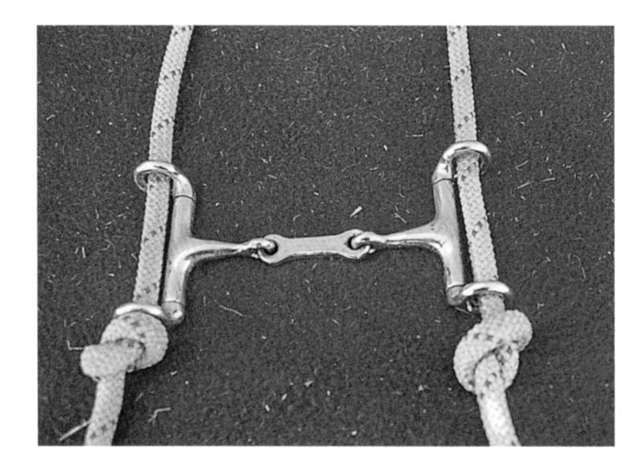

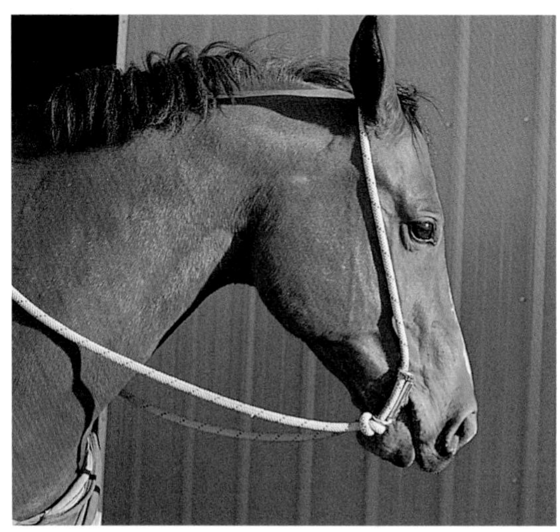

(top & above) Gag bits with "Duncan" cheeks have no rings so it is not possible to use a second set of reins. As with most gag snaffles, the reins, cheek-pieces and headstall act as one continuous unit.

Barrel racing champion Martha Wright prefers to use shanked gag bits with low leverage ratios, when training and competing. (Rick and Kathy Swan Photo)

When the cheeks on a gag bit are loose half rings, a pull on the reins gives some direct snaffle-action as well as gag-action.

GAG SNAFFLES

In the most common types of gag bridles, the reins, cheekpieces and headstall act as one continuous unit. The bit works almost like a pulley. The mouthpiece, usually jointed, floats up and down because the bit is suspended through a cord, cable or reins that run through holes in the cheeks. If the cheeks are rings or half-rings, this type of gag essentially acts like a snaffle bit. It provides direct pull from the rider's hand to the horse's mouth, but with more pressure directed to the lips and poll and virtually none to the bars. The gag snaffle is generally used without a curb strap because, as with an ordinary ring snaffle, it would serve no real purpose in the bit's function.

A simple gag snaffle may increase the rider's control over that gained by using a standard snaffle, yet without proportionally increasing the punishment to the horse's mouth. When tension is applied to the reins, the headstall shortens and exerts pressure on the poll and on the corners of the lips. In effect, some of the pressure which would be applied to the tongue and bars with an ordinary snaffle is transferred to less sensitive tissues. The horse may be less likely to resist it and has the distinct advantage of having more control of its own reward. In fact, some people prefer to start their colts in gag snaffles rather than in ring snaffles for these very reasons.

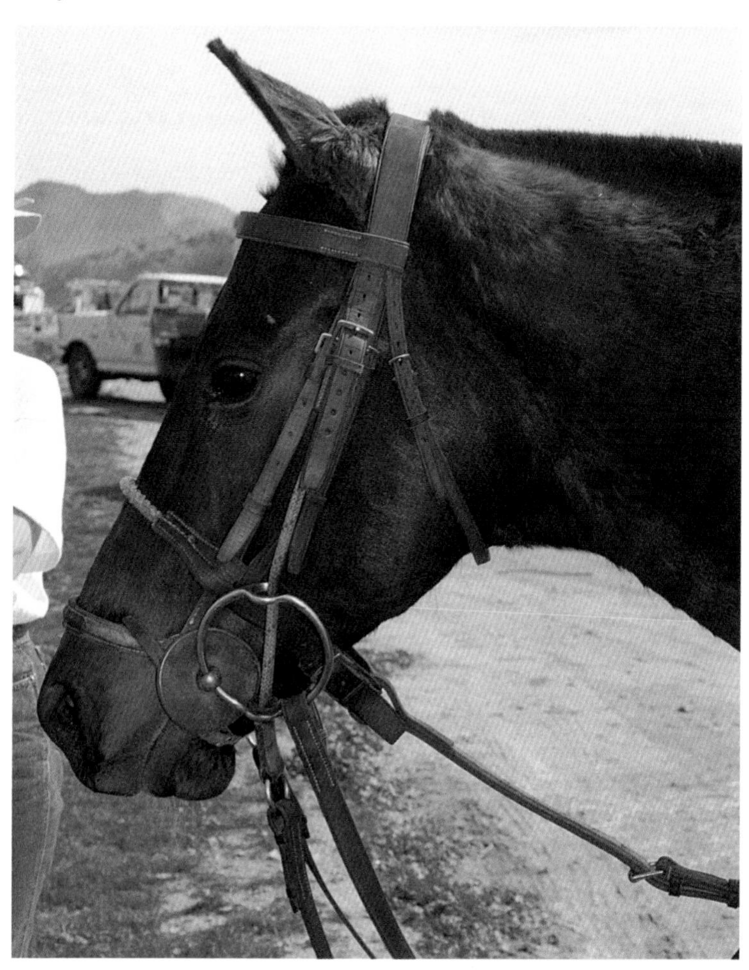

A polo horse with a gag bit with a snaffle rein attached to the rings. Gags are frequently used, as in this case, with standing martingales to limit the horse's ability to raise his head.

SHANKED GAGS

In addition to gag snaffles, there are shanked gags that act as leverage bits. These gags are generally used with curb straps. Typically, the mouthpiece of a shanked gag floats within the cheekpieces, but the cheeks are elongated to extend above and below the corners of the mouth, which alters the line of pull. Generally, there are separate rein and headstall rings to which the bridle and reins attach. The movement of the mouthpiece is restricted by the size and design of the cheeks. In other words, the mouthpiece will slide only so far before being stopped by the parameters of the cheeks. That's when leverage comes into play.

Once the bit is fully engaged, it is essentially like any other curb bit of similar shank and mouthpiece design. As the position of the mouthpiece shifts upwards along the shanks, the more the force is multiplied. For example, a gag bit with 8-inch shanks could go from having a 1:1 leverage ratio when the mouthpiece is positioned dead center in the cheeks, to a 1:7 ratio when the bit is fully employed. In short, some of these bits can become quite severe.

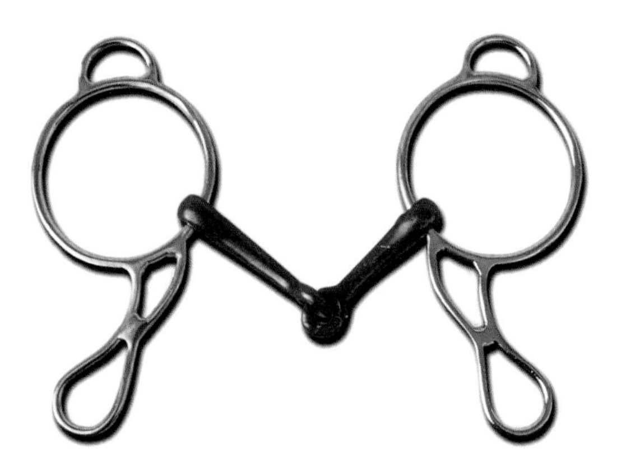

The mouthpiece of the shanked gag floats within the cheekpieces. A gag bit should be so smoothly constructed that the mouthpiece flows like water.

Once the rotation of the mouthpiece is stopped by the cheekpiece ring, the shanked gag becomes a leverage bit.

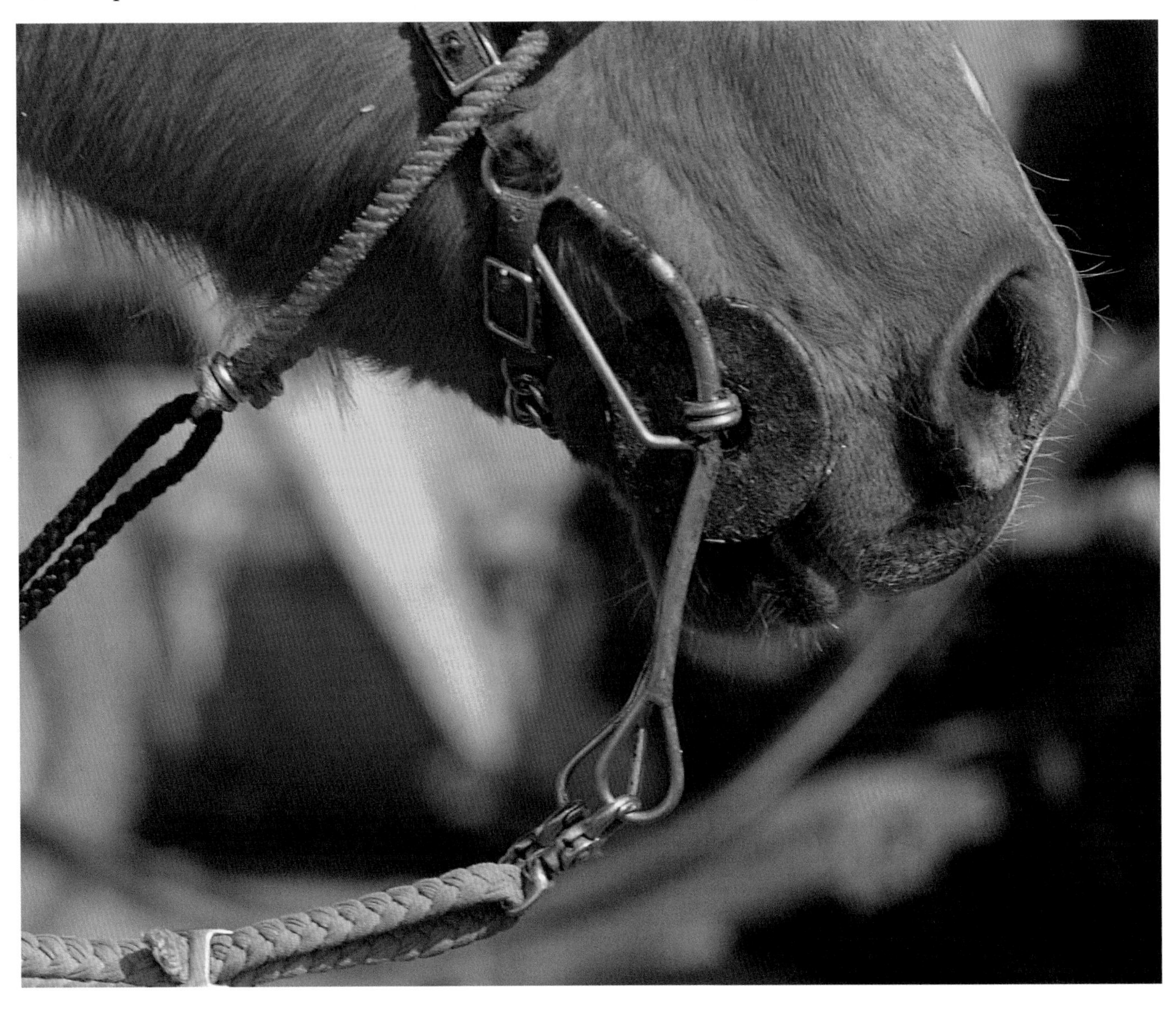

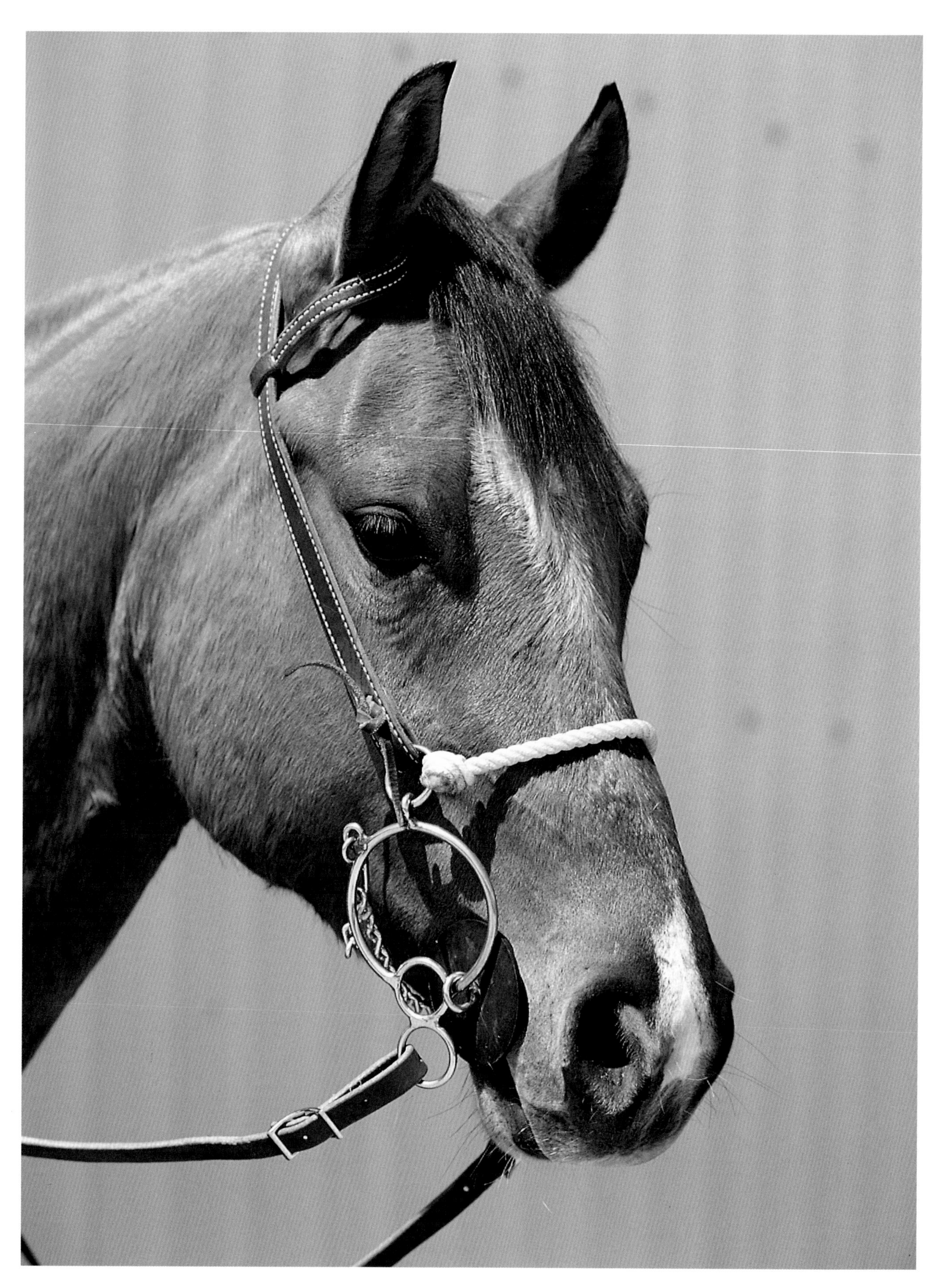

VARIETIES OF GAGS

As with other bits, consider all the features of a gag before you buy one. A gag bit with "Duncan" cheeks has no rings, so it's not possible to use a second set of reins. This feature may or may not be of concern. The size, weight and design of the cheeks may also be a consideration. Some riders favor eggbutt cheeks rather than those with loose, round rings, the idea being that the eggbutt gag drops away more quickly when rein pressure is released.

Shanked gags come in a variety of styles. For example, you might want to consider whether the reins run up through the length of the shanks more in keeping with a gag snaffle, or whether the mouthpiece slides up and down in the cheeks. The former will exert more poll pressure, and the latter will act more as a standard curb bit.

Also consider such things as the length and shape of the shanks (refer to Chapter 8, for more information on shank function). Some gags also allow you the option of attaching the reins in different places, depending on how much leverage you desire. Many such gags can be used with or without a chin strap, depending on the effect you're after. They are useful in certain circumstances, because the bit can have a gag action when equal tension is placed on both reins, but act like a snaffle when tension is placed on only one rein.

There are also any number of combination bits that have gag features, including gag hackamores, sometimes called hackamore bits or barrel racing bits. In addition to having a mouthpiece that slides up and down, these types of bits also include a noseband and chin strap. Some are designed so the gag action affects primarily the nose. Others effect primarily the mouth. While still others do a good job of equalizing the pressure on several points, including, nose, mouth, chin and poll. Advocates of this type of system point out that rein pressure is spread over the tongue, bars, corners of the lips, nose, poll and chin without undue pressure on any one area. However, some gag hackamores are quite severe so use good judgement when selecting one.

In terms of mouthpieces and shank designs, the same rules used to evaluate other bits apply to gags. But there is one additional and critical consideration. The bit must flow like water. If the mouthpiece or cheeks do not glide, leave it on the shelf. The best reason to choose a gag over other bits is to give you and your horse a timing advantage. Make sure the bit is up to the task.

(opposite) A combination gag hackamore. (Glory Ann Kurtz Photo)

"NOT ALL BITLESS BRIDLES ARE CREATED EQUAL."

11

Going Bitless

Many people like the idea of riding without a bit. With certain horses and at particular stages of training, bitless bridles can provide a practical advantage. But not all bitless bridles are created equal. Their quality, construction, design and use will determine whether you've done yourself and your horse a good turn by going to a bitless system.

Traditional bosal hackamores, mechanical hackamores, sidepulls, easy stops, nosebands and even halters fall within the realm of bitless bridles. However, there are important differences in the way each operates. Some bitless bridles provide excellent directional control. Others promote vertical flexion but less lateral control. Some simply give the rider the upper hand because they are designed to inflict pain.

Since there is virtually no padding to buffer or protect sensitive nerves, most horses will react to pressure applied to key points on their heads. Some horses are more sensitive to pressure on their noses, others seem to respond more to pressure on cheeks, poll or jaw. How a horse reacts to the squeeze will depend on the horse. When a mechanical hackamore's curb chain bites into a horse's jawline, for instance, some animals toss their heads in distress. Others are extremely sensitive across the bridge of the nose and may carry their faces well behind the vertical to evade the bump of a heavy or rough rawhide bosal. One may respond readily to the signals conveyed through a soft rope sidepull. Another may not be fazed in the least by the bone crunching effects of an easy stop.

With bitless headgear, you have to use the same considerations that you would with any other bridle, or risk dulling the horse's sensitivity and responsiveness to rein signals. Keep in mind that some devices are better designed for getting vertical control (front to back), while

(overleaf) Even though there is no mouthpiece, mechanical hackamores have metal shanks that attach to a noseband and curb chain. (Gemma Giannini Photo)

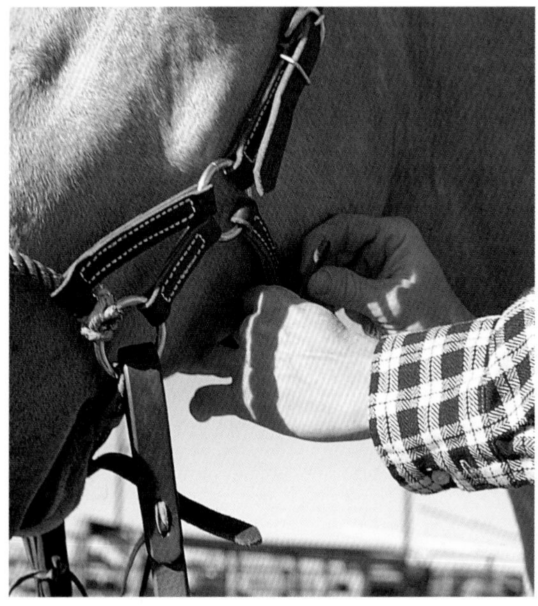

(top) Sidepull nosebands are most frequently found in single or double lariat rope, leather or metal. The stiffer the material, the more bite it carries but the less feel it gives the rider. This is a gentle noseband.

(above) The sidepull is most often used as a training tool because it promotes excellent lateral control without multiplying the effects of the rider's pull.

others promote lateral control (side to side). In this chapter we'll look at several bitless options so you can determine whether any fit into your riding or training program.

SIDEPULLS

The sidepull is one of the least complicated pieces of bitless headgear. It is little more than a hybrid halter. On each side of the noseband, rein rings are positioned in line with the corners of a horse's mouth. A chin strap beneath the rein rings allows the noseband to be snugged up into position. Sidepull nosebands are most frequently found in single or double lariat rope, leather or metal. The stiffer the material, the more bite it carries and the less feel it gives the rider. The sidepull is most often used as a training tool because, like the snaffle, it promotes excellent lateral control without multiplying the effects of the rider's pull.

While it's impossible to trace who developed the sidepull, the device first gained widespread acceptance among cutting horse trainers, then branched out to other disciplines. It's easy to understand why. Stopping, turning and backing are basic skills that any saddle horse must learn. But the number of times a young cutting horse is asked to do them is far greater than the average pleasure horse experiences in a lifetime. The cutter must continually stop, turn and reposition the horse with the movements of the cow in order to teach the horse the rules of the game.

When a horse's head must be handled a lot, the sidepull affords some advantages over a bit. First, it is a relatively mild piece of headgear. The rider can take hold of a horse's nose with the sidepull in order to stop and turn the horse without scaring a colt or totally blowing its concentration. The sidepull provides enough feel and control to help the rider direct a horse through an extensive series of maneuvers without sacrificing its mouth.

Handled roughly, however, a sidepull still has the potential to be harsh. Heavy hands will dull a sensitive nose just as effectively as they can ruin a good mouth. Stiff lariat rope or metal nosebands carry authority. Like a bit, the narrower and less flexible the noseband, the smaller the points of contact with the nose, the harsher the sidepull will be.

Of course, the sidepull's most significant advantage is the lateral control it gives a rider. It mimics the action of a snaffle bit because the reins are attached to the noseband directly on each side of the horse's face. When pressure is applied to either rein, it literally leads the horse's nose in that direction.

In comparison, on a traditional hackamore, the reins attach directly beneath the horse's jaw, so directional signals are less clear. A pull on the hackamore reins applies pressure to the top of the nose as well as beneath the jawline, which may be somewhat confusing to the horse.

A secondary advantage of the sidepull is that it encourages a horse to keep its head low. One reason is the way a sidepull fits. Many trainers adjust the headstall so the noseband sits two to three inches above the nostrils with the rings close to the corners of the mouth. (Some trainers say the lower the better.) We recommend that the noseband rest no lower than the bottom end of the nasal bone to prevent pain and to keep the noseband from interfering with the horse's breathing. The chin strap should be adjusted snugly enough to keep the nosepiece from shifting or sliding when the reins are pulled. Because the pressure is exerted low on the nose and there is no counterpressure exerted under the jaw (as with a bosal), the horse tends simply to follow the pull without raising its head. To further enhance this effect, many riders use a sidepull with a running martingale.

A short-coming of the sidepull is that it does little to promote vertical flexion or to shift the horse's weight to its hindquarters. The stiffer nosebands, such as the metal ones, may be more useful in getting the horse to transfer its center of balance rearward when both reins are pulled.

To avoid soring a horse's nose or dulling its responses to the sidepull, the noseband should be moved up or down periodically. You may even want to adjust it during a long riding session to keep the horse from becoming numb in one spot. The idea, of course, is to preserve a light feeling in the horse's face just as you would if you were riding with a bit.

BOSAL HACKAMORES

The traditional or true hackamore is a bitless bridle that includes a headstall, bosal (noseband), mecate (a combination lead rope and reins) and, in some cases, a fiador (throatlatch). American cowboys inherited the hackamore from early Spanish/Mexican horsemen, and its use has spread far and wide. Most of the terms associated with hackamore horsemanship have their origin in Spanish words. The term hackamore comes from the Spanish word la jaquima, which means headstall. Because the hackamore has such historic and ongoing significance in western riding and training, we have dedicated an entire chapter to the traditional hackamore, and it is there that we will take a comprehensive look at it.

MECHANICAL HACKAMORES

While mechanical hackamores are indeed bitless bridles, they are probably misnamed. Because of the way that they function, mechanical hackamores more closely resemble a curb bit than they do a true hackamore. Even though there is no mouthpiece, mechanical hackamores have metal shanks that attach to a noseband and curb chain. The shanks amplify the force on the nose, chin and poll in the same way that a leverage bit works on the mouth, chin and poll. When the rider takes up on the reins, pressure comes to bear, sometimes with great force.

Many competitive, endurance, trail, pleasure (not show) and speed event riders like mechanical hackamores because they do provide a good measure of control without risk of injury to the horse's mouth. They also provide a horse an opportunity to eat and drink without interference from a bit when riders stop for a break.

Many trail and distance riders like to ride with mechanical hackamores, because they allow leverage and control without a mouthpiece.

Mechanical hackamores have the potential to be severe. Many feature extremely long shanks. And the longer the shanks, the more the force is multiplied when the reins are pulled.

Of equal consequence is the type and position of the noseband and chin strap. The wider and softer the noseband, the milder the bridle will be because pressure is dispersed over a greater surface area of the horse's face. Harsh nosebands of narrow-gauged metal or chain link are sometimes disguised by rubber tubing or leather, so look beneath the cosmetic covering before you buy. It's also important to fit the headstall so that the noseband sits high enough on the horse's face to rest firmly on the nasal bone rather than on the soft cartilage lower down toward the nostrils. It's less likely to do permanent damage or cut off the air supply if the rider exerts too much muscle.

A definite downside of the way many mechanical hackamores are constructed is that when the noseband is in the proper position, the chin strap isn't. Unless special design considerations have been made, the curb chain will likely contact the jawline back behind the chin groove where the bone divides into two sharp narrow branches. Whenever the curb chain engages, it's likely to pinch. That's why some horses that are ridden with mechanical hackamores get into the habit of flipping their heads when the reins are pulled. One solution might be to exchange the chain curb for a smooth leather strap that lessens the bite and makes the animal more content with its headgear.

Before purchasing a mechanical hackamore, examine it closely. Look at how the shanks connect to the noseband and chin strap. Some poorly manufactured shanks have sharp, jagged or protruding joints or surfaces that dig into the cheeks whenever the reins are pulled.

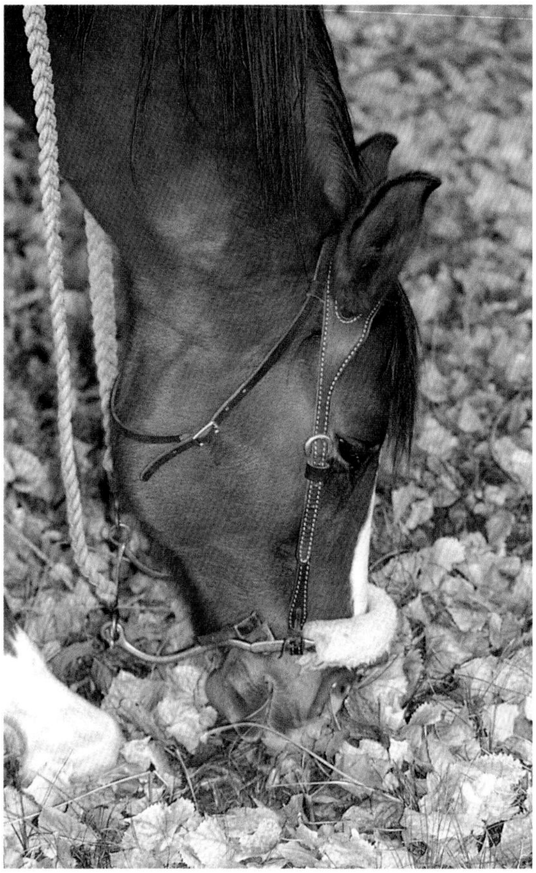

Mechanical hackamores are practical for riding long straight distances, but have limited application for teaching horses lateral maneuvers. Like other shank-type bits, pressure applied to one rein tends to affect both sides of the horse's face equally. In fact, most of the theories that apply to other shanked devices apply to them. They're best when used with light give and take signals, and are most effective for horses who have been taught to neck rein. Mechanical hackamores may be a good choice for horses who operate best with leveraged control but whose mouths have been injured or who are afraid of or overly sensitive to the bit.

One advantage of all bitless bridles for trail and endurance riding is that there is nothing in the horse's mouth to interfere with eating and drinking.

EASY STOPS

An easy stop is a severe modification of the hackamore. It acts much like a winch on a horse's face. Easy stops generally incorporate a stiff rope noseband which connects to a metal rod beneath the chin that forks into shanks. There are several variations of this device, but essentially how it works is this: When the reins are pulled, the metal chin rod presses into the lower jaw while the nose is compressed in a vise-like squeeze.

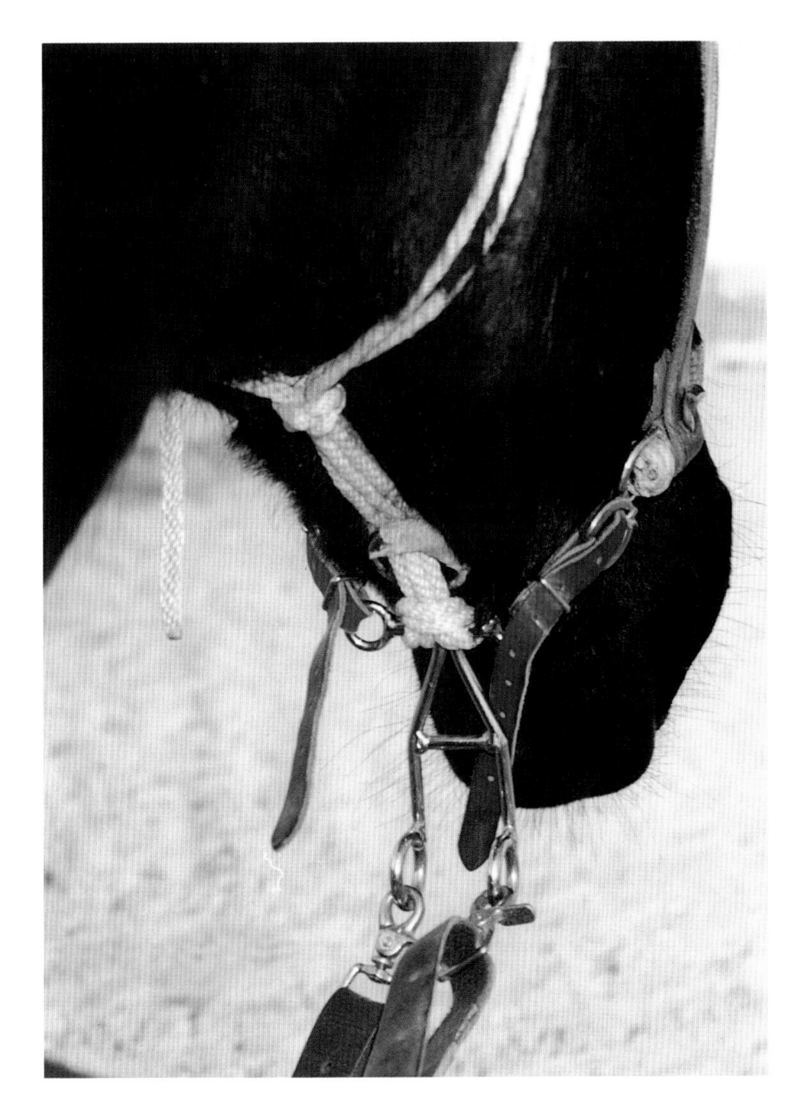

(left & above) The easy stop is a potentially severe bitless bridle, which is capable of applying crushing force to the horse's lower jaw.

Easy stops are essentially designed to intimidate horses into compliance or submission. A little pull goes a long way. Handled roughly, they're capable of breaking jawbones. When a rider decides to use an easy stop, it is generally a method of last resort. That's generally when muscle becomes a substitute for time and better training ideas. Unfortunately, at one time easy stops gained a measure of popularity when some trainers began promoting them as a quick way to get extreme vertical flexion. However, easy stops, and other such instruments, are never a good substitute for patient, humane training, and they are prohibited in almost all judged events.

"CONSTRUCTION, QUALITY AND FIT ARE IMPORTANT TO THE WAY A BOSAL FUNCTIONS."

12

The Traditional Hackamore

While not every horse is an ideal candidate for the hackamore, few things are more beautiful than a finely crafted bosal on a striking, confident and responsive athlete.

The true hackamore is a combination of headstall, bosal (nosepiece), mecate (horsehair reins and leadrope), and sometimes a fiador (throatlatch). Modern hackamore horsemanship evolved from Spanish vaquero traditions. At one time hackamores were used almost exclusively by West Coast reinsmen, but today the hackamore knows no geographic boundaries.

The late Tony Amaral of Byron, California, and Al Dunning of Scottsdale, Arizona, represent two different generations of hackamore horsemen. They shared their enthusiasm for the tool and explained how it can best be used to train exceptional athletes. These men have won countless titles in reining, working cowhorse, cutting, roping and other events.

Amaral came from a California ranching background and learned to use the hackamore from some of the great oldtime vaqueros — men who started their horses in hackamores and often spent several years training them in the hackamore before putting them into a bit. Amaral was widely regarded as one of the best hackamore reinsmen ever. Al Dunning represents a newer breed of hackamore enthusiast. He grew up showing horses in Arizona, and he, too, learned from some top hands, including Don Dodge. Dunning adopted the more modern use of the hackamore, that of a transitional tool between the snaffle bit and the bridle.

Both Amaral and Dunning explained that the bosal conveys certain training advantages not available with other head gear, and shared their knowledge in this chapter.

(top) The traditional hackamore.
(above left) Detail of a well-made bosal, with fine strands used in the cheeks, each strand beveled to make the edges lie smooth.
(above right) The base of the heel knot shows that this bosal's core is made of rawhide.

(overleaf) Al Dunning has achieved excellent results with reining horses using the hackamore. The sensitivity of the horse's nose is central to control in the hackamore.

CONSTRUCTION, QUALITY AND FIT

The heart of the hackamore is the bosal, historically a braided rawhide, leather or hitched or twisted horsehair noseband formed around a rawhide core. While some manufacturers market aluminum and synthetic bosals, the most respected hackamore reinsmen don't recommend them, nor are they permitted in the show ring.

Bosal, (correctly pronounced bo-SAUL, but commonly said bo-zelle, bozzel or bo-zal) comes from the Spanish word bozal, meaning muzzle. Construction, quality and fit are important to the way a bosal functions. What's inside is equally important. The bosal is typically braided around a rawhide, nylon or metal cable core. A rawhide core is preferable because it provides greater flexibility and feel. And it is the bosal's "feel" or "life," which gives the hackamore its special advantage.

Rawhide cores will vary greatly in their stiffness and flexibility. The thicker or the more twists to the rawhide, the firmer the bosal will be. An advantage of a rawhide core is that the bosal can be easily molded to fit the horse's face. To modify or shape the opening, the leather or rawhide can be dampened and the bosal placed around a cylindrical object to dry. (Be careful to use a form that won't discolor the noseband). Cable and synthetic cores don't provide this luxury. They tend to hold their original shape no matter what you do. Metal and nylon cores also tend to make the bosal stiffer and less yielding, thus more severe. Bosals with metal cable cores are generally not permitted in the show ring. You can usually (but not always) tell what the core material is by looking at the butt, or heel knot of the bosal.

The bosal has four parts: the nose button, which sits across the bridge of the nose; the side buttons, which hold the headstall in place; the cheeks, which contact the sides and jaws of the horse's face; and the heel button or heel knot, which is the counterbalance to the nosepiece.

The number of strands used in the braidwork (known as plaits) affects both the quality and price of the bosal. The number will also affect its weight and balance. The tightness and smoothness of the braiding are also considerations in judging quality. The number of plaits is

Most bosals naturally arc in one direction, due to the braidwork. The arc should curve downward, toward the chin.

The heart of the hackamore is the noseband or bosal. Bosals come in a variety of sizes, textures, and weights.

determined by counting around the circumference of the cheekpiece rather than the nose button. Sometimes consumers are misled into thinking that the plait count is a combination of the strands in the cheek- and nose-pieces, but this isn't so. Standards within the industry are 8, 12, 16 and 24-plait bosals. Sixteen plait bosals are perhaps the most common in show tack. Some craftsmen are even commissioned to produce 32-plait bosals, but that's unusual and very costly due to the complexity of the braiding.

The intricacy of fine braiding is certainly valuable as an art form, but a bosal with a moderate number of plaits might be more practical and comfortable for the horse, Amaral noted. When a bosal gets sweaty and dirty, the edges of each strand can stand up and become rasplike and irritate the horse's nose and jaw. On the finest made bosals, the edges of the rawhide and leather strands are beveled prior to braiding so they lay perfectly flat. It's also important to keep the bosal clean and conditioned so that dirt and sweat don't cause ridges to develop. Saddle soap and leather conditioner or even beeswax can be used to keep the braiding smooth.

Dale Chavez, a respected tack manufacturer, recommends that newcomers to hackamore horsemanship use what he calls a "safety" bosal. This is a bosal woven of smooth, soft latigo leather over a pliable rawhide core. Such a bosal has less bite and reduces the risk of chafing. On rawhide bosals, the Chavez Company has taken another precaution. The rawhide is woven with the hide inside out. That way the abrasive hair follicles don't rub the horse's face raw.

SIZE VARIATION

Training bosals usually come in 5/8 to 3/4-inch diameters as measured in the cheekpieces. But bosals can range in size from as narrow as 5/16 (known as pencil bosals or bosalitos) to as wide as 1 inch. (Remember, we're talking about cheek diameters. In most bosals, the nose buttons will be larger than the cheekpieces). The appropriate size will depend on the horse's sensitivity and stage of training.

The quality and life or feel of the bosal is determined by the core and the number and make-up of the plaits.

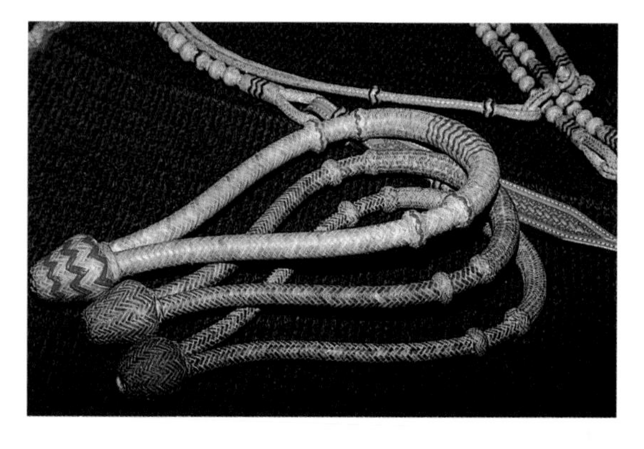

Generally speaking, the larger and heavier the bosal, the more pressure it exerts on the nose when resting and when the reins are pulled. For an uneducated horse, the added signal makes the rider's request clearer and more urgent. As the hackamore horse progresses, the rider uses lighter and lighter cues, and moves from thicker to thinner bosals, perhaps in several steps. Smaller bosals tend to be lighter and more pliable than larger ones and are usually less severe. However, a bosal with a small diameter that is exceptionally stiff and unyielding tends to concentrate pressure on a given point, much like a bit with a small mouthpiece, increasing the severity.

The size of the bosal from the top of the nose button to inside the heel knot is also important. Fit can be adjusted somewhat by the number of wraps taken when tying the

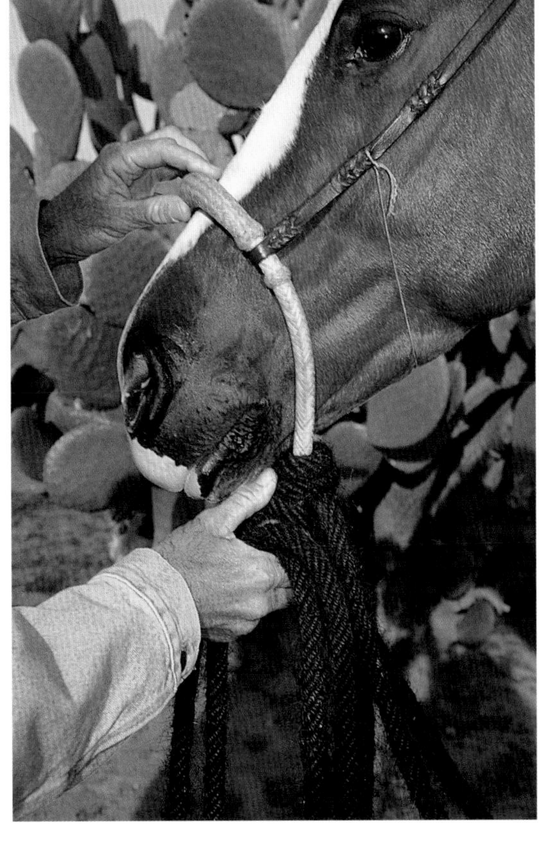

(above) It is important that the bosal be fitted to the horse so that the heel knot curves towards the horse's chin.

(left) There needs to be an inch or more space between the mecate knot and the jawline, so the bosal moves freely.

mecate — as long as the bosal is not too small to begin with. The industry standard is 12-14 inches (although 10 inches is sufficient for some of today's refined, small-muzzled horses). The extra inch or two may be needed to accommodate larger horses. When the headstall is fitted and the mecate is tied, the mecate knot should hang at least an inch below the horse's jawline when the reins are released.

The heel knot and wraps of the mecate balance the entire hackamore and should be of sufficient weight to allow the bosal to drop forward away from the jaw the instant rein pressure is released. A fiador can help balance the heel knot, keeping it off the chin. It will also stabilize and secure the headstall. However, a fiador which is too tight may prevent the bosal from dropping away from the jaw when pressure is released, and some trainers, such as Amaral and Dunning, prefer to omit it. Instead, they rely on the natural balance and stability of the bosal and a simple headstall to keep the hackamore in position. A thin latigo or rope jowl strap is often used to prevent the headstall from riding up into the horse's eye.

THE MECATE

The traditional mecate is a 21 to 22-foot-long horse hair rope which is tied around the heel knot of the bosal to form one continuous rein and lead rope. The weight of the mecate in combination with the weight of the bosal's heel button acts as a counterbalance to the nose button and allows the hackamore to disengage swiftly when the rider releases his rein hold.

The mecate is also called falsariendas (Spanish for false reins) because it is not a permanent part of any one hackamore and is periodically taken from one bosal and put on another. Most horsehair mecates come in diameters ranging between 3/8- to 3/4- inch thick. Riders should choose the size most comfortable to their hands and which complement the size of the bosal. Too often, people simply follow the recommendation of someone else rather than going by what feels right to them. However, working with reins that are too large or bulky can inhibit horsemanship.

Also, the smaller the bosal, the finer the horsehair reins that are used with it. This becomes especially important when the bosal is used under the bridle during traditional vaquero training. Finer reins make it easier for the horseman to deal with a double set of reins (known as riding a two-rein), with one pair attached to the bosal and the other to the bit.

Traditional mecates are generally made from either mane or tail hair or a combination of the two. Mane hair ropes are softer and therefore preferable to tail hair mecates,

but they are also more expensive. Light hair also tends to be finer than dark hair. It's been said that some oldtimers used to prefer the pricklier ropes, and would even make them from oxtails because the coarse hair would irritate or sore the horse's neck and make the task of teaching the horse to neck rein easier. Not everyone buys this theory. Amaral said the truth of the matter was that good horse hair ropes were simply hard to come by. And because many of the ropes available in the past were so coarse, it was common for traditional reinsmen to wear gloves when showing hackamore horses.

Learning to correctly tie the mecate is important. It takes knowledge and practice to achieve the proper result. When finished, the knot, reins, and lead rope should be one smooth, snug, well-balanced unit.

Many bosals have a distinct front and back. This can make a difference in how they will hang on the horse. When the bosal was woven, the braider's braiding pattern (left to right, or right to left) may have caused the bosal to arc slightly in one direction. If there is a discernable arc, it's important that the heel knot of the bosal curve toward the horse's chin. As you tie the mecate, this slight bow may become more pronounced. This is fine, as long as the heel knot does not rest against the horse's chin.

Also, decide whether you want your lead rope to extend toward the front or back of the heel knot. When the hackamore is being used to ride in open range country and will also serve as a halter (usually with a fiador), it's probably advantageous for the lead rope to extend to the front. For training and showing purposes, the bosal may remain in better balance if the lead rope and reins all exit to the rear, toward the horse. That way, when the lead rope is secured around the saddle horn, it does not cause the bosal to twist on the horse's nose.

There are several ways to tie the mecate. We've included the method preferred by Al Dunning, at the end of this chapter. The true test of the hackamore's fit won't come until you've put the bosal on your horse's head. Remember, there should be at least an inch of space between the horse's chin and the mecate knot. The bosal should balance lightly on the horse's nose with only light contact with the cheeks and no contact beneath the jaw. If it doesn't, start again. Take fewer or more wraps, depending on the horse's size.

When riding, the lead rope can be tucked loosely into your belt, wrapped around the saddle horn and secured with a half hitch, or even coiled and tied to the front saddle strings. Traditionally, when a cowboy was riding a broncy colt, it behooved him to tuck the mecate lead into his belt or pocket so that if he parted company with his horse, he'd still have a hold of it. It probably spared the buckaroo many a walk home. Also, note that the traditional vaquero way of holding the hackamore reins is with a small loop in the left hand, allowing the rider to vary his rein length depending on his needs. However, this custom is seldom honored anymore.

(opposite top) Louis Ortega was known as one of the masters for braiding bosals with tremendous feel. This Ortega belongs to hackamore enthusiast Al Dunning.

(opposite bottom) The proper and traditional way to hold the hackamore reins is with a small loop held in the left hand.

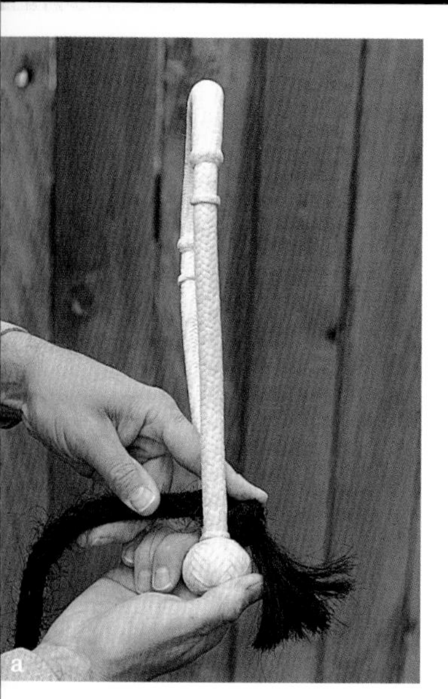
a

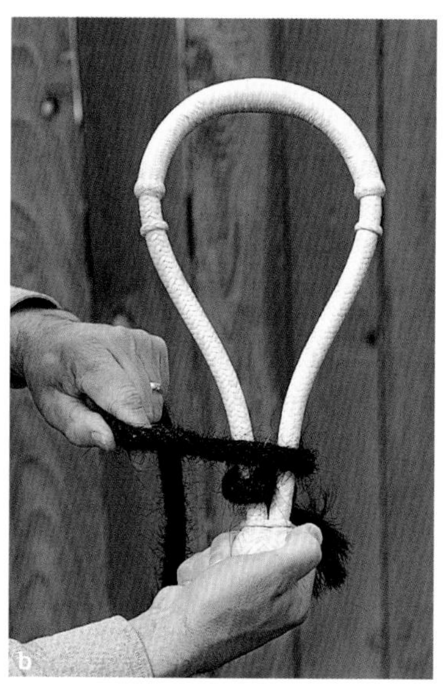
b

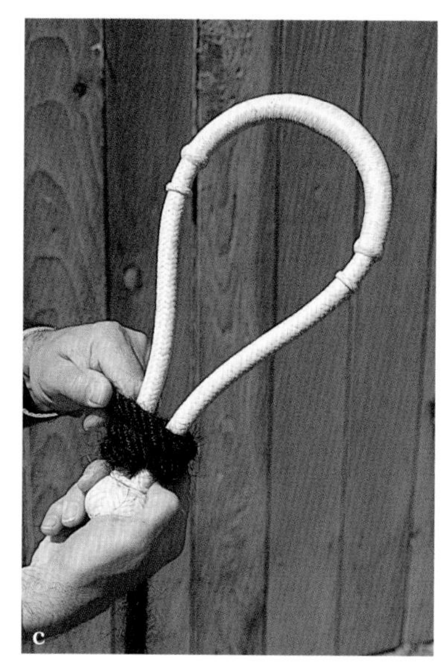
c

d

a. Start by turning the bosal so it arcs away from you. Remember, the heel button should curve toward the horse's chin, not toward the jaw. Thread the tail knot of the mecate between the branches of the bosal so the tail points away from you. If you can, snug it into place against the heel button. If the space is too tight, the mecate may not fit all the way down into the groove without damaging the bosal. Don't force it. Simply take your first wrap below it. Keep the tail short so it won't hit the horse in the face.

b, c, d. Take two to three clockwise wraps (left to right) around the cheekpieces. The number of wraps will be determined by the size of your horse's nose. The first wrap may need to be below the mecate's tail knot to fill the space between it and the heel button. Spiral upward, laying one wrap neatly on top of the other, snugging and straightening the rope as you go. Use your thumb to help keep the wraps flat and tight.

e, f. On the next wrap, form the reins by pulling a loop of the mecate toward you through the center of the cheek branches.

g. Adjust the rein length for horse and rider. You can approximate using the span of your arms, or by actually slipping the bosal and mecate on the horse for an exact fit. With a slight drape to them, the reins should reach just behind the saddle horn with enough slack to allow the rider to take a small loop in the rein which is held in the left hand. Six to eight inches of slack behind the horn should be enough.

Before continuing, smooth out any wrinkles or kinks that may have developed in the rope so the reins will hang smoothly.

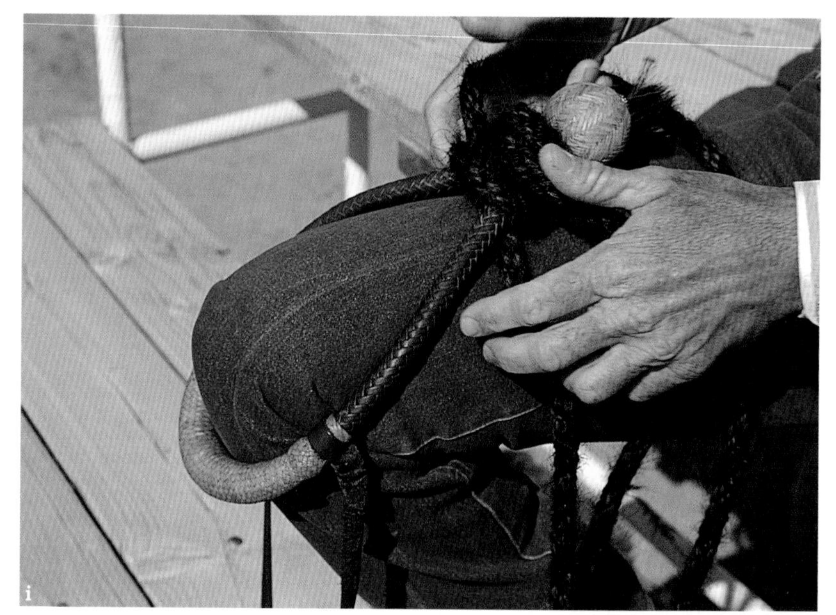
i

k

e

f

g

h

j

h. Keep the strands of your rope side by side between the branches of the bosal to ensure a definite left and right rein, and take another wrap. Again gently snug it down.

i. You can keep your knee through the center of the bosal, so the cheek branches do not close up and become too tight for the nose.

j. To secure the reins and create a lead rope, take at least one more full wrap around both cheeks. Begin another wrap around the left cheek branch, then thread the loose end through the middle and tuck it beneath the previous two layers so that the lead rope exits to the rear through the center between the reins. If you want the lead rope to extend to the front of the bosal, continue to wrap the mecate around the right cheek, then tuck the end of the rope beneath the previous layers so it extends in the opposite direction of the reins.

k. Snug the coils one more time, holding the bosal open with your knee or foot, making sure the mecate forms a flat, smooth bar beneath the horse's chin and jaw.

Check the hackamore's fit by putting it on the horse. Remember, there should be at least an inch of space between the horse's chin and the mecate knot. The bosal should balance lightly on the horse's nose with only light contact with the cheeks and no contact beneath the jaw.

The fiador (which runs from the heel knot of the bosal back along the jawline to the throatlatch and up over the poll) helps to balance the bridle, keeps the bosal in place and prevents the horse from slipping out of the headgear.

THE FIADOR

For cowboys who break colts or traditionally ride with a hackamore and rely on it as a halter and lead rope during rest breaks or while working on foot, the fiador is indispensable. The fiador helps keep the bosal in place and makes it difficult for the horse to rub off, pull off, buck off, or back out of its headgear. When properly tied, the fiador forms a throat-latch and bosal attachment which also helps to balance the bridle, support the weight of the heel knot and keep the bosal from resting on the horse's chin.

The fiador is generally made from 16 feet of thin sturdy rope. Quarter-inch nylon, cotton sash cord, or horse hair (horse hair was traditionally used) rope work well. The cord is doubled and tied using hackamore, fiador and sheet bend knots. The hackamore knot is tied three feet from the bight (the looped end). The loop that is formed slips over the bosal's heel knot. The remaining ends, which extend to the back of the bosal, are joined together and tied with a fiador knot (allowing enough rope to run the length of the jawline to the point of the throatlatch). The looped end of the cord will then be passed up through the off-side of the browband loops, around the poll and back through the near (left) side of the browband. When the hackamore is put on the horse, the free ends will be hooked through the loop and secured with a sheet bend knot.

PRINCIPLES OF USE

Many people are under the misconception that the true vaqueros started their horses in snaffle bits, then progressed to the hackamore and then into the bridle. But Tony Amaral, who learned his trade from traditional California reinsmen, emphasized that the use of the snaffle bit is really a modern phenomenon.

It was once common for stockmen to wait until their horses were four or five years of age to start them under saddle. The horses were allowed some time to grow up because cowboys needed horses with the strength and maturity to handle a full day's work. In the vaquero tradition, many of these horses were started in hackamores. Whether by intent or happenstance, such timing coincides nicely with the age at which most horses are cutting their bridle (canine) teeth.

Amaral's friend and contemporary, Don Dodge of Phoenix, is given much of the credit for popularizing the practice of training with snaffle bits before moving a horse into a hackamore. Dodge used the snaffle as a way to preserve a horse's nose so it would have a longer competitive career in the hackamore. Only later did the prestigious event for 3-year-olds known as the "Reined Cowhorse Snaffle Bit Futurity" emerge. It was done to develop a market for younger horses. But it also took a toll on the traditional training methods and popularity of hackamore classes.

The rise of the show horse industry has accelerated the horse's education and made the hackamore more of a transitional tool between the snaffle and the shanked bit. In effect, it still helps eliminate conflicts with teething, and allows trainers to build on the foundation established with the snaffle.

Riders such as Amaral and Dunning explain that they specifically like the hackamore because it helps them get more flexion through the poll, promotes a greater degree of collection and balance, and provides an opportunity to improve stopping power and directional control while staying out of the horse's mouth. A horse's skills can be refined to a high degree in the hackamore before the animal is introduced to a bridle (i.e. a shanked bit).

Perhaps the most important concept that Amaral and Dunning emphasize is that a good hackamore horseman does not rush the training process. By the time a horse graduates out of a hackamore, it should fluidly perform all the maneuvers it will be asked to do in the bridle, including responding to the neck rein.

In the vaquero tradition, when the horse first makes the transition to the bridle, the rider continues to ride off the hackamore reins while the horse learns to carry the bit. According to Tony Amaral, hackamores can be used effectively with either one or two hands on the reins, depending on a horse's stage and level of training. In West Coast reining and working cowhorse competition, hackamore events used to be divided into green and advanced classes. The green horses were shown two-handed, the advanced horses one-handed. Many horse show associations now permit hackamore users to ride with two hands, but this was not always the case. Al Dunning was instrumental in bringing about this change in American Quarter Horse Association competition.

In the early and intermediate stages of training, the hackamore is most useful as a two-handed device. When a hackamore is used two-handed, a direct rein is used to tip the horse's nose in the direction of the turn while being supplemented with a bearing (i.e. supporting or indirect) rein. The indirect rein not only instills the idea of neck reining, it provides stability for the hackamore.

The rider's hands are generally held low and wide. For turning, the direct rein should be used with more sideways than backwards pull. That way the rein provides a visual cue as to which way the horse should turn, and causes pressure to be applied to the side of the face (similar to the pull-through effect of the snaffle). The supporting rein keeps the bosal from tilting on the horse's face. A straight backwards pull on one rein would probably only confound the horse since the pressure would be exerted primarily on the top of the nose and beneath the jaw.

A hackamore is also ill-designed for use with equal pressure on both reins. As with other head controlling devices, unrelenting pressure gives the horse something to push or lean against. Also, because the hackamore contacts some very sensitive points on the face, the horse may become resentful, defiant or overly timid in response to heavy-handed rein pressure. Instead, the bosal should be used with a light bumping action, initiated by gently tugging on one rein at a time. This raises the heel knot, presses the nose button into

Tony Amaral, one of the most respected hackamore horsemen of all time, showed horses in the hackamore two-handed and one-handed, depending on the horse's stage of training.

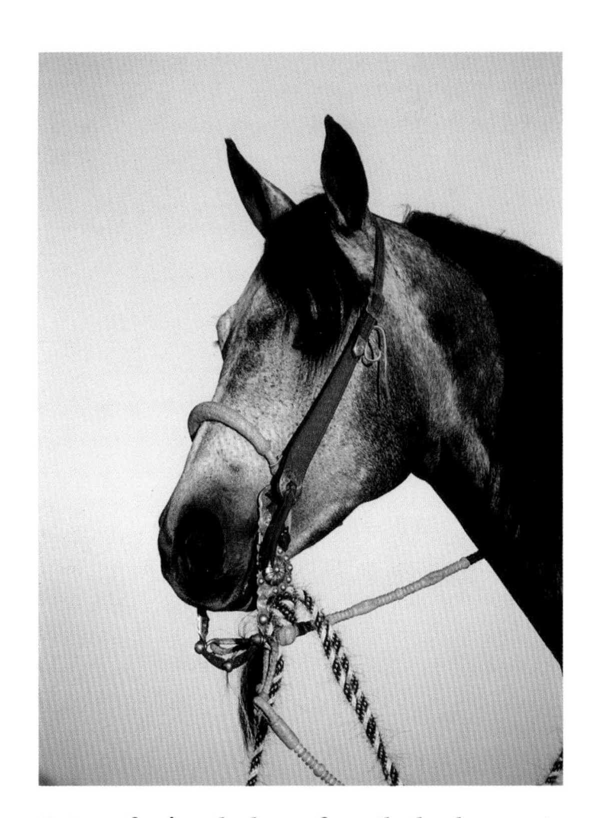

In transferring the horse from the hackamore to the spade bit, the vaqueros added the bit before removing the bosal and gradually transferred control from the bosal to the bit.

the top of the face, and brings the cheekpieces into contact with the sides and lower jaw at the same time. Alternating pulls and releases can be used to ask the horse to flex at the poll and stop. The hackamore is meant to be used with give-and-take action.

The natural rocking action of the bosal when the horse is in motion encourages the horse to flex at the poll and assume a more vertical headset. The heel knot acts as a counterbalance and helps prevent the animal from overflexing. However, an extremely sensitive horse equipped with a heavy or unstable hackamore or ridden with heavy hands may start to carry its nose well behind the vertical to try to avoid the bumping or friction on its nose and jawline. In such cases, it may be wise to evaluate the weight, size and use of the hackamore, or find something more suitable.

"Riders who get too rough with their hands usually make a horse resist," explains Dunning. "They can cause a horse to poke its nose through the hackamore rather than work off it. And the horse's nose is the important part. You never hear a good hackamore man talking about the jaw. When someone says a horse has a`good nose,' it means that when the hackamore rotates on the nose, the horse is sensitive enough to give its head. And if you have a horse that gives its head properly — the old term would be `stays over the knob,' which means the horse keeps its head vertical — you have so much control with the

(below left) Doubling is the practice of pulling the horse's face around to the side in order to take away its speed, direction and forward momentum.

(below right) The tip of the nasal bone is very thin and easily fractured. To prevent injury, the bosal should be placed slightly above the end of the bone. If the bosal is below the bone, the delicate nasal cartilage may be injured.

hackamore, it's unreal. If you have a horse that's not broke and wants to stick its nose through the hackamore, then you have very little control," said Dunning. "But when you have a horse broke right in the hackamore, it's the finest feeling piece of equipment you can use."

Doubling is another technique promoted by oldtime hackamore horsemen to teach horses to stop in the bosal. Doubling is the practice of pulling the horse's face around to the side in order to take away its speed, direction and forward momentum. This same technique is used to turn a horse into the fence in a rollback. If the foundation is laid early in training, doubling can be useful in developing consistent control and a reliable stop in the hackamore.

There is some debate about where the bosal should be placed on the nose. Positioned correctly, it should rest on the bridge of the nose, or just slightly above, where it is supported by the nasal bone. The horse's responses will help you determine the right spot. Resistance may be a sign of painful contact. Check to make sure the bosal fits and is positioned correctly. It is also a good idea to periodically move the bosal up or down a fraction of an inch to preserve responsiveness. While some trainers might suggest that the bosal should be placed low on the nose near the nostrils where bone turns to cartilage, be aware that the lower the noseband sits, the greater the risk of damaging the tip of the nasal bone or cartilage if you pull too hard.

Some misinformed people also promote the idea of intentionally soring a horse's nose and jawline to elicit a better response with a hackamore. However, if you have to resort to such tactics for control, the hackamore is the wrong choice of tack. Callused skin loses its sensitivity and repeated abuse dulls the horse's reactions to your commands. You could also be dismissed from a class for signs of soring.

Accomplished hackamore reinsmen go to extra lengths to preserve a horse's sensitivity. They choose finely crafted bosals with a lot of flexibility and feel. They may even wrap the cheeks of the bosal with electrical tape, latex or lambs wool to make contact softer and more subtle. The bosal should make only light contact with the nose and cheeks. Only when the rein hand is raised should the heel knot be tipped into contact with the lower jaw.

"THE KEY TO SUCCESS WITH A SPADE BIT IS IN ITS SIGNAL."

13

The Spade Bit and Its Relatives

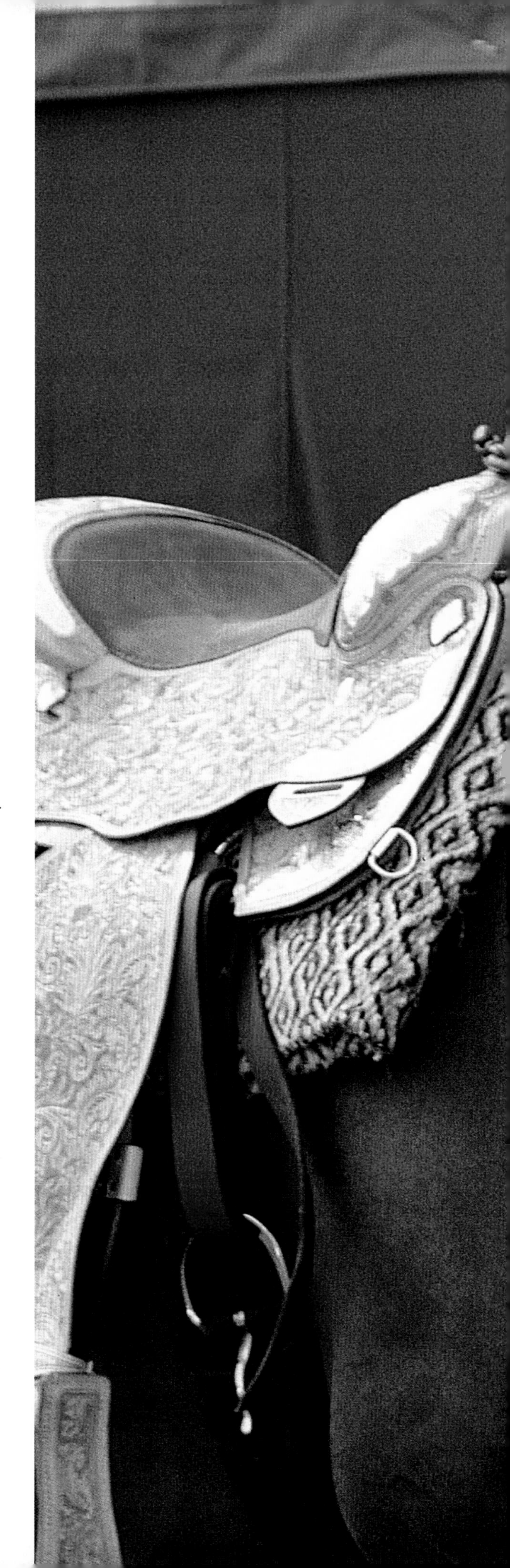

Bits very similar to today's spade bits were probably used in the time of Xenophon in 370 B.C. In more recent times, the vaqueros of old Mexico and California used the spade bit as an integral part of their training and horsemanship, and its influence gradually spread eastward. Today, a handful of men and women have preserved some of the old bridle horse traditions, yet admit that some of the techniques are becoming lost, forgotten or bastardized.

Using the spade, the vaqueros were able to achieve a subtlety and brilliance of performance seldom surpassed. Whether they could have achieved equal results with less severe bits is a valid question. Though potentially severe, the spade allows exquisite communication between horse and rider because of the way it contacts the tongue and palate — the two most sensitive areas of the mouth.

While it has been said that the vaqueros never used a spade bit until the horse was thoroughly trained in the hackamore, oldtimers will tell you that then, as now, riders did what they needed to do to gain their horses' attention and respect. Because not every horse has a sensitive nose, some horses were probably advanced into a bit sooner than others. But typically, the transition to the bridle was made gradually. Further, not every horse went immediately into a spade. There are other California-style bits, such as half-breeds, that provided intermediate steps into the bridle.

As training progressed, a spade bit was often hung in the horse's mouth but left alone while the rider continued to signal the horse via the hackamore reins. Gradually the rider would start to bring the spade bit reins into play, using them in conjunction with the hackamore reins. After being ridden for a time in this two-reined system, the bosal

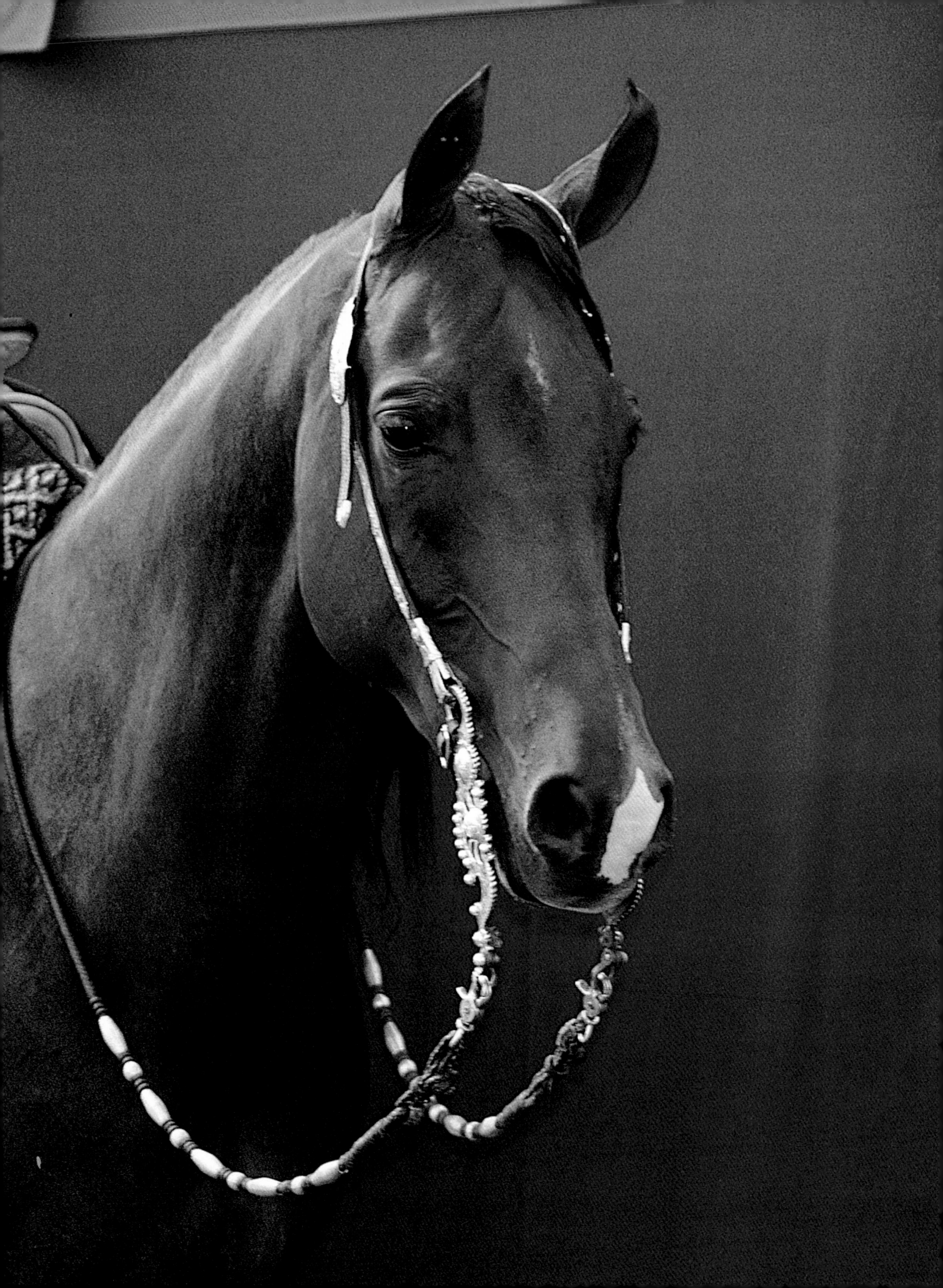

(overleaf) ***This horse is relaxed with his vaquero style bit. Even with no rein tension, the bit encourages the horse to carry his head in an attractive position. The cheeks of California style bits are often wide, heavy and ornate. They should be balanced in such a way that the bit releases contact with the mouth as soon as pressure on the reins is released.***

(above) ***In progressing from the hackamore to the spade bit the horse is sometimes ridden in a two-reined system, gradually transferring commands from the hackamore to the spade bit rein.***

(below left) ***A spoon extending relatively straight up from the mouthpiece makes for a severe bit, giving little signal to the horse.***
(below right) ***A bit with a laid back spoon affords more signal.***

was removed and the horse was ridden with just the bit. The transition to the spade bit alone is know as "putting the horse straight up in the bridle."

SPADE BIT DESIGN AND THEORY

The key to success with a spade bit is in its signal. The swing of the slack, and the laying of rein against neck, rather than the sheer force of tension on the mouthpiece, were behind the vaquero's success. By the time the horse was ridden in just the spade bit, the horse was expected to be so well trained that the slightest of rein movements would elicit a response.

Unfortunately, not everyone has used the spade with such care and finesse. By design, spade bits can be a powerful means of controlling a horse with little regard for its mouth. Over the years, enough riders have abused their horses with spade bits that the bits have been condemned by many. But there are many devices on the market today that are equally dangerous in the wrong hands. Unlike a good spade mouthpiece, they've been intentionally designed to inflict pain.

A spade bit is a shanked (leverage) bit which should be used with a curb strap. The bit has a straight bar mouthpiece with a centerpiece to which a cricket and spoon (or spade) are attached. The spoon is designed to rest against tongue and palate. A well-designed mouthpiece creates a slight suction that helps the horse keep the bit in the proper position. One advantage is that the high spoon makes it virtually impossible for a busy-mouthed horse to get its tongue over the bit. Another is that the cricket may pacify a nervous horse and promote a wet mouth. In fact, many spade bit horses happily work the cricket while holding the mouthpiece in a comfortable position.

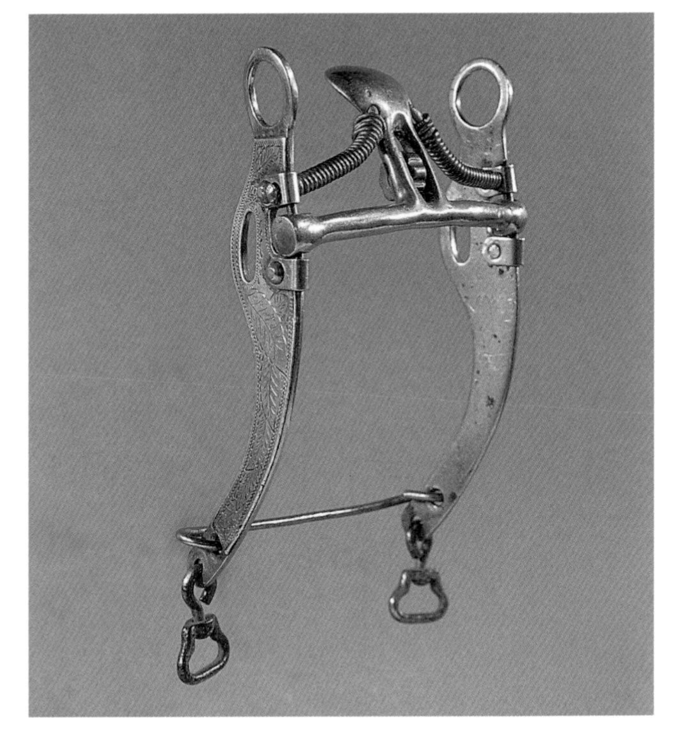

Above the solid bar mouthpiece are braces, also called spacer bars, which connect from the cheeks to the spoon. These are often wrapped with tightly coiled copper wire or copper beads. The spacer bars prevent the bit from shifting too far back into the horse's mouth where it might damage the soft palate. They come into contact with the corners of the horse's mouth, while the straight bar sits lower on the tongue and mouth bars, nearer the middle of the space between the incisors and cheek teeth.

The height, shape and angle of the mouthpiece are of paramount importance. In some spade bits, the spoon extends virtually straight up in line with the upper shanks. This adds to the severity of the spade, as any rotation of the lower shanks would bring the apex of the spoon into sharp contact with the palate. To compensate, the horse will sometimes overflex at the poll and assume a behind-the-vertical headset.

Legendary bridleman Don Dodge points out that the better-designed spades should have high, narrow spoons, never more than two fingers in width and at least 3 inches high. The spade should be smooth and laid back in such a way that it can rest comfortably on tongue and palate, contacting the roof of the mouth far up into the mouth without poking it. Shorter spades, he observes, often lack the stability of the longer ones and may tip or tilt in the horse's mouth when the reins are pulled.

Dodge also notes that straighter spades may tend to put the horse on the defensive, causing the animal to elevate its head. In contrast, the laid back spade encourages the horse to perform with a more natural head and neck carriage. A finely balanced spade hangs in such a way that it is uncomfortable for the horse to carry its head either too high or too low. It also promotes a desirable degree of poll flexion, with the front of the horse's face at or just slightly in front of the vertical. This position is often referred to as having a horse "in the bridle" or simply "bridled." This characteristic head carriage is probably where the term "putting the horse straight up in the bridle" originates. An "overbridled" horse, on the other hand, is one who gets behind the bit to try to avoid contact.

Rein tension on the spade puts pressure on the tongue similar to that of a simple, straight-barred curb bit. There is also pressure on the bars of the mouth and the chin groove due to the action of the curb strap. Because the bit has no port, there is no provision for tongue relief, and a jerk on the reins can simultaneously cut both the tongue and the palate. If not handled delicately, the spade bit is capable of causing significant damage to the mouth.

The cheeks of spade bits are often wide, heavy and ornate. It is usually difficult for the horse to catch them with his lips. As in other leverage bits, the cheeks should be balanced in such a way that the bit releases contact with the mouth as soon as contact with the reins is released. The cheeks will also add greatly to the overall weight of the bit.

(above) This spade bit has a spoon that is well rolled back. Additionally, there is a roller at the apex of the spoon in order to ease the movement of the spoon across the palate when rein pressure is applied. The combination of these features makes the bit relatively gentle.

(below) "Straight up in the bridle." A finely balanced spade bit encourages the desirable degree of poll flexion and encourages the horse to carry his head neither too high nor too low.

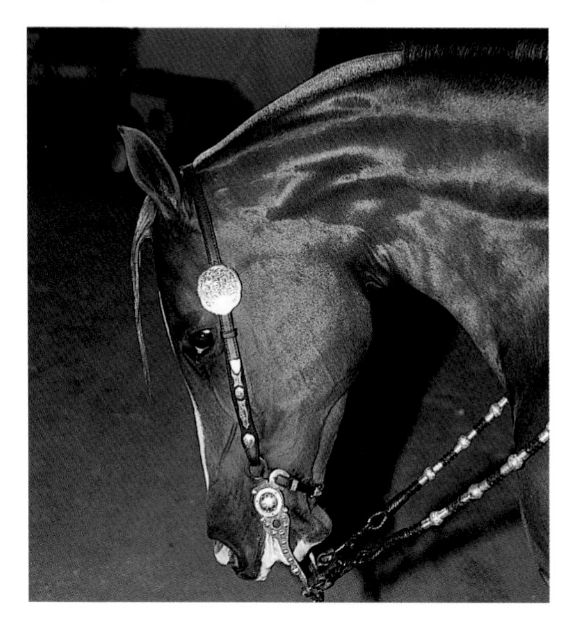

Weight can be both a positive and negative factor. In a spade bit, the weight of the shanks should help balance the weight of the mouthpiece, allowing the horse to carry the bit in the proper position. Additional weight also amplifies the pull on the reins. As Don Dodge succinctly points out, you don't have to hit someone as hard with a lead pipe as you do with a wooden stick to get the same impact. In fact, old spade bit riders commonly added lead shot or ornate buttons to their rawhide bridle reins to multiply the force of the signal: ie. more weight, less hand movement to get the desired response. Metal "slobber" chains which attach reins to bit shanks, as well as metal stabilizer bars or chains (sometimes called shank hobbles or slobber bars) that extend between the bottom of the shanks, also add to the weight of these California-style bits.

Spade bits and their relatives are traditionally ridden with rawhide or braided leather romal reins. Unlike split reins, the two reins join into one at the romal (ro-mel), a flexible quirt or whip. The reins are traditionally held in the left hand with the reins passing through the palm, bottom to top. The romal or quirt is held in the right hand.

According to Don Dodge, the reins can be held in one of two ways: He prefers to pass the reins between pinkie and ring finger, up through the palm of his hand and out through thumb and forefinger. However, the rules of many horse show associations, including the National Reined Cow Horse Association, stipulate that the romal reins must pass to the outside of the pinkie finger. Dodge maintains that by doing so the rider sacrifices some of his grip and feel of the horse's mouth. The reins should be held low over the saddle horn, and should be kept even to prevent the spoon from twisting in the horse's mouth. On a good bridle horse, the rider's hands should never have to move more than an inch or two in any direction. It should take relatively little tension on the reins to get the desired response.

BITS FOR TODAY?

Great bridlemen lament that many of the true bridle horse traditions are all but lost. Tony Amaral and Don Dodge have been mentors to many of today's top reining, cutting and working cowhorse riders, and in this way, have passed on some of the true vaquero traditions. Amaral and Dodge learned from the masters of their day, and point out that the great California reinsmen took years to develop and train their horses. Their show horses were also their working ranch horses, and they saw a lot more hard miles than the horses competing today.

While the vaquero methods tend to be romanticized, Dodge points out that spade bits, half-breeds and other bridles did and do give horsemen more firepower. A seasoned horse, one who perhaps no longer has much respect for the hackamore or a milder bit, is less likely to ignore or challenge a spade bit. And then, as now, the best way for the horse to avoid palate, tongue and bar pressure is to flex at the poll and submit to bit pressure.

Yet an overzealous pull on a palate type bit is likely to cause the horse to raise its head, stiffen up and gape its mouth. Used as a pry bar, a spade bit is unlikely to help any rider win a performance contest. With a spade bit, finesse is the name of the game. It's fair to assume that a horse which works with its ears up and mouth closed is reasonably comfortable with its bit. And, in keeping with the vaquero's art, the traditions and techniques should be passed from the most knowledgeable to the most skilled.

The most basic half-breed is a straight-barred curb bit with a high narrow centerpiece that contains a roller or cricket.

THE CALIFORNIA INFLUENCE

There are several other types of bits which, though not technically spades, borrow some of the features. Many of these have mouthpieces or shanks which have been named after places, people, even horses, and appropriately reflect the Spanish heritage: Las Cruces, San Joaquin, and Salinas mouthpieces, and Santa Barbara cheeks, are just a few examples.

Half-breed bits include several mouthpieces that feature closed ports with crickets. The most basic half-breed is a straight-barred curb bit with a high narrow centerpiece that contains a roller or cricket. Crickets are often made of steel or copper, or a combination of the two. Like the spade, the straight, solid mouthpiece of the simple half-breed effectively removes any tongue relief. The half-breed's name comes from the fact that it is a hybrid between a curb bit and a spade bit. However, it lacks the braces and spoon of a spade and the open port of the curb.

Also included in this group are bits that are sometimes called hooded curbs. This includes the Mona Lisa, Salinas and San Joaquin mouthpieces and several variations. There is often some confusion among these three mouthpieces and they are sometimes mistaken for spade bits. Each mouthpiece has a copper-covered hood over the port and generally a cricket.

Don Dodge originated the Mona Lisa mouthpiece, and explains that it was named after a great reined cowhorse mare that he showed. What sets this mouthpiece apart

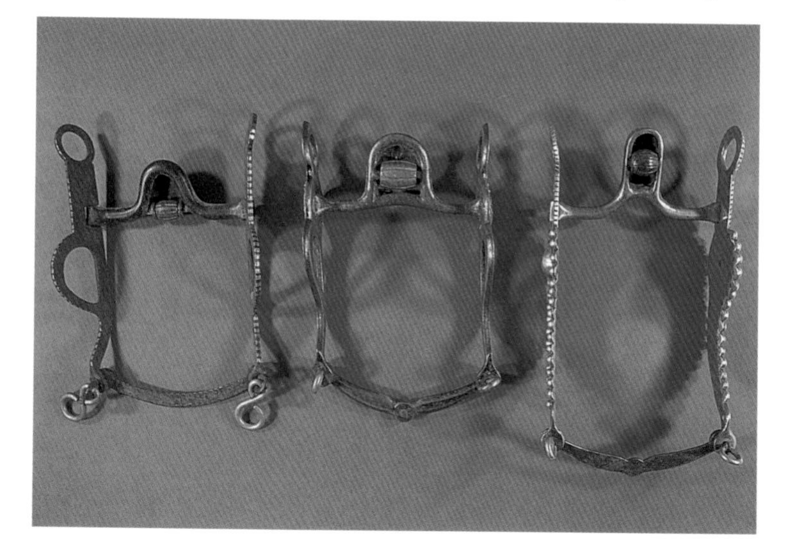

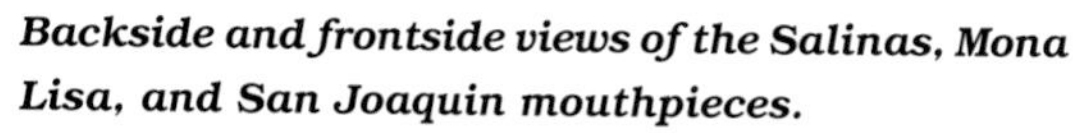

Backside and frontside views of the Salinas, Mona Lisa, and San Joaquin mouthpieces.

from the Salinas is that its steel cricket is tucked well up into the port. The bit bars extend across the width of the mouthpiece with only a slight rise over the tongue. The placement of the cricket within the port improves its wear life, and makes it less likely that a sharp edge will develop along the bottom of the mouthpiece which could cut the tongue. Dodge also notes that such placement of the cricket makes the bit sing a little louder than the Salinas as the horse rolls the cricket with the tongue. In the Salinas mouthpiece, the cricket ties into the bit bars at the bottom of the hooded port. The San Joaquin is usually differentiated from the other two by its higher, narrower, copper-covered port with the cricket placed even higher than in the Mona Lisa.

The so-called cathedral bit has a high, spoon or triangular-shaped port which rises as much as 3½ inches above the mouthpiece. Cathedral bits are generally open at the bottom of the port and lack a cricket. The Las Cruces mouthpiece resembles a cathedral with its flattened and rolled back, A-shaped port, but is much lower.

With any of this family of palate-type bits the pressure on the roof of the mouth may essentially be eliminated by a tightly adjusted curb strap. Certainly the height, width

The cathedral bit has a high spoon over a triangular-shaped port which rises as much as 3½ inches above the mouthpiece. Cathedral bits are generally open at the bottom of the port and lack a cricket.

This particular half-breed bit does not have a hooded port.

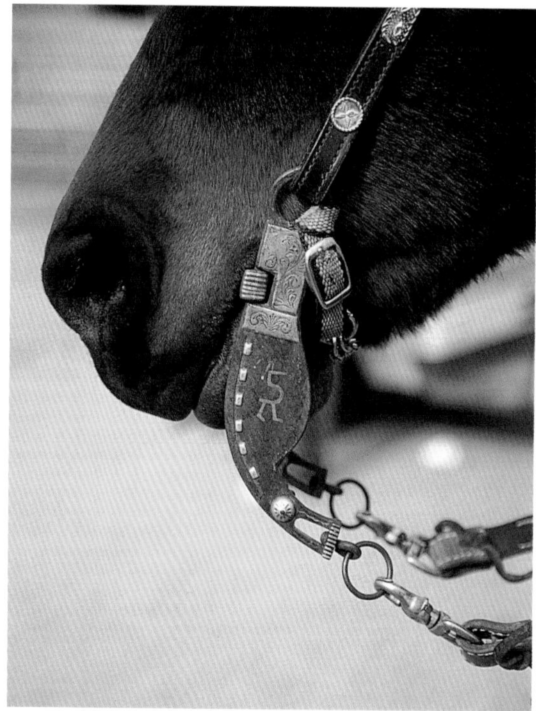

(above) With any of the palate-type bits, the pressure on the roof of the mouth may essentially be eliminated by a tightly adjusted curb strap. (left) A frog-mouthed Santa Barbara bit. This particular bit has been wrapped in latex to provide bar relief.

and curvature of the port, and the angle in which the mouthpiece has been set into the cheeks will affect their potential severity. As with the spade bit, the half-breed, Salinas and Mona Lisa bits put direct pressure on the tongue because their solid, covered port hoods and crickets provide no space for tongue relief. It is also important to realize that any raised port or spoon need not be 2 inches high to contact the palate if there is no tongue relief because the bit does not rest on the bars but rather sits on top of the tongue. This decreases the distance between the high point of the mouthpiece and the palate. Bits with hooded ports are also more likely to contact the palate because of the sheer thickness of the metal in the center of the mouthpiece.

"MANY RESPECTED TRAINERS USE BITTING AND TRAINING ACCESSORIES TO GET RESULTS."

14

Bit Accessories & Training Aids

Although some people think of anything other than bit and reins as gimmicks, many respected trainers routinely use bitting and training accessories to get results in a timely way. Even while your hands, seat and legs will continue to be your most reliable riding assets, learning to utilize accessories knowledeably can enhance training, carriage and performance, and make your job as a rider easier and safer.

NOSEBANDS

There are many types of nosebands. Some people routinely call any and all nosebands cavessons. Other people reserve the term cavesson to identify only the noseband portion of an English bridle. We will use the two terms interchangeably.

The principle purpose of a noseband is to aid or modify the bit's action. A noseband may be used simply as a way to keep the horse's mouth shut, or to prevent the horse from evading contact. For example, a noseband used with a standing martingale (also called a tie-down) can keep the horse from raising its head to avoid the bridle's pressure. A carefully placed noseband, such as a dropped noseband, may also promote a quiet mouth and discourage habitual lower lip flapping as a nervous response.

When the main function of the noseband or cavesson is as a point of attachment for a martingale, the noseband should be fitted relatively high on the bridge of the nose, well above the lower end of the nasal bones. One way to establish placement for this purpose is to measure two fingers width below the front of the projecting cheek bones (facial crests). To ensure that it's not too tight, two fingers should slip easily between the front of the face and the

(overleaf) A roper chases down the calf as his jerk line feeds out of his belt, keeping tension on the horse's bit.

(top) The standard cavesson is a flat leather strap. (above) This wire noseband is thin and has quite a bite. This horse will be unlikely to open its mouth to evade bit pressure.

inside of the noseband. A properly constructed noseband should hang at a right angle with its cheekpieces.

The standard cavesson is a flat leather strap, but western trainers commonly use rolled leather, rope and nylon nosebands as well. There are other types and some are designed to be less than kind, including spiked, chain, cable and even wire. The idea of the severe types is to keep the horse from leaning into them. But many such nosebands are potentially damaging — and especially so if they are adjusted or fitted so tightly that there is no way for the horse to escape their impact. For example, the spiked or spike-nose cavesson has small metal cone-shaped studs embedded in its lining. These are abrasive to the horse's nose. While they may increase control of the head, they can also damage the nerves in the nose, especially if the horse should fall. Rope, cable, chain and wire cavessons pack a more severe bite than their smooth, flat leather counterparts. Some manufacturers may try to reduce the impact of such devices by encasing the core material in leather or plastic, but the effects can still be rough.

Be aware that most horse show associations restrict the types of nosebands that are allowed and the classes in which they are permitted. Some events may require the use of a noseband and standing martingale as safety components. Sheepskin-covered cavessons or shadow rolls prevent the horse from seeing the ground in front of it and are used to prevent shying at shadows or other potentially frightening sights.

One of the most commonly used training cavessons is the simple dropped noseband, usually either of leather or rope. The dropped noseband is fitted just at the lower end of the nasal bones. The lower portion passes below the bit and lies in the chin groove. The dropped noseband should be carefully adjusted so that it does not hang too low where it could interfere with the horse's breathing. It should also be loose enough to permit some movement of the lower jaw rather than requiring the horse to maintain rigid contact with the bit. A mobile jaw will allow the horse to relax and yield more readily to the bit's signals.

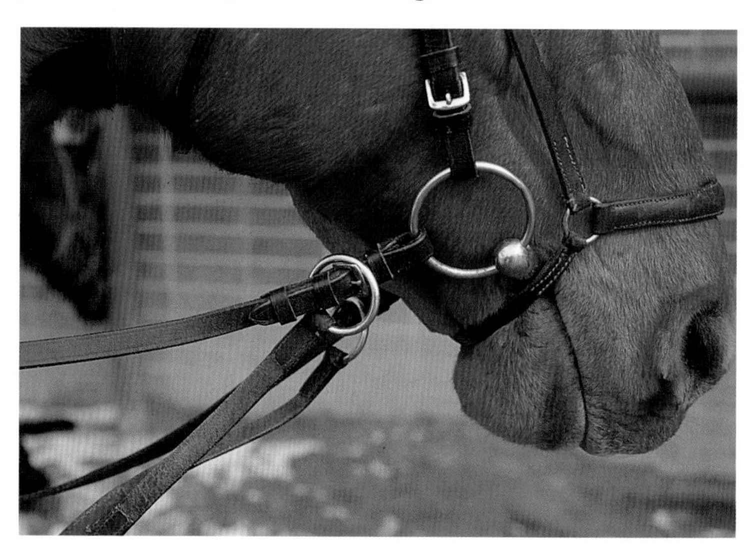

(right) The dropped noseband passes below the bit and functions to keep the bit in position and the horse's mouth closed. If the top strap of the dropped noseband is placed too low it may interfere with the horse's breathing. Notice that the running martingale, without protective stops, has migrated forward and is in danger of becoming caught on the rein buckles.

A common fault with some dropped nosebands is that the nosepiece doesn't allow for proper adjustment. The noseband may be too long in front and too short behind. This causes the front to hang too close to the nostrils and presses the bit into the corners of the lips, not to mention the potential to restrict breathing or damage cartilage.

Dropped nosebands are generally used with snaffle bits. They can be used with shanked bits, but care must be taken. It's wise to introduce the shanked bit first, allowing a period of adjustment before adding the cavesson, because the combination can be startling. You've got increased leverage and no way for the horse to escape or minimize the pull. Adjusted correctly, a dropped noseband encourages the horse to keep its mouth closed, ensures that the bit remains central in the mouth and keeps the horse from crossing its jaws (moving the upper and lower jaws in opposite directions) to evade the bit. The pressure of the noseband assists and strengthens the action of the bit. Tension on the reins is transmitted to the nose as the horse gives its lower jaw. Such pressure causes the horse to drop his head, allowing the bit to press against the bars. In this position, the bit will have the greatest effect. The combination of the snaffle bit and dropped noseband provides control of the horse's head position not possible with the snaffle bit alone.

The "Flash" noseband has an extra strap that attaches to the top of the cavesson and passes below the bit.

The "Flash" noseband, named after a jumping horse who wore it, attaches to the center of the cavesson above the nose. The lower end passes below the bit and lies in the chin groove. Some bridles are made with flash nosebands, but a flash attachment may be obtained separately and buckled to the cavesson. The advantage over the dropped noseband is that the pressure is applied higher on the nose. A problem sometimes seen with flash nosebands is that the lower strap may tend to pull down the front of the cavesson.

The figure 8 or Gackle noseband has a top strap that fastens above the bit and a lower strap that fastens under the bit and lies in the chin groove. The two straps intersect in the middle of the face at about the level where a cavesson would be located. This is where the nose pressure is concentrated. It is useful for horses that pull on the bit and those that work their jaws in a scissor-like way. Both the flash and the figure 8 nosebands have actions similar to the dropped noseband but are less severe and are not as likely to interfere with breathing.

The figure 8 noseband has a top strap that fastens above the bit and a lower strap that fastens under the bit and lies in the chin groove. The two straps intersect in the middle of the face and this is where the nose pressure is concentrated.

There are two opposing schools of thought on the use of nosebands. Some trainers avoid using nosebands, particularly on young horses, because they don't want to interfere with a young horse's ability to mouth or play with the bit. They believe that allowing free jaw movement promotes relaxation and a greater acceptance of the bit. Nosebands are only added if the horse develops a problem, such as not being able to keep the bit in position, or opening its mouth to evade the bit's actions. There may also be some concern that if the horse cannot open its mouth it may panic.

The cheeker lifts the bit in the horse's mouth and prevents the horse from evading its action.

Other trainers routinely begin schooling young horses in nosebands so they never learn to open their mouths to avoid the bit. Once the horse has accepted the bit and is working well, the noseband is removed. Both techniques have produced champions.

CHEEKER

The cheeker, which is usually made of rubber, fits over the bit rings on either side and has straps that run upwards and backwards and join in the lower center of the horse's face. From there a central strap runs up the center of the face and fastens to an attachment on the headpiece of the bridle between the horse's ears. This noseband lifts the bit in the horse's mouth and prevents the horse from evading its action. In addition, for some reason, any strap running up the center of the face seems to discourage horses that tend to pull on the bit.

MARTINGALES

There are basically two kinds of martingales: running and standing. Both types function by discouraging or physically preventing the horse from raising its head too high or extending its nose too far in front of its body. They promote both balance and proper bit action.

A properly adjusted standing martingale will allow the horse to use its head and neck for balance and speed, while maintaining an acceptable headset.

STANDING MARTINGALE

The standing martingale is also known in western circles as a tie-down. It generally consists of a simple strap which runs from the saddle girth to the noseband. A tie-down restricts the range of head and neck movement by exerting pressure on the horse's nasal bones.

Some tie-downs and martingales include a neck strap, known as a yoke, which helps keep the martingale from flopping or becoming a potential hazard such as getting tangled with a foot. A simpler design may be used with a breast collar, whereby the strap connects to or passes through the collar's center ring.

The standing martingale need not be adjusted so tightly as to pull the horse's head down into an unnatural or uncomfortable position. Rather, the martingale should limit the degree to which the horse can raise its head, making it unable to evade contact with the bit when the reins are pulled. The setting should also eliminate the chance that the rider could be hit in the face by the horse throwing its head. In fact, standing martingales are required on polo horses, and are frequently used on roping and other timed-event horses to prevent such accidents. A martingale also provides a brace or balance for the horse to lean against during hard stops and fast turns. In roping, it also helps keep the horse's head out of the way of the roper as he makes his catch.

It is inadvisable to use a standing martingale with a dropped noseband because it puts too much pressure on the nasal bones. Should the action of a dropped noseband be considered necessary in combination with a tie-down, a flash noseband may be used instead. Sometimes standing martingales are attached to the headpiece of the bridle behind the ears. This applies pressure to the poll and is used to pull the head down. Some horsemen condemn this practice as being too forceful.

Martingales should always be used with caution. Some horses panic when their heads and necks are restricted, and may fight against them, injuring themselves or others in the process. Make adjustments judiciously, and alter the settings or your choice of equipment only in a safe, familiar environment to begin with. The heat of competition is no time to be experimenting with your tie-down.

RUNNING MARTINGALES

A running martingale exerts its influence on the bit by engaging the reins whenever the horse raises its head out of position. Like the standing martingale, the running martingale attaches to the girth or breast collar. The running martingale, rather than leading to the noseband, forks into two straps to which rings are attached. The reins run through these rings. There are several variations of the running martingale. Some include neck straps or yokes. Other, more simplified, versions do not. You'll sometimes hear the stripped down versions called training forks or single forks.

The best running martingales are fully adjustable. It should be possible to change the center or cinch strap as well as the yoke and rein straps to fit each horse. Proper adjustment is what makes a running martingale valuable. The bridle reins pass through the rings on the martingale and then to the rider's hands. The rider should be able to guide the horse with direct and indirect

The running martingale doesn't come into play unless the horse raises its head too high, or roots its nose out too far. This allows the rider to maintain the proper headset, without excessive restriction.

rein pressure without undue interference from the martingale. It should become active only when the horse raises its head out of position.

One rule of thumb is to adjust the martingale so that when the rein rings are pulled straight up, they reach the middle of the horse's neck. Others use the base of the throatlatch as a guide when the horse is standing in a relaxed position. What's appropriate will vary from horse to horse, trainer to trainer, depending on the results desired. However, yoke and cinch straps should be adjusted snugly enough so there is no chance that the horse could get hung up in the equipment.

If the rein straps of the running martingale are adjusted too tightly, so that the rein forms an angle between the horse's mouth and the rider's hand, its action (especially with a jointed snaffle) will be quite severe. In fact, the downward pull will change the snaffle's action to that of a leverage bit. The martingale will amplify the force on the mouthpiece, exerting greater pressure on the bars while shifting the pull away from the corners of the lips.

Because it can magnify pulling power, many trainers discourage the use of a running martingale with anything but a true snaffle, meaning a non-shanked bit. As a safety precaution, the running martingale should also be used with leather or rubber rein stops. These protective guards fit tightly on the reins and form a barrier to keep the martingale's rein rings from migrating forward and becoming caught on the rein buckles. They could prevent a nasty wreck.

The Irish martingale is a short leather strap with rings on either end. The reins run through these rings below the horse's neck. There are no straps running from the rings to the girth. This is a safety device to keep the reins from flipping over the neck.

A seldom seen but potentially useful type of running martingale is the pulley martingale. A strap extending forward from the girth ends in a pulley through which a cord is run. The bridle reins pass through rings attached to the cord. This martingale allows the horse to bend his neck in one direction without the restriction against the opposite side of his mouth which may occur with a standard running martingale.

While some horsemen and women disdain the use of running martingales, many riders swear by them and maintain that they can help training progress because they are self-reinforcing: the horse works against itself when it is out of position.

ROPING ACCESSORIES

In addition to standing martingales, most timed calf ropers use what's known as a jerk line. Also called a backup rope, the jerk line is used to cue the horse to maintain tension on the catch rope or lariat as the roper runs to the calf.

The jerk line is a long soft rope which attaches to the bottom of the bit shanks, runs back through a pulley or ring connected to the saddle and is then tucked into the roper's belt. As the roper runs to the calf, loops in the rope which have been tucked into the cowboy's belt pull loose one at a time thus keeping tension on the horse's bit. The pressure encourages the horse to back up and maintain tension on the catch rope. The jerk line should be just long enough to run out as the roper reaches the calf so the horse does not pull the calf away from the cowboy.

Sometimes the jerk line is tied directly to the catch rope and is passed through a neck rope and around the saddle so that it tightens under pressure from the roped calf. Once a horse learns about the jerk line, some ropers prefer not to use it in practice but only in competition because its continuous use can make the horse's mouth sore.

Jerk lines are prohibited in judged roping competitions, because it is the horse's ability to work the rope properly that is being evaluated. However, in top rodeos with major prize money at stake, the calf roper without a jerk line is certainly the exception.

Steer ropers sometimes attach a jerk line to the nose band and allow it to drag behind the horse. When the roper dismounts to tie the steer, he grabs the jerk line to stop the horse. The trick is to be in such a position after dismounting that the dragging jerk line is within reach.

The calf roper may also thread the catch rope or lariat through a neck rope, which encircles the horse's neck. When the calf is caught, the neck rope holds the catch rope in front of the horse under its chin and helps guide the horse straight back away from the calf. Some ropers attach an

(top left) The black jerk line passes from the lower ends of the bit shanks, through a pulley on the saddle and is placed in a series of tucks in the rider's belt. The catch rope passes through a rope around the horse's neck and also through a keeper attached to the tie-down.

(top right) A calf roping horse maintaining tension on the rope while his rider ties the calf. The red jerk line is hanging limp.

additional loop to the noseband through which the catch rope passes to aid the horse in backing straight away.

Calf ropers may carry a second catch rope in case they miss the calf with the first loop. This second rope, rather than passing through the neck rope, passes through a small loop, or "keeper" which is attached to the martingale or tie-down rather than passing through the neck rope. Thus it does not interfere with the first catch rope. According to the rules of the American Quarter Horse Association if a "keeper" is used in calf roping it must be attached to the noseband of the martingale (tie-down) and cannot be attached to the bridle or bit.

DRAW REINS OR RUNNING REINS

What are called running reins in Europe are generally called draw reins in America. Draw reins create a pulley-like effect on the horse's mouth, with the reins sliding through the bit rings. The fixed end of the rein is generally attached either at the bottom ring of the girth, extending up between the horse's front legs through the bit rings and then to the riders hands, or at the cinch rings in the saddle skirts through the bit rings and then to the rider's hands. Depending on where they attach, draw reins provide a great deal of downward torque on the horse's head. The added leverage tends to pull the horse's head in toward its chest.

Used judiciously, draw reins can help a rider develop greater poll flexion and more control of the front of the horse's face. Use of draw reins can help condition the muscles along the crest of the neck making it easier for the horse to maintain a "bridled" frame. However, the system does not allow the horse to find any relief by extending its nose forward from the vertical. Overuse may tend to put the horse behind the bit.

Also, if the horse resists the pressure by stiffening upward against the pull, the horse's topline could begin to exhibit a bowed appearance. People sometimes mistakenly identify this posture as saying a horse is flexing back behind the poll, but, in fact, it is simply due to the overdevelopment of neck muscles. The only true pivot point in the the neck is between the first and second vertebrae behind the poll.

The draw reins' action can have the effect of causing the horse to over-flex and get behind the bit.

Draw reins should be used with strong driving leg cues, and only for those brief periods when a horse resists by stiffening its neck, poll and lower jaw. Draw reins work best when pressure is applied to one side at a time. If both reins are used together to force the horse into a certain position of flexion, it will probably resist. Some individuals use draw reins or running martingales in conjunction with curb bits to force extreme head sets on show horses. This is dangerous because horses may become frightened, mad or frustrated, and a serious accident may result. Draw reins of any type should be put aside when the desired results are achieved.

Another form of draw rein is the "polo" draw rein. A strap runs from the cinch between the horse's front legs to a ring at his chest. A neck plate holds this in position. The reins fasten to the ring and then run through the bit rings to the rider's hands. For horses which tend to stick their noses up or out, the polo draw rein is designed to bring the nose back down where it belongs.

The German martingale is set up much like draw reins and operates on a similar principle. A direct rein attaches to the bit ring just as it would on a regular snaffle. A draw rein then ties into the direct rein, running through the bit rings and back to the girth. In this system, the direct rein takes effect first. The pull is supplemented by a lesser downward pull from the draw rein. Again, this technique works best when the horse is driven forward with strong leg cues to encourage the horse to move forward while flexing and yielding at the poll.

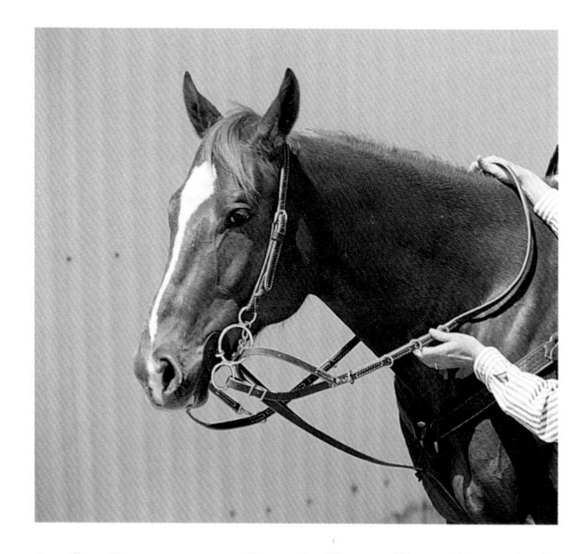

In the German martingale the pull on the rein is supplemented by a lesser downward pull from the draw rein. (Glory Ann Kurtz Photo)

CHAMBON & DE GOGUE

The chambon is a pulley like device that exerts pressure from mouth to poll to cinch rings. It is used to induce the horse to stretch and arc its topline and lower its head carriage. It is used exclusively for longeing exercises. If not properly adjusted, it can be dangerous. The horse should be accepting of a short tie-down before outfitting the horse with a chambon. A relative to the chambon, which is used for riding, is called the De Gogue. Reins run from the hand, through the bit rings up to a poll strap with pulleys. From there the reins extend down between the front legs to the girth. The action is similar to that of a gag snaffle.

A FINAL NOTE

An important word of caution: It is inadvisable to use martingales or any devices that restrict head carriage on horses used for trail or cross country riding. A horse's head is very heavy (as you may know if you've ever cradled one in your lap) and is used as a counterweight to help the horse maintain balance. If a horse is expected to travel up and down steep slopes, he must have the freedom to place his head in the proper position to keep his equilibrium. If he must cross deep water, he must be able to raise his head. There have been tragic reports of horses drowning while wearing standing martingales because they were unable to keep their noses above water.

"BITS CAN HELP YOU MOVE YOUR HORSE UP THE PERFORMANCE LADDER."

15

Bit Progressions and Soft Mouths

Knowledgeable trainers often change bits when they reach different stages of training. For instance, we've talked extensively about the snaffle bit, hackamore, leverage bit sequence. Some bits are considered to be "schooling" or training bits while others are considered to be "finishing" or show bits. Usually, what you see in the warm-up arena never goes through the in-gate. We've seen tackrooms filled with every conceivable type of headgear. Yet most trainers will tell you that they use a handful of bridles on a regular basis and keep the rest in reserve for the odd horse or when there's a problem to remedy.

Sometimes when riders don't know what else to do, they experiment with bits. Sometimes they find an answer. Sometimes they don't. For instance, a horse that constantly lugs on the snaffle may have a complete change of attitude when moved into a curb bit. The horse who fusses with or grabs the shanks of a loose-cheeked curb might be perfectly content in a solid grazing bit. Making a switch may provide better control, a fancier headset, or the hair trigger responses you're after. Bits can help you move your horse up the performance ladder.

MEASURING PROGRESS

Some people start colts in halters, some in hackamores, some in snaffle bits. There are even trainers who start their colts with nothing on their heads at all. But there comes a time when a rider must take control of his horse's face. The common denominator among good trainers is that when they do, they strive to reduce their horses' fear, gain their trust, cultivate respect and make them receptive to what it is they have to teach.

(overleaf) **It's not unusual for professional trainers to have well-stocked tack rooms. Seemingly small differences in bits can have desirable affects, but the solution to training problems often lie beyond the mechanical limitations of bits.**

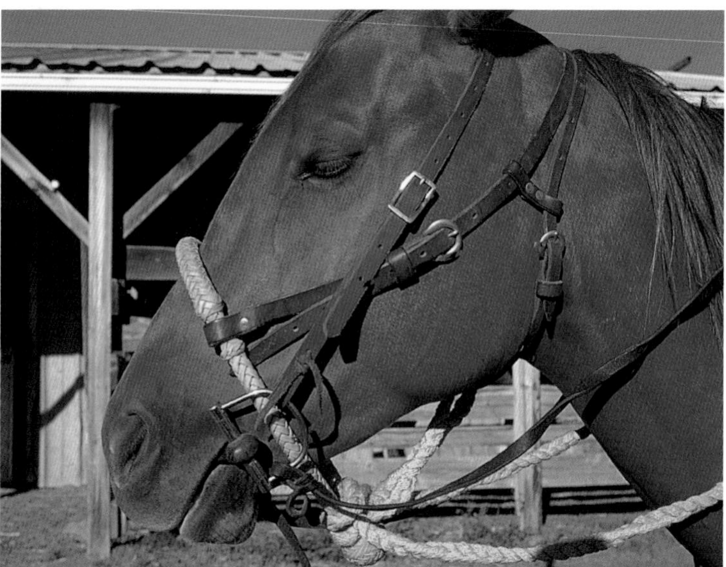

(top) Bits don't come with instruction manuals. A horseman or woman must decide when or if it's time to step a horse into a new bit and how much pulling power is wise.

(center) When progressing from the snaffle bit to the hackamore, many trainers ride the horse with both systems together. They gradually transfer control from the snaffle rein to the hackamore rein.

(bottom) A pelham bit is useful in the direct progression from the snaffle to the leverage bit, especially if the mouthpiece is identical to that in the snaffle. While the horse is becoming accustomed to the bit, as in this case, the rein is attached to the snaffle ring on the pelham. Later the horse will be ridden with a two rein system and, eventually, all control will be transferred to the curb rein.

To our advantage, most young horses tend to pay strict attention to what humans do with them — even if they have no idea how to respond to the actions. There's a whole legion of horse training clinicians who make a living giving demonstrations that capitalize on the horse's natural curiosity and receptivity to learning. What these horsemen show is that psychology — understanding how horses think and react — plays a much greater role in training success than does physical domination.

Smooth-mouthed snaffles, thick bosals, soft rope nosebands and other gentle-by-design headgear allow a rider to guide and teach young horses gently without instilling fear. But sometimes these same tools limit the amount of progress or refinement a rider can achieve with a horse.

In any learning situation, students can get distracted or stop listening to the teacher. This is generally when an instructor needs to take a firmer approach. Even good teachers may raise their voices or clap their hands to get their classes' attention. Once they have it, they resume teaching in a normal voice. However, if a teacher continually yells at a class, the students start tuning that out too.

Bitting is a lot like that. Horses become bored, distracted and even lazy. There may be times when a mild bit and a gentle touch on the reins aren't enough. This is when a trainer may choose to step up the pulling power. But as good trainers remind us, if the choice is to use more bridle, it's wise to use it as a temporary measure. If a strong pull is used every time, the horse soon becomes non-responsive to that, too.

When making transitions, the bits you choose may not be nearly as significant as how you use them and when. Sometimes a simple change in headgear is enough. Horses are very perceptive. If you change bridles, they notice: "Hey, there's something's different in my mouth." The rider creates curiosity. That curiosity is a much better educational mindset than fear. In other words, to keep your program moving forward, you might not need more pulling power as much as you need different pulling power.

Bit progressions work two ways: You can use more force or less. In many cases, experimenting with milder bits is as good a choice as going to something more severe. You can always change tactics if your first inclination fails to improve performance. The ultimate goal is to teach the horse to be lighter to the rein, not heavier. If you always step up in intensity, you work at cross-purposes to the desired result.

First, analyze what your horse's responses are telling you. For example, if your horse raises its head and refuses to open its mouth for bridling, perhaps it associates the bit with pain. If the horse stiffens or seems startled every time you pull on the reins, perhaps you need a bit that provides more signal. If a horse consistently gets behind the bridle, maybe it needs a milder bit or a gentler hand on the reins. If it roots out its nose or tosses its head, maybe your horse is trying to let you know that it's not finding adequate relief from the pressure. Maybe the curb strap is too tight or the

When a young horse is first ridden he tends to jut out his nose, giving the rider little bar contact. As the horse learns, he will begin to yield to the pressure on his mouth by flexing at the poll. With a more vertical face position, there is more pressure on the bars.

This youngster is learning to flex at the poll and yield to the rein. It is rewarded by the release of pressure as soon as it complies.

bit doesn't have enough forward balance to release properly. Or maybe you're too slow to respond when the horse gives to the bit and the horse is starting to fight back or become dull to your rein aids. You have to think about what the horse's reactions mean.

DEVELOPING A SOFT MOUTH

Many riders may hesitate to pull on the reins for fear of hurting their horses' mouths or making them insensitive to the bit. They may cling stoically to their smooth-mouth snaffle bits even though their horses aren't responding well, yet find themselves snatching at the reins in frustration just to get their horse's attention. Part of the problem is a general lack of understanding of how horses becomes "soft" or light in the bridle.

"A big misconception is that people think you keep a horse's mouth soft by not pulling on the reins," says reining horse trainer and veterinarian, Dr. Steve Schwartzenberger. "I believe it's just the opposite. You develop a horse's mouth by pulling on it. You have to ask that horse to give to pressure and teach him to respond without resistance." Steve points out that it is a disservice to allow a horse to push rudely through the bridle. The animal never learns to respect the bit and is certainly no fun to ride, which doesn't set the stage for a happy future for that horse. Who will want it?

Each time you pick up the bridle reins you teach your horse something, good or bad. You establish habits. Even horses who have been handled poorly and have learned bad manners in the bridle can benefit from consistent retraining. A horse with a seemingly "dull" mouth, for instance, may have no physical problem that makes it incapable of being light in the bridle. The nerve receptors in its mouth may be perfectly intact. The horse may simply lack the necessary education.

High level reining competition epitomizes the ability of riders to maneuver their horses with almost telepathic communication. Yet in the earliest stages of training, many reining prospects appear anything but light. They must be pushed and pulled and prodded around, until they start to move and react like reiners. They are conditioned to respond to rein and leg signals in a certain way.

The rider has the responsibility to make a definite connection in the horse's mind between the pull on the reins and how the horse must respond. If a rider pulls on the rein and releases it before the horse has done (or tried to do) what the rider asks, the horse learns nothing. If a light pull elicits no response, a stronger one is in order. When the horse gives, the rider releases. That's how progress is made. The next time the rider asks, it generally takes less of a tug because the horse knows how to find relief.

Bits play an important role in this process. The take-and-give should never turn into a tug-of-war. When the rider pulls, the horse must learn to comply. The rider then thanks his horse by releasing pressure. For some horses, a tug on a thick, smooth-mouthed snaffle might be easy to ignore, while one with a thinner mouthpiece may be less easy to disregard. Force is not used as a substitute for training, but you can't educate the horse if you don't have its attention. "I want to be able to fix my hands and let the horse search for where its head is supposed to be," explains Schwartzenberger. "I let the bit do some of the work. That's why I buy them, to make my job easier."

A rider should never jerk on the reins. If a strong pull is required to get the message across to a horse, the rider should ease the slack from the reins in one fluid motion, making smooth contact with the bit and increasing the force of the pull. Abruptly snatching at the reins will bang the bit in the horse's mouth and instill fear and confusion. Riders who repeatedly jerk on the reins tend to develop horses with bad attitudes, poor self-carriage and bad habits. The horses are always waiting for the next blow. They may adopt defensive strategies such as head tossing, rearing, bucking, sulling up or running away.

A major factor in developing a soft mouth is to break down resistance in the horse's body. This is essential at every stage of training, regardless of bit choice, but becomes especially important when a rider starts moving up the bitting ladder. When horses are moved from snaffle bits into leverage bits, and loose-cheeked bits into stiff-shanked bits, they tend to become stiffer in their responses. Rather than resort to more pressure on the mouth or nose — pressure which is already being amplified by shanks and curb strap — a rider can use leg pressure to encourage forward motion and to ask the horse to yield in the ribcage. This, in turn, eliminates much of the resistance in a horse's jaw and poll.

It's hard for a horse to stiffen and brace against bit pressure when it is in motion. Further, a nudge in the rib cage tends to make a horse break at the poll and turn its

head toward the pressure on its side. Once the horse is slightly off kilter, the rider has a further leverage advantage and can then ask for even greater vertical poll flexion. It is easier to do when the horse is walking, jogging or loping in a circle than when its body is moving in a straight line. However, the rider should avoid pulling back equally on both reins. This would likely create resistance and be counterproductive in getting a greater degree of poll flexion.

Vertical flexion is important because it helps the horse move in a more balanced, collected frame. But the appropriate degree of vertical poll flexion develops over time. The transition to a leverage device can help further that process. However, before making that step, a rider should continue to refine the horse's confidence, flexibility and responsiveness to leg and rein.

Most trainers are not advocates of heavy artillery. Specific bits may be introduced during the training process to promote respect and/or stimulate an interest in the messages being communicated. Specific bit choices depend a lot on individual preferences. Trainers who specialize in particular sports tend to follow established trends. Every now and again new theories emerge and so does new tack. But the things that classify as "gimmicks" tend to flourish for a time, then recede. Those based on sound horsemanship principles seem to stand up to the test of time and cross disciplinary boundaries.

Not surprisingly, many trainers follow a fairly standard bit progression. They start with the mildest bits and increase in intensity as performance demands also increase. Today, more people probably start their young horses in smooth-mouth snaffles than any other device. But most western performance riders usually advance to other bits over time.

Observation is a powerful tool. If riders pay attention, horses often reveal what they need in the way of bits. It often becomes obvious when it's time to make a change. The horse's progress may plateau or even begin to deteriorate. Yet, if a horse stays light and supple in a mild bit, there may be no compelling need to step up to a more forceful one.

However, in western events, horses competing in senior divisions (age 6 and over) are generally required to be shown in curb bits with one hand on the reins. Neck reining is a sign of higher education and increases the level of difficulty in executing the performance. Curb bits tend to provide better one-handed control. The introduction to the curb bit should take place well before the day of the show.

In theory, a horse's responsiveness should improve throughout its lifetime. In some cases it does. But many horses don't get the benefit of consistent, progressive training. And like humans, some horses want to work only as hard as they have to. In essence, they get wise to the bridle and become more difficult to control and guide. They may not have the same ambition to please, and often riders don't have the expertise to keep them finely tuned.

(opposite) Bitmaker, horseman and educator Greg Darnall shows the horse's natural tendency to flex at the poll when a cathedral mouthpiece is installed. The horse automatically seeks a position where the bit fits comfortably, i.e., the bit does some of the work for the rider.

You might hear people comment that a horse "has no mouth left." Even so, most horses can remain safe, serviceable mounts by finding and using the type of bridle they will respond to.

MAKING A CHANGE

When contemplating a change in headgear, there are many options. Here are some of the things you might consider:

1) Use a larger or smaller diameter mouthpiece.
2) Change to a completely different style of mouthpiece.
3) Shift the position of the bit in the horse's mouth.
4) Use a bitting accessory such as a running martingale, tie-down or draw reins.
5) Switch to a gag type bridle.
6) Use a leverage bit.
7) Readjust or change your chin strap.
8) Go to a bitless bridle.
9) Employ a combination type bit.
10) Experiment with a palate type bridle.

While many of us resist the idea of needing a more persuasive tool, you may want to consider Dr. Steve Schwartzenberger's philosophy: "If you have a bit that a horse is more sensitive to, you won't be inclined to use your hands as aggressively as you would otherwise. The only time I get into trouble with a bridle is when I'm using something that is not enough bit for the horse. That's when I tend to pull harder than I should. That's when I run the risk of pinching or bruising the mouth, or scaring a horse. By going to a more persuasive bit I can be lighter with my hands."

The transition to a new bit need not be traumatic. A rider can bit the horse up and turn it loose in a stall or corral and give it ample opportunity to become accustomed to the mouthpiece before any pressure is applied. It may also be wise to ride with the new bit for a week or two, then go back to the previous bit. This can be especially useful when making a transition from a snaffle to a leverage bit.

Trainers often say that the ideal time to move a horse into a shanked bridle is when it is doing everything right in a snaffle. While it may sound contradictory, a step up in bits can sometimes mean a temporary step back in training progress. For example, when a horse moves from a snaffle into a leverage bit, it's common for the horse to become stiff and resistant. The natural instinct of the horse is to move into pressure; we teach the horse to move away from it. With a change in bits, the horse may need to retest the waters and make sure the same rules apply. It may also scare the horse the first few times it feels the chin strap tighten and trap its lower jaw between bit bars and curb strap. And when a horse gets scared, its fight or flight mechanism kicks in. When you change bits, take your time, soften your hands, and help your horse learn that the principles of pressure and release still apply to the new device.

When moving a young horse into a leverage bit, many riders initially try to stay with a mouthpiece that feels safe and comfortable to the horse. The Loomis "shanked snaffle," Tom Thumb and Argentine bits (which are, in fact, curbs) may be popular choices for that very reason. Their mouthpieces are jointed like a conventional ring snaffle so may "feel" familiar to most horses.

But lest you forget, once shanks and a curb strap are attached to this mouthpiece, the bit can pack a wallop. This is particularly true when it is combined with loose shanks. The bit may fold around the soft tissues of the tongue and bars. If pulled hard, the joint can peak and come into contact with the roof of the mouth. The loose-shanked Billy Allen is similar in design, but its three-section mouthpiece, with its short barrel in the middle between the two cannons, allows the bit to flex without collapsing like a jointed mouthpiece. The loose shanks on both bits allow a little greater flexibility for two-handed work.

With leverage bits of any type, you do tend to lose some lateral control. So any change in bits will likely require some patient reschooling to re-establish a given level of flexibility, responsiveness and control. As the horse adjusts to the change, the stage is set to begin a higher level of education.

To meet event deadlines, the training pace that many of today's elite performance horses must undergo requires a little expediency on the part of riders. Yet an accelerated learning program need not be a cruel one. By using the right bits at the right times, and in the right ways, horsemen and women can ease the transitions and reach peak performance in a reasonable period of time.

"THE RIDER'S HANDS MUST LEARN TO FOLLOW THE HORSE'S MOTION."

16

Developing Soft Hands

The highest compliment anyone can pay a rider is to say that he or she has "soft" or light hands. It indicates an uncommon touch, the ability to interact with a horse intuitively, relying on perception not force. Don't be discouraged if you don't think you've got a gossamer touch. Most riders have to work to achieve it. As with virtually all aspects of horsemanship, you can train yourself to have better hands.

Horses and people will be your tutors. Watch, listen, and try to "feel" what it is they have to teach you. Your skills will improve through instruction, imitation, self-evaluation and the determination to be a better rider. To instill good habits in yourself (just as you do your horse), you must think about where your hands are at all times, and make a conscious decision about how hard or soft to pull on the reins.

Without question, it is easier for an inexperienced rider to learn to use his or her hands lightly by riding well-schooled horses than by riding poorly trained ones. A good horse takes a major variable out of the equation. An educated horse knows what the rein cues mean and reacts to them positively when the rider uses his aids correctly. If the animal doesn't respond well, the rider is likely at fault.

This often becomes evident when a trainer can ride a horse and it responds one way, then when a student rider takes over, it responds another. A well-trained horse may overreact when a well-meaning rider pulls too hard. Consequently, the person learns to temper the pressure he or she applies to the reins. A dull-mouthed horse might be indifferent no matter what the rider does.

Riding many different horses will also help you learn to use your hands more effectively. It provides a baseline for comparison. It also forces you to adapt and use your

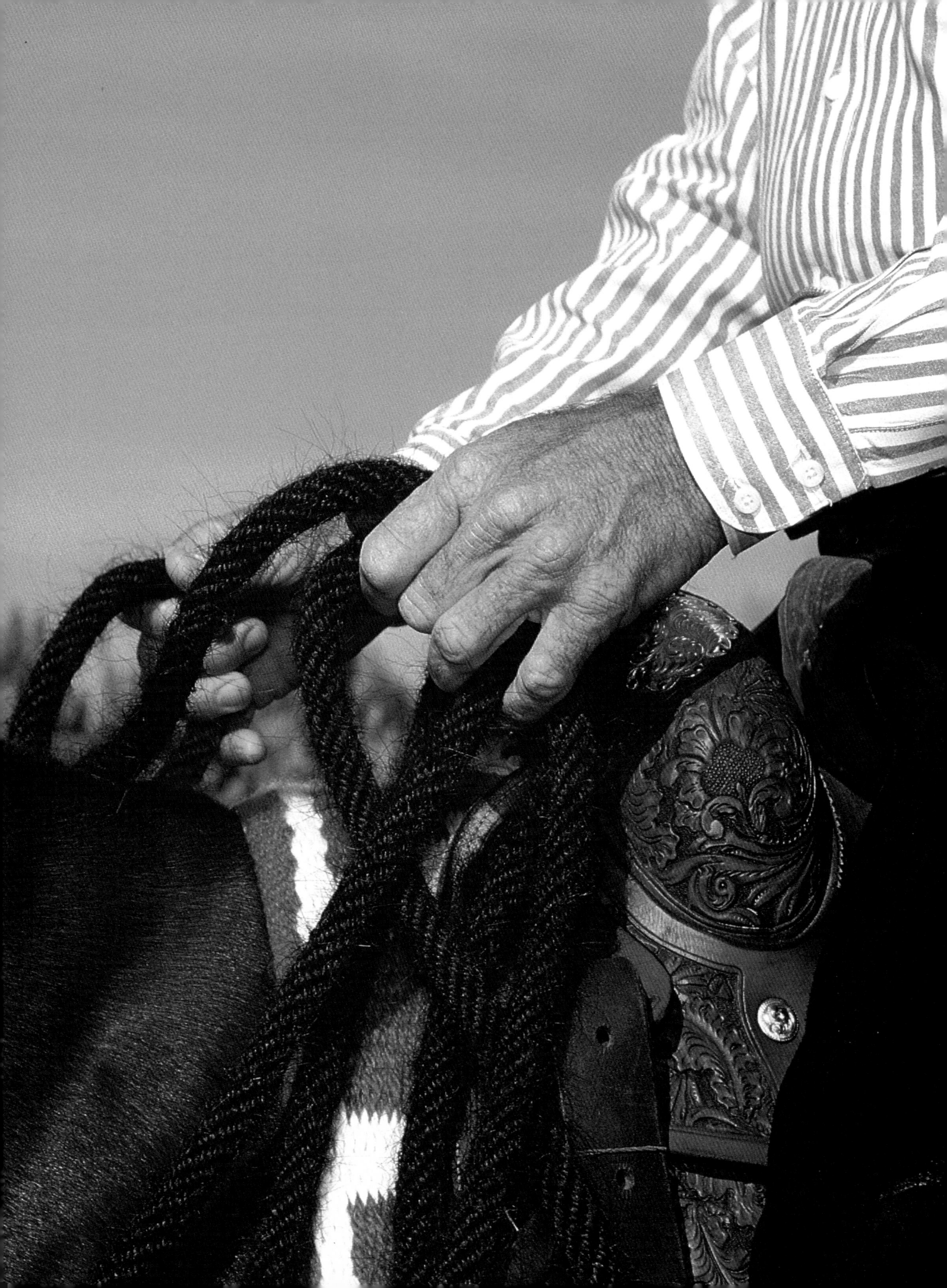

Muscle isn't as important as strategy when it comes to establishing or maintaining control. If a horse becomes too headstrong, a rider can regain control by pulling its head around to the side to take away its forward momentum.

(overleaf) As with virtually all aspects of horsemanship, you can train yourself to develop "soft" hands.

hands appropriately for each individual — which is what developing good hands is all about. Learning to use your reins effectively is a lot like fiddling with the tuning and volume control on the stereo. Sometimes just small adjustments can make everything come in crystal clear.

Good instructors can help students see and feel what they need to do, and demonstrate how to do it: where to hold the reins, the direction of pull, how to use the reins separately and together, and so on.

A GOOD SEAT

The foundation for developing good hands is to first develop a good seat. In a word, what you need is *balance*. But achieving a balanced seat is sometimes easier said than done. Some horses are rough-strided, making it difficult for the rider to stay firmly anchored in the saddle. Other riders lack the physical conditioning and coordination necessary to move easily with their horses' gaits.

A common mistake which inexperienced riders make is to try to steady themselves using the reins. But the reins are not handles. Gripping the reins to help keep your seat will jolt the horse's mouth with every stride it takes and make things worse. Pain in the horse's mouth will cause it to stiffen, hollow its back and become even rougher to ride. Secondly, it may make the horse hard-mouthed and difficult to control because the rein signals are inconsistent and confusing.

To develop a good seat and hands, riders have to learn to assert mind over motion. In many cases it's simply a matter of spending enough hours in the saddle to get physically fit and develop a greater sense of rhythm with the horse. Being able to move in synchronization with the horse is essential. The rider's hands must learn to follow the horse's motion.

The trick is to learn how to influence the horse's movement without interfering with it. Some riding instructors have their students ride reinless while working the horse on a longe line. In this way, riders are forced to rely solely on their seat and legs for balance, without using the reins as a crutch. Sometimes instructors take the exercise a step further by eliminating the stirrups to further improve balance.

When riding, it's important to learn to relax and allow your seat, legs and torso to act as shock absorbers rather than transmit the impact of the horse's stride through your arms and hands. First make sure that your stirrups are adjusted to the proper length. If your stirrups are too long, you'll struggle to keep the stirrup tread centered under the balls of your feet. Any instability in your feet and legs will interfere with your hands. If they're too short, you'll likely be propelled from the saddle with each stride and that, too, will negatively impact your hands. You may find that a simple stirrup adjustment quiets your hands and improves your overall balance almost instantaneously.

Adjusting your stirrups may give you better balance and a greater sense of security in the saddle which will allow you to control your hands better. The proper stirrup length is illustrated by the angle of knee, and degree of heels down.

(below) Trainer Terry Thompson gallops his horse on a loose rein with confidence because he relies on his weight, legs and body position as part of a total guidance system.

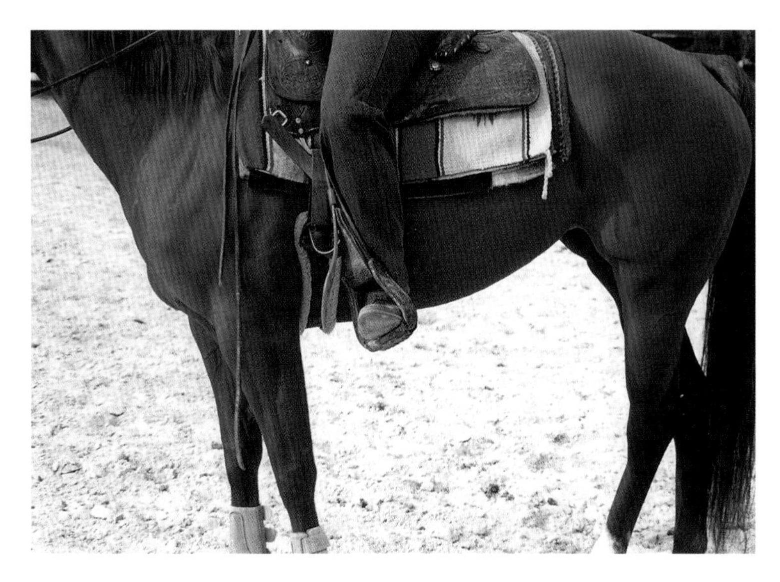

(opposite) You can't develop light hands unless you learn to guide your horse by using your weight and legs. Terry Thompson shows how he moves his mare sideways using his weight and legs to push her to the left. Light contact with the reins restricts forward motion.

(left) Leg pressure, along with shifted weight, is applied to the side you wish the horse to move away from.

Equally important is to concentrate on operating your hands independently of your seat and legs. Relax your shoulders, arms, hands and fingers and allow them to float with the movement of the horse. Focus on using your legs as much as your hands to guide and control the horse. Unless you learn to steer with your weight and legs, you will never achieve light hands, and you will characterize yourself as a perennial beginner.

Intermediate and advanced riders make the transition from being overly reliant on their hands to using their entire bodies to direct and control their mounts. So, if you find yourself pulling harder than you think you should, make the effort to increase leg pressure to break down resistance in the horse's face. This takes work, but you will be well rewarded.

There are many excellent horsemanship books that explain in depth ways to improve both your seat and hands. Riding lessons from a knowledgeable individual are also an excellent investment. An independent observer can watch and analyze what you are doing and offer suggestions of ways you can improve, speeding your progress.

THE RIGHT GRIP

Whether you ride one-handed or two, there are several ways to hold your reins. The best way, of course, is to do what's most comfortable for you. But it's equally important to practice principles of good horsemanship with whatever grip you use. Utilizing good form allows you to communicate more clearly with your horse. For example, keeping your forearm, wrist, and hand in a straight line from elbow to fingertips not only looks nice in a equitation class, it provides a leverage advantage. You will be better able to utilize the strength in your forearm to steady the reins than if you hold them with a floppy, broken-wristed grasp.

For years, western tradition dictated that riders hold their reins in the left hand. There's a practical reason for this. By guiding the horse with the left hand, a cowboy kept his right hand free to throw a rope, open a gate,

(above) No limp wrists please, advises trainer Dave Moore. Keeping a fairly straight line from rein hand to elbow is not only correct for equitation purposes, it provides a good mechanical advantage when neck-reining.

signal a fellow rider, roll a smoke or do whatever needed to be done with his "good" hand. (Keep in mind that most people are right-handed.) Because horses were trained to neck rein, it didn't take a lot of coordination to steer with the less dextrous hand. Many riders continue to adhere to this convention, yet riding etiquette isn't quite as rigid these days. A growing number of horsemen and women have abandoned the tradition, riding and showing with their right hands on the reins, because its more comfortable.

With the growing number of snaffle bit, hackamore and timed event classes, many people in the competitive arena use both hands on the reins, regulations permitting. But before you enter the show ring, be sure to consult the rulebook so you're not disqualified because you failed to conform to the prescribed etiquette.

When it comes to grip, choose the rein hold that makes you most effective as a rider. If you're schooling your horse two-handed, for example, experiment with doubling your reins between the span of your hands or lacing them between your ring and little fingers. Then try holding each rein separately. Does one system give you more control or feel than another? If you're riding one-handed, try placing your index finger between your split reins. Compare that to holding both reins between thumb and forefinger. (At AQHA and other approved shows, putting more than one finger between the bridle reins is cause for disqualification.)

Some riders find that slipping one finger between the reins makes it easier to keep the horse's face tipped into the direction of the turn when neck reining. However, if it feels uncomfortable, don't do it.

Remember, like your horse, you may need a period to adjust to any change, so give the new technique a chance before you reject it. If you're riding with closed (romal style) reins in the show ring, the reins must pass to the outside of the pinkie finger. But for schooling purposes, you may want to experiment with dividing the reins between pinkie and ring fingers. Does one way feel more natural than the other?

When handling your reins, keep in mind that your horse is your partner. There's no need for a death grip. You'll communicate best by taking a light, relaxed hold. Don't hold the reins so loosely that the horse could pull or shake the reins out of your hands, but do keep it soft enough so that you can sense the workings of the horse's mouth much like a fisherman feeling for the vibrations when a fish starts to play his line.

Communication flows two ways. Be sensitive to what the horse has to tell you. When signaling the horse, strive to use less pressure than you'd use to cut soft butter with a knife. If you don't get a response, you can always ask again with a little more conviction. But don't jerk. Break down resistance in the horse's face by asking with your legs. By using your legs more, you'll be able to use your hands less.

Earlier we made the analogy that the reins are the phone lines that run between you and your horse. To keep the connection clear and static free, choose reins that are comfortable and hang quietly until you have something to say to the horse. If you're a petite woman and a three-quarter inch mecate rein is too bulky, go to something smaller. If you're a large man, half-inch soft latigo reins might feel too light and delicate. Heavy harness leather might be a better alternative.

The type of reins should also work well with the type of bit. An ornate California style bit would not only look out of character with light-weight latigo split reins, it wouldn't feel right or function well. Traditional braided rawhide romal reins would be in keeping with the tradition and would better balance the bit, allowing you to communicate more clearly with the horse.

When riding, check from time to time to be sure that your reins are of even length, and are neither too long nor too short. Signals become skewed when one rein is longer than the other and can confound even the best trained horses.

CAN WESTERN HORSES BE "ON THE BIT?"

The term "on the bit" is usually used in English circles because a rider maintains constant contact with the horse's mouth via the reins. It indicates that the horse is flexed at the poll and is willingly moving forward into the bit without pulling against the rider's hands or trying to evade the bit by overflexing and getting behind it. The rein is used as a light, yet continuous physical link.

The term "on the bit" is commonly used in English riding (bottom), but even in western disciplines the result of good training is the same (below). The horse is soft and yielding, travels with collection, and is psychologically ready to comply to the slightest rein signal without resistance.

In western horsemanship, this same principle applies though it is expressed differently. There is a link between horse and rider even when the rider is not making direct contact with the horse's mouth. During training, a western rider constantly takes hold of a horse's mouth to ask for flexion and compliance. The horse is shown what to do, then released until it needs more reinforcement. In this way, the trainer weans the horse from a need for continuous contact on the bit and gets control on a loose rein.

With time and education, constant physical contact gives way to psychological contact. The horse becomes soft and supple, remains flexed at the poll, maintains its frame or collection, and is ready to respond to the weight of the reins and pressure of the bit at any moment. In effect, the horse remains mentally "on the bit," even though there is no constant pressure being applied to its mouth.

As with the dressage horse, the communication between horse and rider becomes so subtle that the physical nature of it becomes secondary. To the observer, the cues seem non-existent. During the training phases, however, there is much more obvious interaction between horse and rider via bridle, reins and legs, and it is more apparent that the horse is physically "on the bit."

PRACTICE MAKES PERFECT

It is often said that you should take hold of the reins as though they are attached to the bit by gossamer threads that can be easily broken. That's an ideal to help you visualize just how light communication can be. However, not every horse responds to that level of sensitivity. It may be more realistic to think about trying to pull with the same degree of force needed to stretch a rubber band without snapping it. In fact, we know of one riding instructor who actually does connect the reins to the bit with rubber bands for students who need to learn to use their hands more slowly and sensitively.

Another analogy that's easy to relate to is to take a hold of the reins as though you're squeezing water from a sponge. The motion is fluid rather than harsh or abrupt. You have to educate your mind to control your hands. You have to control your body to control your hands. With practice, your responses will become automatic.

The bits you choose can also help you develop better hands. By using a mild bit — although not so mild that the horse will ignore it — the novice rider can perfect his or her timing and skill without unduly punishing the horse. It's best to start with a bit that allows some room for error. That means bits with mild mouthpieces, little or no leverage, and lots of signal.

Once you feel you're in better control of your hands, seat and legs, you can experiment with different head gear. You can move up in stages as a way to test and challenge yourself. Find out just how lightly you can use your hands and still get the responses you want. You can experiment with different bits as a way to develop more finesse as a rider, but never to the detriment of the horse. Horses are forgiving, but they also have long memories. The way your horse responds will be either humbling or exhilarating, and will let you know whether you're really learning to use your hands effectively.

Developing soft hands, of course, takes more brain than bit. To be light-handed, you have to think about being light-handed. If you are not getting the responses you want, first analyze what it is you are doing. Keep it in that perspective. The horse's behavior simply reflects the signals that you are giving it. Horses can be retrained to be lighter in the bridle, but only if you retrain yourself first.

Finally, bits should never be used as weapons or as mechanisms to punish. Hold your temper. You can sore a horse's mouth or scare the animal enough to make the animal lighter in the bridle — at least temporarily — but you haven't gotten to the root of the problem. Whenever you encounter resistance (which you invariably will), work through the problem mentally first. Then apply brain, not brawn. That, of course, is the real key to developing soft hands.

"PREVENTING PROBLEMS IS ALWAYS EASIER THAN CORRECTING THEM."

17

Problems, Solutions and Safety

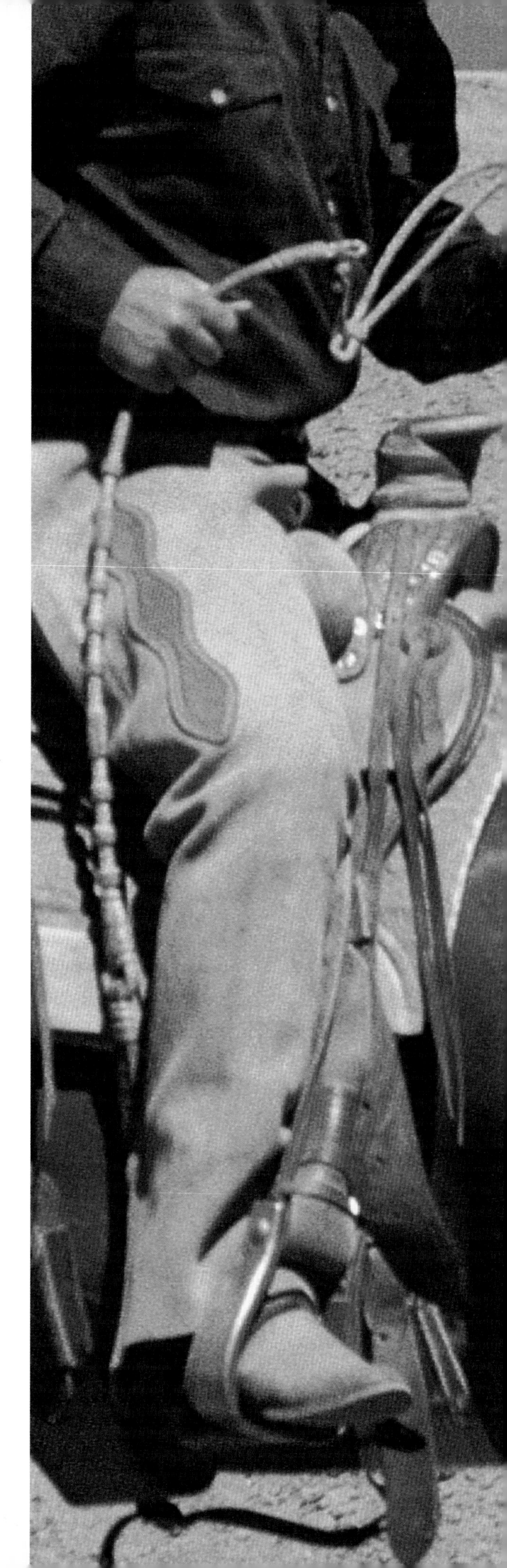

Bitting problems are not uncommon. Most, of course, are man-made. Riders may use too much or too little bit or allow their tempers or ignorance to get in the way of treating their horses' mouths courteously. In this chapter we'll look at what can go wrong in the bitting equation, how to avoid and/or solve some of the most common problems, and provide some additional safety tips.

SYMPTOMS OF PROBLEMS

Horses have a variety of ways to let you know that something is wrong with their bits or the ways in which you are using them. Some symptoms are immediately obvious. Others are more subtle and will take some close observation and interpretation on your part.

You know your horse best. It will be up to you to determine what specific behavior means. While we might presume that a horse with its mouth closed and ears up is relatively content with its bit, or that a horse with its tongue sticking out is trying to say the pressure on its tongue is uncomfortable —neither is true based on face value alone. For instance, we know of one gelding who sticks out his tongue to demonstrate his quirky personality. He does it even while standing in his stall bare-headed.

As for frustration, horses can show their displeasure in many ways and it may appear to be totally unrelated to the bridle even when it is. So if performance or attitude aren't up to par, take stock of the horse's headgear while you're assessing its health, environment and other factors.

Be aware that apparent resistance to the bit may actually be caused by pain somewhere other than the mouth. For instance, a horse may become difficult to stop, turn, roll back or put into a collected frame, due to soreness

in its back or hocks. The horse may become heavy on the forehand and consequently, heavy on the bit. Similarly, a horse with forefoot problems such as laminitis, navicular disease, a stone bruise or abscess, may attempt to stay off of its front end. Such horses might become stiff, or difficult to turn in one direction or the other.

Be sure to rule out any medical basis for the "bitting" problem before you head to the tack room. It would be unfair to put something more severe in the horse's mouth when it is already trying to cope with physical pain elsewhere.

Horses are frequently started under saddle as long yearlings and two-year-olds, which coincides with when they are teething. Their mouths may be especially sensitive. If a problem develops, consider postponing bitting until the mouth heals or use a bitless bridle instead.

EVASION TACTICS

A horse may take a number of steps to evade a bit. For instance, if you bang the horse's teeth every time you insert the bit, it won't take long before the horse begins to resist being bridled by raising its head and clenching its teeth.

When a horse is said to "take the bit in his teeth," he is actually extending his nose, getting ahead of the bit, and retracting the corners of his lips. The bit ends up resting against the lower cheek teeth, where contact with the mouth is painless.

When a horse is said to "spit out the bit" he is tucking his chin against his chest, getting behind the bit, to avoid the bit's pressure. He may brace his lower lip outside on the shank of a curb bit thus taking the pressure off the bars. He can also turn the bit in his mouth with his tongue, sometimes called "scissoring," thereby avoiding its pressure. A horse may continually nod or toss his head in an attempt to adjust the position of the bit in his mouth, so that it will be more comfortable.

HEAD TOSSING & STAR GAZING

Head tossing, in particular, is a problem which should be addressed without delay. It may become a habit that is nearly impossible to break — even after the initial cause is remedied. The first step should be a thorough veterinary examination. Diseases of the eyes, ears, nose, mouth, brain or guttural pouches, or injuries to the neck or spinal cord, may be involved. Less complicated, and more obvious, causes are such things as harassment by flies.

Signs such as sneezing, snorting, coughing, nasal discharge and watery eyes which accompany head tossing may hint as to the cause. It may be a seasonal phenomenon, suggesting an allergic reaction such as allergic rhinitis or a reaction to insects. Certainly, the most troublesome is the horse that shakes its head not only when bridled but when stalled or pastured as well. Inflammation of the nasal passages should be considered.

Whatever the cause, treatment should begin without delay. Such things as insect control, moving a stalled

COMMON SIGNS OF BITTING PROBLEMS

* Pulling on the bit. *
* Head tossing. *
* Excessive head nodding. *
* Ear pinning. *
* Tongue lolling. *
* Gaping of the mouth. *
* Bit champing. *
* Tail swishing or wringing. *
* Failure to travel straight. *
(sometimes mistaken for lameness)
* Difficulty in guiding and stopping. *
* Dropping feed. *
(if the mouth is sore)
* Excessive salivation. *
* Abnormal head carriage. *
(such as overflexion or over extension)
* Sores on the tongue or gum bars. *
* Sores on the corners of the lips, nose or chin. *
* Cuts in the mouth. *
* Bleeding from the mouth. *

(opposite) A horse that sticks his tongue out the side of his mouth may be unhappy with his bit or, as in this case, he may simply be relaxed.

(pages 164-165) When too much bit is used with too much muscle, it's likely the horse will be worrying about his mouth, not his job. Pinned ears and a gaping mouth are sure signs of an unhappy horse.

horse to pasture or providing the company of other horses (or even of a non-equine companion such as a goat), may be helpful.

In the majority of cases, veterinarians fail to find any medical reason for head tossing. If a horse tosses its head only when bridled and ridden, both the bitting system and the way the rider uses it should be evaluated.

Some horses toss their heads because they are unhappy with the restrictions placed on them by the rider's hands on the bit. It may be a sign of discomfort or simply one of impatience. Some barn sour horses toss their heads when they're in a hurry to get back to their stalls or stablemates.

It takes patience to resolve head-tossing. You may need help in analyzing the situation. Among the things you can try are adjusting the position of the bit in the horse's mouth and experimenting with different bits. Better to start with less rather than more. Try changing to a milder bit or to a bitless bridle. Overbridling can frighten a horse — particularly one that may already resent the confinement it feels in the bridle — and cause it to rear up and go over backwards.

You may also need to change your riding tactics. Use your hands softly and consistently, and be sure to provide your horse a zone of relief. Allow the horse to assume a head position that's natural and comfortable. If all else fails, consult a professional who has dealt successfully with such problems. The horse may need patient retraining to learn to accept and carry a bit.

Only as a last resort should a more forceful measure, such as a standing martingale, be used. A tie-down should be used with caution and it should never be adjusted too tightly. There is always the possibility that a horse may react violently to having its head restricted. A tie-down is not a good permanent solution. Used in combination with other retraining methods, it may help correct the problem of head-tossing.

Once a horse develops the habit, it may be very difficult to resolve, which is why the importance of getting the horse off to the proper start cannot be overemphasized. Also be aware that even the best trainers occasionally encounter head shakers that develop the habit for no apparent reason and defy nearly all attempts to remedy it.

A less common problem is the horse that is always ahead of the bit. In extreme cases of high-headedness, the horse is called a "star gazer." Again, a veterinary examination is indicated. If no medical reason can be found, the same progression of adjustments suggested for the head-tosser may be helpful.

RUNNING THROUGH THE BIT

Certainly, some horses are born with less sensitivity than others and may need more pulling power to be sufficiently responsive to the rider. But as a rule, horses become hard-mouthed as a result of poor training and riding. Consider, too, that horses who consistently pull on or "run through" the bit, may as likely have sore mouths as insensitive ones. Fear, confusion and pain can make a horse oblivious to the meaning of the bit signals and cause the horse's mouth to go "dry." Contact with the bit becomes even more uncomfortable because there is even more friction between the bit and the mouth.

Whenever there are bitting problems, it is always best to change to a milder rather than a more severe bit — at least at first. If a rider then deems it necessary to step up in severity, it should be regarded as a temporary measure. When the horse's responses improve, the rider should revert back to a milder bit. Always reward progress. Mild bits with tongue toys can also improve natural lubrication by stimulating the flow of saliva.

SOLVING ODD PROBLEMS

Some horses have a tendency to get their tongues over the bit. This can be disastrous, because tension on the reins presses the bit against the very sensitive frenulum below the tongue. Proper adjustment of headstalls, nosebands and chin straps make this unlikely, but for problem horses there are various types of lollering bits which have wide mouthpieces or attachments in the centers which keep the tongue in place.

This racehorse is rigged with blinkers, a racing ring (Dexter) bit, and a gauze tongue tie which functions to prevent the horse from retracting his tongue.

Tongue ties, made of either strap, gauze or cloth may be used to keep the tongue beneath the mouthpiece. The material loops around the tongue and ties beneath the chin. There is also a W-shaped metal tongue controller that attaches to its own headstall and chin strap and holds the tongue down. Some people shudder at the idea of a tongue tie, but most horses do not seem to mind it in any way. However, all horses certainly react adversely when their tongues are over the bit.

A horse that continually chews on his bit may also be helped by adjusting the cheekpieces of the headstall or tightening the curb strap. Sometimes a dropped noseband or a lollering bit may correct the problem. Some trainers have cured horses of chewing on the bit by wrapping the mouthpiece in cloth soaked in something tasty such as sugar water.

For horses that have a tendency to bear or pull to one side, there are regulator or sidelining bits and bit burrs. Sidelining bits have an extension on one side. When the rein is attached to this extension it gives the driver (usually used on cart horses rather than riding horses) extra leverage to straighten the horse. In the slip-mouth sidelining bit, the center of the mouthpiece is hollow; a bar, which is a few inches longer than the bit, runs through the mouthpiece and out each side. When a horse bears to one side, the bar slides to the opposite side and gives the rider more leverage with which to straighten the horse.

A bit burr is a circular piece of rubber or leather with short stiff bristles that fits on the mouthpiece just inside the rings or shanks. In theory, it discourages the horse from pressing on the burr side — although it often fails to achieve the desired result.

A slip-mouth sidelining bit.

TREATING BITTING INJURIES

Bitting injuries may be apparent as soon as they occur because of bleeding or the horse's obvious reaction to the pain. Be aware that horses do not generally "scream in pain," even in severe situations. Seldom, in fact, does the horse vocalize its discomfort. The general response to sharp pain is a sudden attempt to escape from the source. In the case of a mouth injury, a horse might suddenly jerk its head or react any time the reins are touched. However, the signs of injury may be more subtle. The horse may simply not respond to the rider's signals. Indeed, many injuries will not be apparent until the bridle is removed.

As soon as an injury becomes apparent, the bit should be removed from the mouth. If there is profuse bleeding (and there may well be, because the mouth is extremely well supplied with blood vessels) or an obvious cut, veterinary assistance should be obtained. Prompt attention to a cut tongue or palate may hasten healing and prevent long term complications or defects.

Topical medications do little to help speed the healing of pressure sores on the bars or corners of the lips. If the sores are severe, the horse should not be bitted until they heal. A horse who is forced to perform with a sore mouth, may develop fear of the bit or form bad habits such as head tossing. Continued irritation may also lead to destruction of nerve endings and a loss of sensitivity to the bit. Obviously, the rider should determine why the injury occurred and make appropriate changes in bitting or riding to avoid future injury. Prevention is certainly better than cure.

Repair of severe mouth injuries, especially cut tongues, frequently requires general anesthesia and major surgery. The expense alone is good reason to avoid them, to say nothing of the pain to the horse, the set-back in training, and the possibility that the horse may never

Replacing a bit which is damaged is highly recommended. Even something as seemingly minor as flaking chrome can cause chronic injury.

return to the previous level of performance. It is fortunate that most mouth injuries heal well, and that most horses are reasonably forgiving.

AN OUNCE OF PREVENTION

Preventing problems is always easier than correcting them. A few safe bitting practices can make a big difference in your horse's continued comfort and acceptance of the bit.

- ➤ Clean and check bits regularly for defects which might injure the horse's mouth. Replace any faulty tack.
- ➤ Never tie a horse with the bridle reins. Use a halter so that if the horse pulls back, it won't damage its mouth.
- ➤ When leading a bridled horse, hold both reins or tie the second rein securely around the saddle horn so there is no chance of it dropping and getting stepped on.
- ➤ Never leave a horse bitted up (tied back) so long that its neck muscles become fatigued making it difficult for the horse to keep the pressure off its mouth.
- ➤ Never leave a horse alone when it is bitted up.
- ➤ Avoid using a running martingale with a shanked bit.
- ➤ When using a running martingale, be sure to use reins stops to keep the rings of the martingale from becoming caught on the rein rings of the bit.
- ➤ Adjust a tie-down (standing martingale) with enough slack so the horse can stand comfortably, and use its head and neck effectively for balance during performance.
- ➤ Avoid letting a horse eat or graze while wearing a bit.
- ➤ Have a routine veterinary and dental examination every six months.
- ➤ Make sure the bit fits and that the headstall and all accessories are adjusted properly.
- ➤ Be considerate when bridling. Handle the horse's ears gently and be careful not to bump the bit against the horse's teeth when inserting it into the mouth.
- ➤ Never punish the horse by jerking on the reins and avoid banging its mouth with the bit.
- ➤ Make it a habit to check the horse's lips, gums, bars and tongue for signs of tenderness or injury.

"IF YOU SHOW OR COMPETE, IT'S IMPORTANT TO CONSULT THE CURRENT RULEBOOKS."

18

Bitting And Competition

Virtually every breed and horse show organization has developed rules or guidelines for the types of bits, bridles and accessories that are permitted in competition. The rules are there to protect horses from abuse and provide judges a way to fairly evaluate and compare the entries. Certainly no show committee can devise regulations for every circumstance. So most organizations have broad-based rules that cover humane treatment, which can be applied to bitting practices.

Fortunately, most people don't choose equipment with the intent to harm their horses. It is the rare individual who wants to win at any cost and is only prevented from using harsh bits by the existence of rules.

In this chapter, it is not our intent to recite show rules, but rather to consider them in the context of why they're developed. If you show or compete, it's extremely important to consult the current rulebooks for approved tack and how it is to be used. Bit and tack recommendations are continuously being evaluated and changed. Also, the rules are extremely divergent from one organization to the next. What one association may allow, another may prohibit.

For instance, a 5/16 inch snaffle bit that's legal in an American Quarter Horse Association western pleasure class would be cause for disqualification in a National Snaffle Bit Association event. Peruvian Pasos are shown in Peruvian bits with shanks no longer than 6 inches. The Peruvian bit is a relatively mild, low port curb, which would be legal in almost all western classes. However, it is traditionally coupled with a Peruvian curb chain that would be prohibited in most western breed associations.

Most rules specify that curb straps may be either leather or chain but must be at least a half-inch wide and lie flat against the chin. No braided, rawhide, rolled, wire, metal

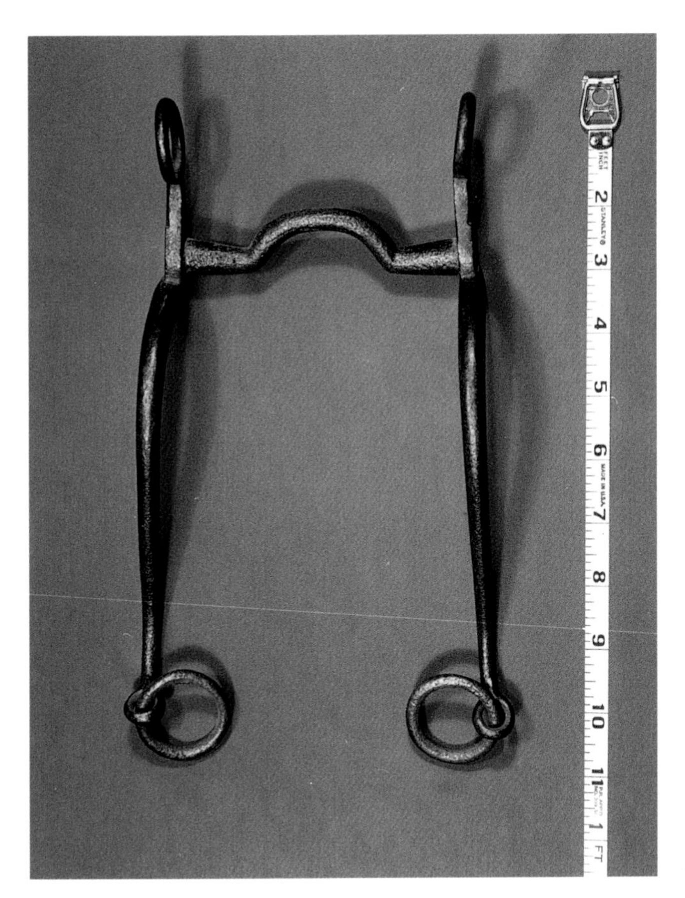

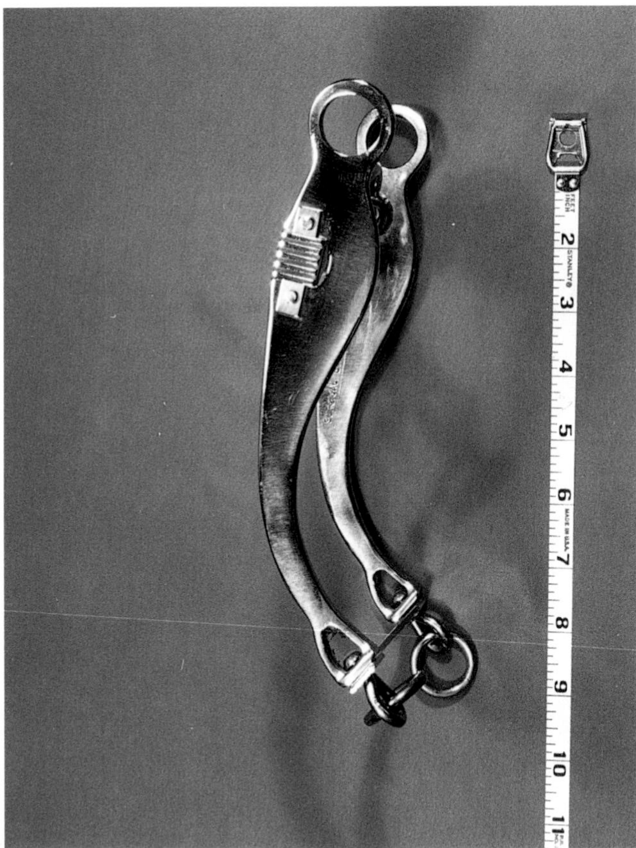

Horse show associations stipulate the allowable length of bit shanks, with 8½ inches commonly being the maximum length allowable. However, some associations measure the entire shank from the bridle loop to the rein loop while others measure from the mouthpiece to the rein loop.

or other substance can be used in conjunction with, or as part of, a leather chin strap or curb chain.

Most stock horse breeds allow curb bits with shanks up to 8½ inches long. But it's important to note how the shank is to be measured. For instance, the American Horse Shows Association (AHSA) stipulates that Paso Fino bits can have shanks no longer than six inches. Yet the shanks are measured from the mouthpiece to the bottom of the rein rings. The length of the shank above the mouthpiece is not considered — even though it makes a substantial difference in the pulling power of the bit. A bit with 1 inch above the mouthpiece and 6 below is much more severe than one with 2 inches above the mouthpiece and 6 inches below. (Refer to Chapter 8 for a more complete discussion of leverage).

The AQHA, on the other hand, measures bit shanks from the inside top of the bridle loop to the middle of the rein ring,allowing 8½ inches total, (also regardless of the position of the mouthpiece). In most of the western divisions, AHSA conforms to the 8½ inch rule as well. But why would these associations stipulate measuring shanks from the center of the rein ring rather than the bottom of it? Probably because that's the position where the rein engages the bit when the slack is taken up by the rider.

So, are longer shanks and a milder curb chain more acceptable than a bit with less leverage but more bite to the curb chain? Probably not. But these are some of the dilemmas with which rules committees have to contend when making up show regulations. Incidentally, Peruvian Paso riders may

(overleaf) Almost every equestrian discipline has its own set of standards for bits and bridles. When you get to this level of competition, you generally know what the requirements of the sport are. Often, bit choices depend as much upon tradition as function. And in the English realm, traditions change slowly.

choose to use flat curb straps with their Peruvian bits rather than the traditional Peruvian curb chain.

Even within an association what is permitted in one class may be cause for disqualification in another. For example, many associations allow higher ports, longer shanks, and gag-type bits to be used in timed-event classes such as barrel racing, roping and team penning, yet prohibit these bits in rail classes such as western pleasure or horsemanship. There's actually a certain irony to this. The rationale is that timed-event competitors need bits that provide greater control because the horse is performing at speed. There is probably a grain of truth to this. Yet these same rules also open the door to abuse. In a race against the clock, riders are psyched up and asking for maximum performance. When a rider takes hold of the reins to stop a horse hard or turn it fast, a more severe bit provides far greater opportunity to damage the mouth than exists, say, in a western pleasure class. The pleasure horse is simply asked to walk, jog and lope, reverse directions, go through its paces once again, and back up. The pulling power of the bit is hardly a factor.

Following that same thought, an association which allows 3½ inch ports in the senior western divisions may prohibit English horses from being shown in bits with ports that exceed 1½ inches. The differences may conform to the traditions of the disciplines but may not necessarily be based on the logic of humane use.

The rules make more sense if you consider that the mature western horse is supposed to be guided with one hand and a certain degree of slack in the reins. Yet, when that same bit is permitted to be used two-handed in an event like team penning, where the horse may be pulled and stopped repeatedly and forcefully — the rules may be worthy of reconsideration.

No matter what event we're discussing, a horse's responsiveness should be paramount to its ability to win. But that responsiveness should depend on the training done prior to the show rather than on the hardware that is permitted in the arena.

To their credit, almost all event organizations specify a minimum diameter for the mouthpieces that can be used. That's because the severity of the bit ties directly to its size and texture. The smaller and rougher the mouthpiece is, the more it concentrates the force of the pull and the greater the potential for cutting the tongue or bars. The National Snaffle Bit Association, a specialty organization for the pleasure horse industry, requires that snaffle mouthpieces be smooth and at least ⅜-inch thick or larger measured one inch from the bit rings. The distance of one inch from the rings or butt of the mouthpiece is important because that's where the bit comes into contact with the mouth bars.

The American Horse Shows Association, which sanctions approximately 2,500 events each year and has more than 60,000 members, uses the same standard, as does the National Reining Horse Association, the National Reined Cow Horse Association and others. These same associations

The Peruvian bit is relatively mild, but its curb chain would be prohibited in most western breed associations. (Gemma Giannini Photo)

allow shanked bits to have slightly smaller bit bars, 5/16 of an inch. That, too, gives pause for thought since leverage bits can exert even greater force on a smaller surface area than a direct pulling bit, such as a snaffle. Perhaps for simplicity sake, the Quarter Horse, Paint and Appaloosa associations allow a minimum of 5/16-inch bit bars for both snaffle and leverage bits.

Snaffle bit rules usually limit the size and shape of the bit rings as well. O-rings, D-rings and egg-butt snaffles are generally permitted with cheeks 2-4 inches in diameter. Interestingly, with a direct pulling bit, ring size has little effect on the force of the pull. However, it can influence the pull-through effect (see Chapter 6 for more on snaffle bits). The size, shape and connection to the mouthpiece do, of course, effect the bit's signal. The larger the rings, the more signal the bit provides (especially with loose-ringed bits). The ring size restrictions do, however, provide for greater uniformity within the class.

Many organizations also state a maximum size for the bit bars, usually no larger than 3/4-inch in diameter. Greater dimension not only adds weight but also bulk to the bit and may make the mouthpiece heavy and uncomfortable. This rule also makes such things as the broad, flat "polo" mouthpiece, or "Rutledge Roper" bit illegal, although such mouthpieces, if well-designed and smoothly constructed, may not be especially severe (see Chapter 7). Polo mouthpieces may, in fact, be milder than some standard curbs because they spread the force of the pull over a greater surface area of tongue and bars. When the shanks swivel, the mouthpiece should remain flat on the surface rather than allowing the narrow edge to roll and dig into soft tissue.

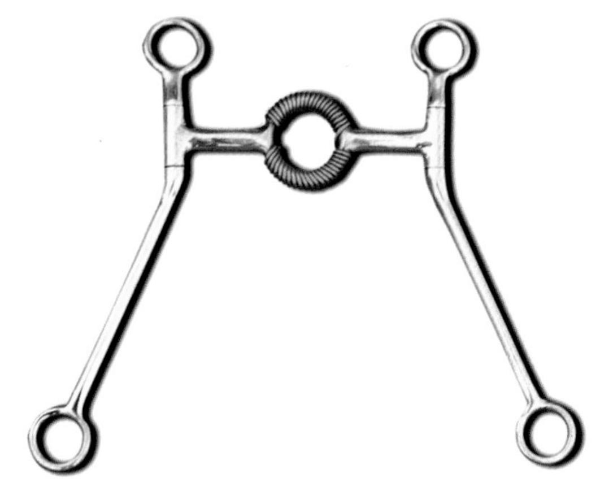

Most associations prohibit bits with anything that extends below the bars of the mouthpiece. The configuration of the donut mouthpiece gives the tongue no relief at all, so the bit is quite severe.

Most associations prohibit bits with anything that extends below the bars of the mouthpiece. Prong-type bits or those with solid donuts, (round, closed ports that protrude well below the bit bars) are severe because the extensions can gouge the tongue or tissues below the tongue as the bit rotates in the mouth. In the case of a donut mouthpiece, the tongue has nowhere to go. As of this writing, a few associations still permit donut mouthpieces to be used in speed events, roping and team penning while prohibiting prong-type bits.

There is a certain degree of latitude to such rules. Some correction type bits have smooth, rounded rivets that extend slightly below the bit bars, and these are usually permitted. Also, some jointed mouthpieces with center rings connecting the cannons are allowed, and some of the rings are slightly larger than the bars. Usually the rules require that the ring be no larger than 1 1/4 inch in diameter and lie flat in the mouth. Some allowance is also given to bits with rollers or crickets in the port, which may extend slightly below the bit bars (see Chapter 7).

Mouthpieces made from twisted or edged bar stock are also generally restricted regardless of the size, shape or texture of the bit. The reason may be to keep western exhibitors from using something unnecessarily severe. Yet many of the same associations allow slow twist, corkscrew, and double and single-twisted wire snaffle bits in their English classes. Such inconsistencies are sometimes hard to fathom.

Chain mouthpieces are also generally prohibited. However, the rules may be more broad-based than that. For example, they may restrict bits with more than three segments to the mouthpiece, or prohibit any mouthpiece with rough, sharp, or edged surfaces. Even so, some chain mouthpieces can be relatively mild provided the links are well designed and have been tumbled smooth so there are no burrs. (People often wear necklaces and bracelets and play with or tug on them with no ill effects.) Yet poorly designed or intentionally rough mouthpieces, such as bicycle or saw-tooth chains, are outlawed for good reason.

Gag bits, mechanical hackamores, nosebands, martingales, draw reins and other accessories are usually limited to timed-event or specialty competition. Such equipment is generally regarded as training tack or artificial aids. In the show ring, judges are trying to determine the degree of training. But sometimes the tack is actually more misunderstood than it is severe.

Gag bits are a case in point. Design can make a great deal of difference in how severe the bit actually is. Many smooth-mouth gag snaffles, for instance, are in fact quite mild. They simply act on different regions of the head and mouth than a standard snaffle — more on the lips and poll than on the tongue and bars. However, shanked gags, in which the mouthpiece slides up and down the length of the cheeks, can be fairly severe — particularly if the shanks are long.

Remember, the leverage increases as the mouthpiece slides up the length of the shanks toward the bridle rings. Without question, such bits can provide additional control in barrel racing, pole bending and other gymkhana events in which a rider needs maneuverability and the ability to rate the horse. Shanked gags are generally allowed in timed competition, as are mechanical hackamores, even though they are restricted elsewhere.

While many associations tend to focus on port height and shank length, it is perhaps an oversimplification of the problems involving bit design. A 3½-inch or higher spade bit that has been properly contoured and rolled back may be much less damaging than a half-breed bit with a straight-up 2-inch port.

Most associations have rules that apply to hackamores as well. The National Cutting Horse Association, for example, permits only traditional rawhide or rope noseband hackamores. They must be adjusted so that two fingers can be slipped easily between noseband and nose on all sides. Interestingly, NCHA does not restrict the type of bits that can be used. Once the cut is made, the cutter drops his rein hand and lets the horse have its head to work. The reins are not picked up until the rider "quits" the cow, so the type of bit a horse is shown in is critical only to the degree that it provides "mental" control.

Competitors in reining and working cowhorse classes are routinely asked to drop the bridle so an equipment judge can ensure that the bit adheres to the event standards and has not caused any damage to the mouth.

The standard used by most stock horse breed associations is to permit only traditional braided leather or rawhide bosals with cheekpieces no larger than ¾-inch. Most associations prohibit bosals with metal or cable cores because they add to the severity of the gear, and fly in the face of tradition. Some rules allow the cheekpieces to be wrapped with a smooth, non-grabbing material such as electrician's tape, which helps keep the jaw from being rubbed raw. But in classes where aesthetics matter, you rarely see a wrapped bosal.

Most rulebooks give the judge or the stewards the ability to use their discretion when it comes to evaluating whether tack is humane or not. The people assigned to check equipment should not be intimidated by exhibitors or be reluctant to blow the whistle on abuse when they see it. Another problem is that there is a general lack of knowledge on the part of riders and officials concerning bits and bridles. The AHSA provides judges and show stewards with a handbook on western bits and tack to help educate them and alleviate confusion when making judgement calls. At National Reining Horse Association events, equipment judges check every horse at the out-gate. Rules are stringently and fairly enforced. One particular year, for example, several exhibitors were disqualified during the reining futurity because they violated chin strap rules. In an event that costs over a thousand dollars to enter and pays more than $100,000 to the winner, having overlooked something as simple as a twist in a curb chain (chains are required to lie flat against the chin) became a very expensive lesson.

At almost all shows, any evidence of blood, or broken or raw skin in or around the horse's mouth, nose or chin — no matter how minor — is cause for immediate disqualification. The National Snaffle Bit Association allows the show steward to use his or her discretion in permitting the exhibitor to switch from a snaffle bit to a bosal, or a bosal to a snaffle bit, if there is evidence of minor soring.

Not all organizations spell out their limits quite so clearly. The Professional Rodeo Cowboys Association (PRCA), for example, has broad rules concerning the humane treatment of animals, but does not restrict the use of any bits or accessories based on their potential severity. But because PRCA contests are judged by the clock and the fastest time wins, riders utilize gear that provides every split-second advantage. Calf ropers, for instance, almost universally use jerk lines to put pressure on the bit to keep the horse working the rope.

Tie-downs of all dimensions and textures are used. It's not uncommon to see metal or cable nosebands in place as a serious reminder for the horse to keep its head down and out of the way of the rope, and to prevent it from evading the bit. Bits and mechanical hackamores with extreme leverage action are also frequently used to keep the horse stopping hard and fast once the catch has been made.

At most horse show ropings, jerk lines are prohibited because it is the horse's skill that is being judged. A trained calf roping horse has learned to maintain tension on the rope without the necessity of being reminded by a pull on the jerk line. AQHA and other show associations also prohibit wire or cable nosebands or chin straps. In fact, they prohibit wire or metal of any kind in contact with the horse's head. Sawtooth bits, tack collars and tack hackamores are also among the items that are specifically listed as illegal equipment.

In recent years, breed and horse show organizations have been making an extra effort to educate judges and members regarding bits and bitting practices. Some of the rules have been rewritten to take the pressure off young horses and trainers. The AQHA, for example, used to define junior horses as those four and under. The division has been expanded to include five-year-olds as well. This gives a horse another year in which to be ridden two-handed in either a snaffle bit or hackamore if the rider so chooses. However, they may also be shown in curb, half-breed or spade bits with one hand on the reins.

AQHA hackamore class rules used to stipulate that only one-hand could be used on the reins, but the rules were rewritten to permit two hands. Also be sure to pay attention to all the rules regarding reining techniques. Incorrect rein holds or hand positions can be cause for penalties or elimination. Senior western horses are still required to be shown in the bridle — meaning a western type curb bit. In American Horse Shows Association competition, junior horses are still those under five years of age. Younger horses which have been shown in a curb bit are no longer eligible for two-handed snaffle bit and hackamore classes.

Sport organizations, such as those for competitive and endurance riding, don't restrict or regulate headgear either. Rather they leave it up to competitors to determine what's best for their horses. The American Endurance Ride Conference publishes an Endurance Riders Handbook that promotes the use of safe, comfortable headgear, which allows the horse to eat and drink with minimal interference. In long distance treks, the ability to refuel is

Easy stop type mechanical hackamores are prohibited in horse show competition by almost every association.

extremely important to the health and well-being of the horse. Short-shanked, mechanical hackamores are especially recommended, while long-shanked bits and hackamores are discouraged because the shanks can get in the way of the horse eating and drinking.

Snaffle bits and mechanical hackamores are the most common kinds of headgear used by distance trail riders, acknowledges saddle and tack maker Sharon Saare, who has long been associated with distance riding programs. But Saare also emphasizes the need for safety and control. When endurance horses become extremely fit, they can become hard to handle. Sometimes a halter or simple ring snaffle is not enough to keep an eager horse under control. "I've been run away with in three different countries riding horses outfitted in snaffle bits," she laughs. Saare recommends that for safety sake, riders should choose head-gear that affords some leverage advantage. Her preference is a well-constructed mechanical hackamore — and she takes one with her whenever she travels.

Much of the headgear that is permitted in the competitive arena today is dictated by tradition and special interest groups. Horse show exhibitors often lobby for either more relaxed or more stringent rules depending on current styles and public sentiment. But just because you're allowed to use certain gear doesn't mean you should. Use what works.

Learn the rules for your breed or event. Get involved with the rules committees especially if there is need for reform or improvement. Not all of today's show rules have been written with the horse's best interest at heart. Remain open-minded. Study how bits work before making a judgement. Sometimes a bit's design can fool you. Also try to gain an appreciation for the performance requirements of certain events. Factor in the potential for abuse. Then strive to make recommendations that competitors and officials will be willing to abide by without compromising the horse.

ABOVE THE BIT: When a horse fails to yield to bit pressure or refuses contact with the bit, usually characterized by extending its nose well in front of vertical. Also "ahead of the bit."

ACCESSORIES: Includes all apparatus not directly associated with the bit or bridle such as martingales and nosebands.

AHEAD OF THE BIT: When a horse fails to yield appropriately to the bit so that its nose extends far forward. The bit may be pulled back against the corners of the lips or lower cheek teeth where contact with the tongue and bars of the mouth is lost.

AIDS: The cues the rider gives the horse with his or her legs, hands, weight, voice or an accessory (such as a crop) which asks the horse to respond.

ARCADE: A row of upper or lower teeth.

ARGENTINE BIT: A broken-mouthed curb bit with short, slightly curved lower shanks, usually with snaffle rings located at the level of the mouthpiece. Is sometimes called an Argentine "snaffle," because of its jointed mouthpiece, however, it is not a true snaffle.

ATLANTOAXIAL JOINT: The junction in the horse's neck between the first cervical vertebra (the atlas) and the second cervical vertebra (the axis), which allows the horse to flex its head toward its body.

BACKUP ROPE: A long accessory rope used by calf ropers to keep the horse applying tension to the catch rope. The back-up rope attaches to the bit shanks, runs through a pulley or ring on the saddle, and is looped and tucked under the rider's belt. When the roper dismounts and runs to the calf, the loops pull loose from the belt one at a time and puts pressure on the bit. This encourages the horse to back away from the calf thereby keeping tension on the catch rope. Also called a jerk line.

BALANCE OF A BIT: The natural position in which a shanked bit hangs in the absence of rein pressure. Balance relates to the degree of bit and chin strap pressure on the horse's mouth and chin groove when the bit is at rest, and how quickly the bit returns to a neutral (disengaged) position when rein pressure is released.

BAR BIT: A straight or only slightly curved, solid, unbroken mouthpiece; usually a snaffle or direct-pulling bit.

BARS OF THE BIT: The parts of the mouthpiece which extend directly in from the cheeks. In a ported mouthpiece the portion to either side of the port.

BARS OF THE MOUTH: The gap in the lower jaw between the incisor and cheek teeth or molars where there are is only gum or a solitary tooth. In males, and a few females, part of this space is occupied by the canine teeth. The mouthpiece of the bit fits in the bars of the mouth. Also called the interdental spaces.

BEARING REIN: Indirect rein pressure used to either balance a direct rein air or to help teach neck-reining.

BEHIND THE BIT: When the horse overflexes in response to rein pressure thereby positioning its nose behind the vertical in an effort to evade the action of the bit.

BICYCLE CHAIN MOUTHPIECE: A severe mouthpiece consisting of several links which resemble a bicycle chain. Sometimes called a mule bit.

BIGHT: The slack part or loop in a rope.

BILLY ALLEN MOUTHPIECE: A broken mouthpiece which has a smooth, short barrel or cylinder-shaped segment which encircles the center joint or has been hinged in such a way as to allow only limited flexion of the mouthpiece. Design attributed to the horseman Billy Allen.

BIT BARS: The parts of the mouthpiece which extend directly in from the cheeks. In a ported mouthpiece the portion to either side of the port.

BIT BURR: A circular piece of rubber or leather with short, stiff bristles on the inside that fits on the mouthpiece just inside the rings or shanks. Its purpose is to discourage the horse from pressing on the burr side.

BITE ALIGNMENT: The way the upper and lower teeth fit together. With proper bite alignment chewing is efficient.

BIT GUARDS: Circular pieces of rubber or leather which fit at the ends of the mouthpiece between the cheeks and bars to keep the horse's lips from being chafed.

BIT PROGRESSION: Moving from one bit to another more advanced bit in stages as a way to advance training. For example, changing from a snaffle or hackamore to a curb.

BIT SEAT: When floating the horse's teeth, the place which is created by rounding the front of the first upper and lower cheek teeth and removing the wolf teeth. This is done to allow the bit to act properly without pinching the lips or cheeks.

BITTING RIG: The apparatus, usually comprised of surcingle, side reins and bridle, which is used for bitting up a horse.

BITTING SYSTEM: The total combination of elements used to control the horse's head, including such things as headstall, bit, noseband, reins, and any other accessories.

BITTING UP: The practice of accustoming the horse to bit pressure without interference from a rider or handler, usually done by tying or attaching reins to the saddle, a surcingle or the horse's tail.

BLUED STEEL: Steel which has been chemically treated to give it a shiny blue-black color.

BOSAL: The noseband band of a hackamore, traditionally made of braided rawhide, leather, horsehair or rope.

BOSAL HACKAMORE: A traditional bitless bridling system with a bosal (noseband), headstall (jaquima) and mecate (rope) reins. Used instead of a bit to guide the horse.

BOSALITO: A very narrow bosal, generally with cheeks 5/16 inch in diameter.

BREAST COLLAR: Strap which passes around the front of the horse's chest and attaches to each side of the saddle to keep the saddle from sliding backwards during riding.

BRIDLE: The entire apparatus used to guide the horse including the headstall, bit and reins.

BRIDLED: Refers to a horse, generally being ridden in a curb or spade bit, that exhibits a degree of poll flexion such that the front of his face is at or just slightly in front of the vertical. Also, a horse which has been taught to maintain this degree of poll flexion without constant rein pressure.

BRIDLE HORSE: A horse which has been trained to respond to a leverage bit. Sometimes refers to a spade bit or vaquero style horse, usually five years old or older.

BRIDLE LEATHER: A light weight leather with an extremely fine, lustrous finish often used for bridles and other show tack.

BRIDLE TEETH: The canine teeth. Very sharp, tusk-like teeth found generally only in males, but occasionally in females, which erupt in the interdental space between the incisor teeth and the cheek teeth. When canine teeth are present, the effective mouth bar space which a rider can take advantage for bitting purposes, is reduced.

BROKEN MOUTHPIECE: A mouthpiece which is jointed in one or more places.

BROWBAND: The part of the bridle that rests across the horse's forehead in front of the ears.

BUCKAROO: Cowboys of the West and Northwest who adopted and modified many of the traditional vaquero methods of horsemanship. Sometimes refers to bronc busters.

BUSY MOUTH: Refers to a horse who is constantly playing with the bit in its mouth.

BUTT OF THE MOUTHPIECE: The junction of the bit bars and the cheeks.

CALIFORNIOS: The cowboys of Mexico and old California who perfected the use of the hackamore and spade bit. More often called vaqueros.

CANINE TEETH: Very sharp teeth found generally only in males, but occasionally in females, which erupt in the interdental space between the incisor teeth and the cheek teeth. When canine teeth are present, the bar space available for bitting purposes is reduced. Also called bridle teeth.

CANNONS: The two separate bars of a bit with a broken mouthpiece.

CAP (DENTAL CAP): A retained deciduous (baby) tooth which is in the way of an erupting permanent tooth.

CATCH ROPE: In roping events, the lariat or rope with a loop at its end which is used to lasso the calf or steer.

CATHEDRAL BIT: A bit with an extremely high port, which may have a spoon, designed to contact the palate. The cathedral mouthpiece, in contrast with the spade and half-breed, has an open port which provides some tongue relief.

CAVESSON: Noseband.

CERVICAL VERTEBRAE: The bones of the spinal column in the neck. In the horse, as in other mammals from the human to the giraffe, there are 7 cervical vertebrae.

CHAMBON: A unique bitting system in which the reins run from the rider's hands, through the bit rings to an attachment at the top center of the bridle's crownpiece. The chambon is used to induce the horse to extend his head and neck downward and forward.

CHEEKER: A bridling accessory, usually of rubber, which fits over each side of the bit rings with straps which meet in the center of the horse's face and connect to a central strap that extends to the crownpiece of the bridle. It functions to lift the bit in the horse's mouth so the horse cannot evade the bit's action.

CHEEKS: Refers to the part of the bit or bridle that contacts the horse's cheeks. In a direct pulling bit, (ie. snaffle,) it may refer to the rings or ends of the bit which connect to the mouthpiece, or may refer just to the prongs which originate from the rings and extend above and/or below the mouthpiece. The term "cheeks" is also used to refer to the shanks of a leverage bit, and is sometimes reserved specifically for the upper shanks where the headstall attaches. Also refers to the lower branches of the bosal which contact the sides of the horse's face and jaw.

CHEEK TEETH: The back teeth which are used for grinding. In the adult horse there are 12 premolars and 12 molars (6 upper and 6 lower of each). In many horses (especially males) there is an additional small, nonfunctional tooth, the first premolar, or wolf tooth, immediately in front of the first upper grinding tooth.

CHIN GROOVE: The depression on the underside of the jaw just behind the incisor teeth. The narrow indentation just behind the fleshy chin. It is the area in which the curb strap should fit.

CHIN STRAP: A strap which attaches to the bit and fits under the horse's jaw which stops the rotation of the bit. Also called a curb strap.

CINCH: The strap or girth which passes under the belly to hold the saddle on the horse's back.

COLD ROLLED STEEL: a commercial grade of steel (an alloy of iron and carbon) which is often used in bit manufacturing. Its chemical composition makes the metal more porous than stainless steel. It tends to rust, which many horsemen believe makes the mouthpiece more palatable to horses.

COLLECTION: The state of the horse in which it has shifted its weight and center of gravity back toward its hindquarters, is yielding lightly to the bridle, rounding its spine and driving itself forward with impulsion from the hind legs.

COMBINATION BIT: A bit that combines the features of 2 or more different types of bit. For example gag and mechanical hackamore combinations are common.

CORRECTION BIT: A severe type of loose-shanked curb with a hinged-port mouthpiece which usually ties into the bit bars at right angles. The number of moving parts allows the bit to collapse and localize pressure on the sides of the tongue and mouthbars. Some correction bits have additional joints within the port itself.

COWBOY SNAFFLE: A curb bit with a broken mouthpiece.

CRICKET: A roller, often made of copper, incorporated into the port or mouthpiece of a bit. Called a cricket because of the chirping noise it may make when the horse plays with it with its tongue.

CROWN PIECE: The portion of the bridle that passes over the horse's head just behind the ears.

CURB BIT: A leverage bit consisting of the mouthpiece and upper and lower shanks, and usually used with a curb (chin) strap.

CURB CAVESSON: A noseband with chains under the jaw connecting it to a curb bit's curb strap hooks. Functions to transfer rein pressure onto the nose.

CURB CHAIN (or STRAP): A chain or strap which attaches to the bit and fits below the horse's jaw in the chin groove which halts the rotation of the mouthpiece when the reins are pulled. Aids in the application of leverage.

CURB (OR CHIN) GROOVE: The narrow indentation on the underside of the jaw just behind the fleshy chin. It is the area in which the curb strap or chain should fit.

CUTTING BIT: A bit used on a cutting horse, usually refers to a grazing bit with lightweight (usually aluminum) shanks which have been swept back away from the chin.

CYLINDER BUTT: A bit in which a metal tube connects the mouthpiece to the rings or shanks. D-ring, egg butt and Don Dodge snaffles are all examples of cylinder butt bits.

D-RING BIT: A snaffle bit in which the rings are shaped like a capital letter D.

DANGLERS: Loose pieces of smooth metal which hang in the middle of a mouthpiece for the horse to work with his tongue. Sometimes called tongue toys.

DECIDUOUS TOOTH: A baby tooth. A tooth which will be shed and replaced by a permanent tooth.

DEEP MOUTHED: Refers to a horse with a relatively long distance from the front of its muzzle to the corners of its lips. The distance generally correlates to the length of the bar space and may affect choice of bits as it relates to fit.

de GOGUE: A bitting system in which the reins run from the rider's hands through the bit rings up to a poll strap with pulleys and then extend down between the front legs to the girth. The action is similar to that of a gag snaffle.

DIRECT PULLING BIT: A non-leverage bit, whereby the pull of the rider's hands is translated pound for pound through the reins in a straight line to the horse's mouth. A snaffle bit.

DIRECT REIN: Pressure exerted on one rein to turn the horse's head in that direction. The left rein is pulled to turn the horse's head to the left, the right rein is pulled to turn the horse's head to the right. When using a direct rein, the rein should be pulled backward toward the rider's hip.

DIVING INTO A STOP: The horse attempts to stop on his front legs rather than using its his hind legs.

DR. BRISTOL BIT: A snaffle bit with a long flat link between the cannons of the mouthpiece. Sometimes incorrectly used to refer to any mouthpiece with a link between the cannons.

DON DODGE SNAFFLE: A cylinder butt snaffle bit in which the rings are offset to the outside of the cylinders thus increasing the intensity of the rein cues by focusing pressure on a more sensitive area of the face.

DONUT BIT: A curb bit in which the mouthpiece, rather than having an open port, has a solid ring of metal which extends both above and below the level of the tongue. The donut bit is very severe because it puts excessive pressure on the tongue when the reins are pulled.

DOUBLE REINED: Any bitting system which incorporates two sets of reins. In many cases there are two separate bits such as a snaffle and a curb, a snaffle and a bosal or a curb and a bosal. In the case of the pelham bit there are two sets of rein rings attached to a single mouthpiece.

DOUBLING: A method of taking away a horse's forward momentum by sharply pulling its head around to one side.

DRAW BIT: A bit designed to rise in the horse's mouth when the reins are pulled, exerting pressure on the corners of the lips and also applying pressure to the poll. A gag bit.

DRAW REINS: Reins which are set up to act on a pulley system rather than as a fixed link between hand and bit. Draw reins are often attached to the cinch rings at either side of the saddle, or to the girth between the front legs, run freely through the rein rings (sometimes pulleys are attached to the rein rings), and then to the rider's hands. Sometimes called running reins.

DROPPED NOSEBAND: A noseband designed to fit below the bit which functions to keep the bit up in the mouth and encourages the horse to keep its mouth closed.

DRY-MOUTHED BIT: A bit which does not enhance the production of saliva in the horse's mouth.

DUNCAN CHEEKS: Cheeks on a gag bit which have holes through which the reins pass but no rings. It is not possible to attach a second (non gag) rein to this type of gag bit.

EAR BRIDLE: A bridle which is held in place by a piece(s) that encircles the horse's ear(s). Ear bridles come in single, double and split ear types.

EAR PIECE: A piece that helps to hold the bridle in place by encircling one or both of the horse's ears.

EASY STOP: A type of bitless bridle in which a fork-shaped piece of metal exerts pressure beneath the jaw while compressing the noseband onto the face when the reins are pulled. Can be severe.

EGG BUTT: A type of fixed ring snaffle bit in which the butt of the mouthpiece where it joins the rings is barrel or egg-shaped. This design eliminates the chances of the lips being pinched by the rings.

ELEVATOR BIT: A leverage bit with upper and lower shanks of equal or approximately equal length primarily used to control vertical positioning of the horse's head while keeping the horse's head in a raised position.

EWE NECK: A neck which is concave along the top line almost as though the neck has been attached upside down..

FACIAL CRESTS: The projecting cheekbones below and forward of the horse's eyes.

FAST TWIST: Refers to a mouthpiece in which the metal bar stock has been twisted numerous times, creating a rough or bumpy surface. The severity of the mouthpiece will be effected by the number of twists and whether the bar stock was round, square or triangular to begin with.

FIADOR: A throatlatch and bosal attachment of lightweight rope or cord which helps to balance the hackamore, supports the weight of the heel knot and prevents it from resting on the horse's chin, and keeps the hackamore from being bucked, rubbed or pulled off.

FIGURE 8 NOSEBAND: A noseband with a top strap that fastens above the bit and a lower strap that fastens below the bit and lies in the chin groove. Also called a Gackle noseband.

FINISHED HORSE: A horse which is trained to a high level of western performance, usually indicating a willing response to the neckrein, and one which is generally being ridden in a leverage bit.

FINISHING BIT: A bit which is used to perfect a horse's responses to neck reining, yielding of face and poll. A leverage bit.

FIXED RING: The rings of a snaffle bit are attached to the mouthpiece in such a way that they cannot rotate.

FIXED SHANKS: Shanks which are solidly attached to the mouthpiece so they do not have any play, give or rotation independent of the mouthpiece. Solid shanks, not hinged.

FLASH NOSEBAND: A separate strap attaching to the cavesson above the nose with the lower end passing below the bit and lying in the chin groove.

FLOAT: An instrument for filing the points off of the horse's teeth. Also the act of filing off the points of the teeth.

FORWARD BALANCE: A bit in which the lower shanks tend to fall forward in the absence of rein pressure thereby releasing pressure on the chin groove. An extremely forward balanced bit may encourage a horse to carry his nose forward of the vertical.

FRENCH SNAFFLE: A type of snaffle bit in which a short, flat link joins the cannons of the mouthpiece. The link rotates so that it always lies flat over the tongue.

FRENULUM: A thin vertical piece of tissue which attaches the bottom of the tongue to the floor of the mouth.

FROG-MOUTHED BIT: A bit with an oval-shaped port in which the opening of the port is narrower than the width of the port itself, sometimes with rather sharp corners at the junction where the bars come into the port.

FULL-CHEEKED BIT: A snaffle bit with prongs that extend both above and below the mouthpiece at the point where the rings attach.

FULL-MOUTHED: A horse which has all of his adult teeth, generally a 5-year-old. The usual number of teeth in the full-mouthed horse is 36 to 42.

FULMER SNAFFLE: A full-cheeked bit in which the cheeks are set inside the attachment of the rings thus reducing the chances of pinching the corners of the lips.

GACKLE NOSEBAND: A noseband with a top strap that fastens above the bit and a lower strap that fastens below the bit and lies in the chin groove. Sometimes called a figure 8 noseband.

GAG BIT: A bit with a sliding mouthpiece designed to rise up in the horse's mouth when pressure is applied, and then automatically releases when the horse yields to the pressure. In the most common type of gag bit, the bit floats up and down on a cord which runs through the cheeks and becomes part of the headstall and reins, acting as one continuous unit. When rein tension is applied, the headstall shortens, the bit rises and pressure is exerted simultaneously on the poll and the corners of the horse's lips.

GAG HACKAMORE: A head controlling device that combines a gag action leverage bit with a noseband and chin strap. Pressure is simultaneously distributed over the tongue, bars, lips, nose, poll and chin when tension is applied to the reins. Sometimes called a hackamore bit or barrel racing bit.

GERMAN MARTINGALE: A rein system which is set up similarly to draw reins and operates on similar principles. A direct rein attaches to the bit ring just as it would on a regular snaffle. A draw rein then ties into the direct rein, running through the bit rings and back to the girth. The draw rein only comes into play when the horse extends its nose up and beyond the influence of the direct rein. Sometimes called a Market Harborough.

GRAZING BIT: A forward balanced leverage bit in which the lower shanks are swept well back behind the vertical. So-called because the shank design allows a horse to put its head down to graze without the lower shanks hitting the ground.

GROUND DRIVING: Guiding and teaching the horse to stop, turn and back up using long lines which the handler operates from the ground rather than from in a saddle or a buggy.

HACKAMORE: A bitless bridle that developed from Spanish (la jaquima) traditions. The traditional hackamore includes a bosal (noseband), mecate (rope reins and leadrope combination), and fiador (throatlatch), or in the absence of a fiador, sometimes a jowl strap. The mechanical hackamore is a bitless leverage device that relies on a noseband attached to shanks and with a curb strap.

HACKAMORE BIT: A head controlling device that combines a gag action type leverage bit with a noseband and chin strap. Pressure is distributed to the tongue, bars, lips, nose, poll and chin when tension is applied to the reins. Sometimes called a hackamore bit or barrel racing bit.

HALF-BREED: A leverage bit which combines attributes of vaquero style spades and American style curbs. The simple half-breed is a straight bar bit with an upright centerpiece that contains a cricket. It looks like the basis of the spade without the braces or spoon. Other half-breeds are characterized by their closed, hooded ports and crickets, including the Salinas, Mona Lisa and San Joaquin bits.

HALF-CHEEKED BIT: A snaffle bit with prongs that extend either above or, more commonly, below the rings.

HALTER: Headgear which does not include any bit, noseband, etc. for guiding a horse. Halters are generally used for leading and tying rather than for riding.

HARD MOUTH: Refers to a horse's mouth which is insensitive and unresponsive to the bit.

HARNESS LEATHER: A heavy leather that's been tanned in such a way as to make it especially strong and resilient. Ideal for tack that gets a lot of use.

HEADGEAR: Apparatus used on the horse's head.

HEAD SET: The position in which the horse carries its head when it is ridden, driven or turned loose. Basically refers to the degree of poll flexion and the elevation of the head and neck. Can be natural or man-made.

HEADSTALL: The bridle exclusive of the bit.

HEADSTALL RING: The ring on the bit to which the headstall is attached. On a leverage bit, it is at the end of the upper shank.

HEEL BUTTON: The braided knob at the bottom of a bosal where the cheek branches terminate. Also called the heel knot.

HEEL KNOT: A braided knot at the lower end of a bosal which functions to balance the bosal on the nose and helps the underside drop away from the jawline.

HIGH PORT BIT: A bit with a port more than 2 inches high.

HOCK HOBBLES: A bitting rig in which the reins are attached to straps which encircle the hocks of the horse.

HOOD: A solid cover over the port of a mouthpiece.

HOOKS: Projections coming down on the front of the first upper cheek teeth and up on the back of the last lower cheek teeth. Hooks form because the horse's upper jaw generally is set slightly forward of the lower jaw so that the there are no opposing tooth to wear them off.

ILLEGAL BIT: A bit which is prohibited by the rules of a particular show or association.

INDIRECT REIN: Rein pressure which is opposite the direction of intended travel. It is used to control the degree of bend and also is the start of neckreining. Sometimes called a supporting, stabilizing or bearing rein.

INTERDENTAL SPACES: The gum space between the incisors (front) and cheek teeth where there are no teeth. Also called the mouth bars. The interdental space may sometimes contain a canine (bridle) tooth.

INCISOR TEETH: The front teeth, 6 upper and 6 lower, which are used for biting.

INSIDE REIN: The rein which coincides with the direction the horse is turning or traveling. If a horse is circling to the left, it is the left rein, and vice versa.

JERK LINE: A long accessory rope used by calf ropers to keep the horse applying tension to the catch rope as the roper dismounts and runs to the calf. The jerk line attaches to the bit shanks, passes through a pulley or ring on the saddle, and is looped and tucked under the rider's belt. When the roper runs to the calf, the loops pull loose from the belt one at a time and puts pressure on the bit. This encourages the horse to back away from the calf thereby keeping tension on the rope. Also called a backup rope.

KEEPER: A small loop of leather or rope which serves to keep the bit or other portion of the tack in place. Keepers are used between the noseband of the bridle and the upper cheeks of full cheeked snaffle bits to keep the prongs from rotating into the horse's face. In calf roping the catch rope may be passed through a keeper which is attached to the noseband thus serving to keep the horse facing the calf.

KEYS: Dangling pieces of smooth metal attached to the middle of a mouthpiece for the horse to work with its tongue.

KIMBERWICK: A pelham bit with a very short upper shank and a D- shaped snaffle ring in which the bulk of the D is below the mouthpiece. The kimberwick generally features a solid, low port mouthpiece, but it may also have a mullen (gently curved) or broken mouthpiece. It is generally used with only a single set of reins, though some Kimberwicks have slots in the D's that allow for the use of more than one rein. With a single rein, when the reins are held normally, it functions as a snaffle, but when the hands are lowered, or a running martingale is used, the action is that of a curb. (Also spelled Kimblewick or Kimberwicke.)

LAMINITIS: Inflammation of the laminae which attach the hoof to the foot. Also called founder.

LAS CRUCES MOUTHPIECE: A mouthpiece resembling a cathedral with its flat, A-shaped port, but is much lower.

LATIGO: Leather that has been tanned to be extremely soft, smooth, supple, and strong, usually with a characteristic burgundy color. Latigo is often used as the tie strap for the saddle cinch because of its strength, but is also used in the manufacture of other tack.

LEG CUES: Cues the rider gives to the horse with his legs to elicit a response. Used alone or in addition to other signals, such as pressure on the bit.

LEVERAGE BIT: A bit that utilizes the principles of leverage to increase the pressure a rider applies to the reins. Provides a useful mechanical advantage. A shanked bit. The shanks of the bit act as the arms of the lever while the mouthpiece acts as the fulcrum. Leverage bits are generally used with a chin (curb) strap.

LEVERAGE RATIO: The proportion of upper to lower shank length as determined by the position of the mouthpiece used to quantify a bit's relative mechanical advantage. A bit with 6 inches of shank below the mouthpiece and 2 inches above the mouthpiece is said to have a leverage ratio of 3:1. That means that each pound of pressure applied to the reins will be multiplied by three.

LIFESAVER: A type of leverage bit which has a broken mouthpiece with an extra link in the center in the shape of a ring or Lifesaver.

LIP GUARDS: Circular pieces of rubber or leather which fit at the ends of the mouthpiece to prevent the lips from being chafed by the rings or shanks.

LOLLERING BIT: A bit with a wide flat metal piece in the center of the mouthpiece which prevents the horse from getting its tongue over the bit.

LONGEING: Exercising the horse in a circle with a long line.

LONGE LINE: The long line used in longeing the horse.

LONG-SHANKED BIT: Bits with cheeks that are 8 inches or longer.

LOOMIS BIT: A pelham bit popularized by reining horse trainer Bob Loomis with 7 1/2 inch shanks and a broken mouthpiece.

LOOSE-JAWED: A leverage bit in which the shanks are not solidly joined to the mouthpiece. Hinges or swivels allow the shanks to move independent of the mouthpiece providing more signal and greater flexibility to act on one side of the horse's face at a time.

LOOSE-RINGED: The rings of a snaffle bit which rotate freely in ends of the mouthpiece.

LOOSE SHANKS: A leverage bit in which the shanks are attached to the mouthpiece via hinges or swivels.

LOW PORT BIT: A bit with a mouthpiece with a port from 3/8 to 1/2 inch high.

LUGS ON THE BIT: Refers to the horse which leans into or pulls on the bit.

MARTINGALE (IRISH): A short leather strap with rings on either end through which the reins run. Is used below the horse's neck as a safety device to keep the reins from flipping over the neck.

MARTINGALE (RUNNING): An accessory which applies pressure to the bit via the reins when the horse raises its head out of position. There are several designs, but basically a strap connects to the girth or breast collar, and divides into two branches with rings at the end through which the reins are passed.

MARTINGALE (STANDING): An accessory strap which connects to a noseband and then to the girth or breast collar which is used to keep the horse from raising its head beyond a certain point.

MECATE: An 18 to 22-foot-long horse hair rope which is tied around the base of a bosal just above the heel knot to form a continuous rein and lead rope.

MECATE KNOT: The wraps used to secure the mecate to the bosal to form perfectly balanced reins, leadrope and counterweight.

MECHANICAL HACKAMORE: A bitless bridle with a noseband, metal shanks and curb chain which utilizes leverage to multiply the pressure applied to the nose, chin and poll.

MEDIUM PORT BITS: Bits with ported mouthpieces from 1/2 inch to 2 inches high.

MODERATE LEVERAGE: The amount of leverage provided by a bit with lower shanks 3 times as long as the upper shanks.

MONA LISA MOUTHPIECE: Mouthpiece developed by horseman Don Dodge and named after his great show mare Mona Lisa, whom Dodge first used it on. The bit has a hooded port similar to a Salinas mouthpiece, but the roller is tucked up high into the port so as not to be visible from the front of the bit. In the Salinas mouthpiece the roller is placed in the bottom of the hooded port near the level of the bit bars.

MONKEY MOUTH: An improper bite alignment in which the lower front teeth (incisors) extend beyond the uppers.

MONTE FOREMAN BIT: One of several bits popularized by the late trainer, coach and clinician Monte Foreman, but usually refers to a western type pelham with large D-shaped snaffle rings and curved back shanks.

MOUTHING BIT: A bit that is constructed to encourage the horse to continually move it with his tongue. Sometimes refers to a thick soft, rubber bit that is used to introduce a horse to a bit because it is so mild in texture.

MOUTHPIECE: The part of the bit which fits inside the horse's mouth.

MULE BIT: A name sometimes given to a bit with a bicycle chain or saw-toothed mouthpiece.

MULLEN MOUTH: A gently curved, portless, solid mouthpiece.

MYLER SHANK: A cylindrical shank attachment with internal bushings that allow the upper and lower shanks to rotate independently of one another.

NASAL BONE: A bone which extends down the middle of the horse's face and terminates in a point a few inches above the nostrils.

NAVICULAR DISEASE: Inflammation of the navicular bone which is located just above and behind the hoof.

NEAR SIDE: The left side of the horse. Since many common handling techniques, such as haltering, bridling and mounting, were traditionally done from the left side, it became known as the "near" side.

NECK REIN: The signal the rider gives his horse to turn by laying a rein against its neck. The horse is taught to move away from the rein contact. A right rein signals the horse to go left, and vice versa. Neck reining allows a rider to ride with the reins in one hand.

NECK STRAP: A strap passing around the lower part of the neck of the horse and through which the straps of a martingale are passed. The yoke keeps the martingale from flopping around and becoming a potential hazard. Sometimes called a neck yoke.

NIPPERS: The front or incisor teeth.

NOSEBAND: Any strap, rope, cable or other material which encircles the nose. It may be a portion of the headstall or a separate piece. A noseband may serve as a point of attachment for an accessory, such as a martingale, or may be used to encourage a horse to keep its mouth closed around the bit.

NOSE BUTTON: The part of a braided rawhide or leather bosal which sits across the bridge of the nose and tends to be larger than the cheekpieces.

O-RING BIT: A snaffle bit in which the rings are round and generally free-moving through the mouthpiece.

OFF SIDE: The right side of the horse. Since many common handling techniques, such as haltering, bridling and mounting, were traditionally done from the left side, the opposite side became known as the "off" side.

ON THE BIT: A horse is in contact and communication with his rider through the bit and the reins. He is ready to respond to cues, generally noted by moving forward into the bridle with adequate poll flexion. Yielding to the bit without overflexion.

OPPOSING REIN: Indirect rein. Rein pressure used to balance a direct rein cue. Also called rein of indirect opposition.

OUTSIDE REIN: The rein on the side opposite from the direction in which the horse is turning.

OVERBITTING: Using a bit which is more severe than is required to guide the horse. A bit which frightens or intimidates a horse.

OVERBRIDLED: Refers to the horse which is behind the bit.

PALATE: The roof of the mouth.

PALATE BITS: Bits which are intentionally designed to contact the roof of the mouth when pressure is applied to the reins. Such bits include many half-breeds, cathedral and spade bits.

PALATE PRESSURE: Refers to the contact a bit makes when it engages the roof of the mouth.

PARROT MOUTH: An improper bite alignment in which the upper front teeth (incisors) extend beyond the lower incisors.

PELHAM BIT: Any shanked bit which has a second set of rein rings situated at the level of the mouthpiece so that the bit may be used with two sets of reins, a curb rein and a snaffle rein.

PENCIL BOSAL: A very narrow bosal, generally with cheeks 5/16 inch in diameter.

PERFORMANCE HORSE: A horse which is required to demonstrate skill at some specific tasks such as reining, cutting or roping. The performance horse is ridden with a less vertical headset than the pleasure horse.

PICK UP THE REINS: To apply sufficient pressure to the reins that the horse knows it is being asked to respond.

PLAITS: Strands of leather used in braidwork as of a bosal.

PLEASURE CLASS: A show division in which the entries are evaluated for the quality of their movement such as at the walk, jog, and lope, (as in western) or walk, trot and canter (as in English), with the judges rewarding the horses which appear to be the most enjoyable to ride (or drive). Entries may be required to back up and/or perform extensions of their gaits.

PLEASURE HORSE: A show horse that is used to compete in classes that emphasize the quality of motion, training and tractability. The term "pleasure horse" is also used for horses that people keep for recreational rather than competitive purposes.

POINTS ON TEETH: Sharp edges which usually develop on the outside of the upper cheek teeth and the inside of the lower cheek teeth.

POLL: The highest point of the horse's head between the ears.

POLL FLEXION: The pivoting action between the first two bones of the horse's neck at the junction known as the atlantoaxial joint. A horse does not really flex "at the poll", but rather at this joint behind the poll. What we observe as "poll flexion" is a yielding of the face toward the horse's body, which helps to contain forward motion and shifts weight toward the hindquarters.

POLO DRAW REINS: Running reins which attach to a ring at the center of the horse's breast collar, pass through the bit rings and then to the rider's hands and act in a pulley-like fashion to encourage the horse to bring its head down and in toward the body.

POLO MOUTHPIECE: A flat metal mouthpiece an inch or more in width which rotates in the shanks so as to always lie flat across the tongue. A bit with such a mouthpiece which is commonly used on roping horses is sometimes called a Rutledge Roper.

POPPER: A flat leather extension at the end of a romal. A quirt. Used to encourage speed or obedience.

PORT: An upward bend in the center of a mouthpiece. The usual purpose is to provide tongue relief.

PULLEY MARTINGALE: A running martingale which is set up to slide left and right beneath the horse's neck, thus lengthening and shortening from side to side, thereby allowing the horse greater lateral movement with its head and neck than a conventional running martingale allows.

PULLEY SYSTEM: A set up that uses a pulley (a wheel or sheave) that changes the direction or point of application of a pulling force such as with a rope or cord, and which increases the force applied to it.

RATIO: Refers to the comparative proportions of something, such as "bit ratio" which compares the length of the lower and upper shank. In a curb bit in which the lower shanks are 3 times as long as the upper shanks, the bit is said to have a 3:1 ratio. In general, the lower the ratio, the less leverage the bit exerts and the milder the bit.

RAWHIDE: Untanned cattle skin.

REINING: Exerting pressure on the reins to obtain a desired response from the horse. Also the word for a highly specialized sport or discipline in which horses are asked to perform high level western maneuvers and patterns that include lead changes, sliding stops, roll backs, spins and speed control utilizing neck reining and subtle body control.

REINS: The pieces of leather, cotton, nylon, horse hair or many other strong, flexible fabrics which pass from the bridle to the rider's hands and are used to guide the horse.

REIN RINGS: The rings on the bit to which the reins attach. The rings on an accessory such as a running martingale through which the reins pass.

REIN STOPS: Leather or rubber rings which fit tightly onto the reins to form a barrier that keeps the rein rings on a running martingale or other accessory from migrating forward where they could become caught on the bit rings.

REVERSE BALANCE: A bit which is weighted in such a way that the upper shanks tend to fall forward toward the nose and the lower shanks tend to shift backwards toward the body. In acutely reverse balanced bits, the curb strap may not readily release pressure on the chin groove even in the absence of rein contact. Such bits tend to encourage more vertical head carriage or even a behind- the-vertical headset.

RIDING AGED HORSE: Generally a horse two years old or older.

ROLLED (BACK) MOUTHPIECE: A bit in which the port or spoon in the mouthpiece has been curved or laid backwards from the vertical. If the port or spoon is high enough to contact the palate, rolling it prevents it from doing so at its apex, making the contact smoother and less damaging.

ROLLER MOUTHPIECE: A mouthpiece with a small wheel incorporated into the port or centerpiece generally made of steel or copper. Rollers, especially those that make a characteristic singing sound, are commonly called "crickets".

ROMAL: A round, braided leather rein extension where the left and right reins form into a single rein, and quirt which includes a flat leather popper.

ROMAL REINS: Round, braided rawhide or leather reins which are joined together by a romal. Vaquero or West Coast style closed reins are held with the reins passing from pinky (or between the pinky and ring fingers) through the palm and fingers and exiting between the index finger and thumb, while the romal is held in the opposite hand.

ROOTING: Refers to a horse which extends its nose forward or pulls against the bit to evade contact or compliance.

ROPING BIT: Although there are many different types of bits used on roping horses, this term usually refers to a bit in which the lower shanks have been fused together into a single rein ring centered beneath the horse's chin.

ROPING REIN: A rein which is a single continuous strap attaching to each side of the bit.

RUNNING REINS: Reins which slide through the rings of a bit without actually attaching to the bit. Also called draw reins.

RUNNING THROUGH THE BRIDLE/BIT: When a horse ignores the pressure of the reins on the bridle. Failing to respond to rein signal.

RUTLEDGE ROPER: A bit having a flat metal mouthpiece an inch or more in width which rotates in the shanks so as to always lie flat on the tongue. Also called a polo mouthpiece.

SAFETY BOSAL: A bosal woven of smooth, soft latigo leather over a pliable rawhide core which has been specially constructed to help prevent the soring or chafing of nose or jaw.

SALINAS MOUTHPIECE: A mouthpiece with a smooth, copper-covered hooded port of medium height containing a cricket which connects into the bit bars at the base of the port.

SAN JOAQUIN MOUTHPIECE: Similar to the Salinas and Mona Lisa mouthpieces but having a higher, narrower, copper-covered, hooded port.

SAW-TEETH MOUTHPIECE: A severe mouthpiece consisting of several links which resemble saw blades with serrated edges. Sometimes called a mule bit, or bicycle chain.

SCAMPERDALE PELHAM: A pelham bit which has the mouthpiece turned back to prevent chafing the lips.

SCHOOLING BITS: Bits used during the training of a horse though not necessarily for showing.

SCOTCHING: The rough, jilted action of a horse in a sliding stop, either because it is getting hung up in bad ground or is making a half-hearted attempt to stop correctly during a slide.

SEASONED: A bit which has been allowed to rust.

SEGUNDA BIT: A full-cheeked, frog-mouthed, direct pulling (snaffle) bit.

SHADOW ROLL: A sheepskin-covered cavesson which prevents the horse from seeing the ground in front of him and help prevent shying at shadows or other potentially frightening sights.

SHALLOW-MOUTHED: Refers to a horse with a relatively short distance from the front of the muzzle to the corners of the lips. A horse with a small or shallow mouth may require special bitting considerations in order to wear a bit comfortably.

SHANKS: The portion of the curb (leverage) bit which extend above and below the mouthpiece. Sometimes refers only to the portions of the bit cheeks below the mouthpiece.

SHANKED GAG: A leverage bit designed to allow the mouthpiece to slide up and down in the cheeks thus giving it gag type action. Leverage comes into play once the movement of the mouthpiece is stopped within the shanks.

SHANKED SNAFFLE: Euphemism for a curb bit with a broken mouthpiece.

SHOEMAKER BIT: A type of bit with S-shaped shanks, designed to prevent the horse from grasping the shanks in its lips.

SHORT-BARRED: Refers to a mouth with a relatively small distance between the incisors and the cheek teeth.

SHORT-SHANKED BIT: A leverage bit in which the entire length of the cheekpieces is less than 6 inches.

SIDE BUTTONS: The short, thick braided pieces on the cheeks of a bosal which hold the headstall in place.

SIDELINING BIT: A bit with an extension on one side for the attachment of the rein. The extra length of one side gives increased leverage to control the horse that bears to one side.

SIDEPULL: A bitless bridle in which the rein rings are positioned on either side of the horse's face, generally in line with the corners of the horse's mouth, allowing the rider to utilize direct rein pressure on the nose and cheeks to guide the horse in the appropriate direction without undue pressure to the jaw, and no impact on the mouth.

SIDE REINS: Reins which are attached to the saddle or bitting harness (surcingle) on either side of the girth to keep the horse's head in the proper position when it is being longed or driven.

SIGNAL: The amount of play in the bit that provides the horse with the clues or warning that the bit is about to engage. The split second lag between when the rider picks up on the reins and the bit exerts pressure on the horse's mouth.

SLACK REIN: Loose reins. No apparent contact between the bit and the hands.

SLIP BITS: Sometimes refers to gag bits. Also refers to bits with hinged cheeks that allow some front to back as well as up and down play.

SLIP-CHEEKED: The shanks rotate front to back as well as slide up and down a few millimeters in the mouthpiece.

SLOBBER BAR: A solid piece of metal connecting the lower ends of the shanks of a bit. Sometimes called a stabilizer bar.

SLOBBER CHAINS: Chains which attach reins to the bit shanks. Their original purpose was to keep the leather reins from being damaged by repeated exposure to water when a bridled horse drinks.

SLOP: Refers to the amount of play in the joints of a bit.

SLOW TWIST: Refers to a mouthpiece in which the stock has been twisted just a few rotations creating a ridged surface that can greatly increase the severity of the bit depending on weather the bar stock was round, square or triangular to begin with.

SMOOTH MOUTH: A mouthpiece which is smoothly rounded. A horse 8 years or more of age.

SNAFFLE BIT: A non-leverage bit, in which the reins attach to the bit in such a way as to form a straight line from the horse's mouth to the rider's hands so as not to significantly alter the pressure applied to the horse's mouth. A direct pulling bit. Usually the cheeks are rings of some type to which both the reins and headstall attach. In some western circles, the term "snaffle" is applied to any bit with a simple, broken mouthpiece.

SNAFFLE MOUTH: When "bit seats" have been created to keep the horse's mouth comfortable, especially when wearing a snaffle bit, by rounding the fronts of the first upper and lower cheek teeth and by removing the wolf teeth. This is done so the snaffle does not pinch the lips or tongue against the teeth.

SOFT IN THE POLL: Used to describe a horse that is compliant to the pull of the reins, characterized by a relaxation of the jaw, flexing of the upper neck (at the atlantoaxial joint), and bringing of the nose in toward the body. A horse which shows no resistance to the bridle.

SOFT MOUTH: Refers to a horse's mouth which is sensitive and responsive to the bit.

SPACER BARS: Curved metal braces, often wrapped with copper wire, situated above the straight bar mouthpiece of a spade bit and which connect to the spoon. The spacer bars provide support and stability for the spoon and prevent the bit from shifting too far back in the horse's mouth where it might damage the soft palate.

SPADE BIT: A complex leverage bit with a straight (portless) bar, high centerpiece (usually containing a roller), and a spade or spoon above it. Braces or spacer bars are located above the straight bar and connect from the cheeks to the spoon.

SPIT OUT THE BIT: Refers to a horse which avoids contact with the bit by overflexing at the poll and tucking its nose behind the vertical.

SPIKED CAVESSON: A noseband with small cone-shaped studs placed in the lining which are harsh and abrasive to the horse's nose. Used in order to promote greater control over the head.

SPLIT EAR BRIDLE: A heastall in which the crownpiece has been split in order to accommodate the ear rather than having a separate ear piece. Also called slit or slot-eared bridles.

SPLIT REINS: Reins which are two separate straps, a left and a right.

SQUAW REINING: A combination of direct and indirect reining used when the horse is first being taught to neck rein.

STABILIZING REIN: The rein on the opposite side from the rein on which the pressure is exerted. Sometimes called a supporting or indirect rein.

STABILIZER BAR: A solid piece of metal connecting the lower ends of the shanks of a bit. Sometimes called a slobber bar.

STABILIZER CHAIN: A chain connecting the lower ends of the shanks of a bit. Also called shank hobbles.

STAINLESS STEEL: an alloy of steel with chromium and sometimes another element (as nickel or molybdenum) that is practically immune to rusting and ordinary corrosion.

STAR GAZER: A horse that carries its head with its nose pointed toward the sky.

STOCK: The metal rod from which the mouthpiece of a bit is fashioned. Also short for "livestock."

STOCK HORSE: A western horse, especially one used in cattle events, such as cutting and working cowhorse. The term "stock horse" originated from the type of horses used by cowboys on western ranches.

STONE BRUISE: Injury to the sole of the foot caused by stepping on a hard or sharp object such as a rock.

STRAIGHT-SHANKED: A leverage bit in which a straight line may be drawn through the upper and lower shanks. Shanks with very little sweep or curve.

SUPPORTING REIN: Rein pressure applied to the opposite side of the face from the direct rein in order to limit the amount of arc or bend the horse makes with its face and neck. Sometimes called a stabilizing or indirect rein.

SURCINGLE: A rig or girth strap which encircles the horse's barrel behind the withers. It is frequently used as a place to attach the reins when accustoming the young horse to the bit or through which to run long reins when ground driving a horse.

SWEET IRON or SWEET STEEL: Steel of a porous nature that is often used in bit making. Its chemical structure allows it to rust, as opposed to stainless steel.

SWEETWATER MOUTHPIECE: A mouthpiece with short bars with the central portion rising in a long, wide arc over the tongue.

SWEPT BACK SHANKS: A leverage bit in which the lower and upper shanks angle toward the rear.

SWIVEL PORT: A port which is jointed or hinged on either side where it joins the bars, so that the port rotates or swivels in the horse's mouth.

SYNTHETIC MOUTHPIECES: Generally refers to plastic, nylon and other nonmetal mouthpieces.

TACK: All of the equipment used on the horse including saddles, brides, halters and accessories.

THREE PIECE BIT: A bit which has a broken mouthpiece with an extra link in the shape of a flat plate, ring or quarter moon in the middle.

THROATLATCH: The area on the underside of the neck where the neck joins the head. Also a portion of the bridle which attaches to the crownpiece and encircles the throat from behind the ears.

TIE DOWN: Accessory, including a strap and noseband, that keeps the horse from raising its head and neck beyond a certain position. also called A standing martingale.

TOM BALDING: A bitmaker, specially known for patenting a smooth ball hinge that is used to join the mouthpiece to the cheeks or shanks of his bits to prevent pinching.

TOM THUMB SNAFFLE: A curb bit with a broken mouthpiece and short, straight shanks.

TONGUE RELIEF: The amount of space or consideration a bit provides for the tongue so that pressure on it is reduced or eliminated. The term is generally used in regard to the height and width, and angle of the port. Many tongue relief bits transfer pressure away from the tongue and onto the bars of the mouth.

TRAINING AIDS: Apparatus used to encourage or enhance a given response during the horse's education but which will be discarded once the desired response has been obtained.

TRANSITIONS: Progressing from one bit to another, such as from a snaffle to a curb. Also used in riding or driving when referring to changes in gait or pace.

TWISTED-WIRE MOUTHPIECE: A broken mouthpiece made of twisted wire or light gage bar stock. There are also double twisted-wire mouthpieces in which he joints of the 2 mouthpieces are off center, one to the left and one to the right.

U.S. MOUTHPIECE: A mouthpiece with an upside-down, U-shaped port, usually 2 inches high, which rises at right angles to the bars of the bit, and which may or may not be rolled back at its apex.

UXETER PELHAM: A kimberwick bit in which the D-ring cheeks are slotted at various levels for the reins. The slot to which the reins are attached determines whether the bit functions as a direct pulling bit (snaffle) or as a leverage bit.

VAQUERO: The Spanish-influenced horsemen and cowboys of Mexico and old California who perfected the use of the hackamore and spade bits. Sometimes called a Californio.

VAQUERO BITS: Generally refers to the spade bit and its relatives, such as the half-breed, Salinas, Mona Lisa, San Joaquin, and others.

VERTICAL FLEXION: The pivoting action between the first 2 cervical vertebrae, the atlantoaxial joint. The horse in vertical flexion has pulled its nose in toward its body which helps to transfer weight to the hindquarters.

WALKING HORSE BIT: A leverage bit with very long, swept-back, S-shaped lower shanks and a very high ratio of lower to upper shank lengths.

WET MOUTH: A mouth in which there is ample production of saliva for the proper function of the bit.

WHOA BIT: Sometimes used to describe a curb bit with high, A- shaped port.

WOLF TOOTH: The first upper premolar, a vestigial and nonfunctional tooth, found in many horses immediately in front of the first upper grinding tooth. It is generally recommended that these teeth be removed by a veterinarian, because they have no known function and may interfere with the action of the bit.

W-MOUTH: A bit with two broken mouthpieces with the joints of the mouthpieces being off center, one to the left and one to the right.

YOKE: A strap which encircles the base of the horse's neck used to keep a martingale in position, preventing it from becoming a potential hazard. Sometimes called a neck strap.

Abscess 167
Allergic rhinitis 167
Amaral, Tony 95, 112, 122, 123, 130
American Endurance Ride Conference 180
American Horse Shows Association 174, 175, 179, 180
American Quarter Horse Association 123, 172, 174, 180
Argentine snaffle 93, 153
Atlantoaxial joint 26–27
Balding, Tom 86
Bars of the mouth. *See* Interdental spaces
Billy Allen bit 73, 153
Bit bars 38
Bit burr 169
Bit guards 22, 44
Bit ratios 83–84
Bit seats 34
Bit selection 69–70
  and changes in teeth 25
  and interdental spaces 20–21
  and mouthpiece design 75–77
  and teeth 31
  tongue relief 75–77
  and tongues 22
Bits
  adjusting 22, 70–71
  Argentine snaffle 93, 153
  balance of 88–89, 92–93
  Billy Allen 73, 153
  bit bars 38
  calculating ratios of 83–84
  California style 95
  cannons 38
  cathedrals 24, 132
  cheeks 38
  contact with lips 22
  correction bit 77, 92
  curb bit 21, 39, 80–87
  double twisted wire 71–72, 74
  Dr. Bristol 58, 74
  elevator bit 84
  fitting 26, 68–69
  French snaffle 74
  gag bits 26, 98–105, 177
  gag snaffles 102
  gogues 26
  grazing bit 38, 40–41
  half-breed 20, 24, 131, 132, 133
  jointed 72–74
  Loomis shanked snaffle 153
  low-port 74
  materials used in 41–42
  medium port curb bit 14
  Mona Lisa 133
  mouthpieces 36–38, 71, 131–133
  moving parts of 93–94
  mullen mouthpiece 75
  Myler bit 94
  O-ring smooth snaffle 12
  parts of 36–38
  Paso Fino bit 174
  pelham 96, 146
  Peruvian bit 172
  Pessoa gag bit 100
  port height 24
  racing ring (Dexter) bit 169
  roping bit 86
  Rutledge Roper 77, 176
  Salinas 76, 133
  Santa Barbara 78, 133
  sawtooth 74
  segunda 74
  shanks 38, 85–86, 87
  signal 85, 86–87
  single twisted wire 71–72
  slip-cheeked 86
  Slip-mouth sidelining bit 169
  snaffle 21, 38–39, 53–54, 56–64
  spade bits 12, 14, 20, 24, 40, 76, 96, 126–132, 177
  straight bar 74
  sweetwater 75
  Tom Thumb 93, 153
  tongue relief 23
  U.S. mouthpiece 76, 92
  W-mouthed 74
  Walking Horse bit 83, 87
  weight of 40–41, 94–95
  western pelham 97
  Weymouth bit 85
Bitting
  changing bits 144–148, 152–153
  chewing on the bit 169
  and competition 172–181
  "getting ahead of the bit" 167
  "getting behind the bit" 167
  getting the tongue over the bit 169
  head tossing 167–168
  injuries from 170–171
  introducing the bit 48
  preventing problems 171
  proper bridling 51
  pulling to one side 169
  resistance to bit 164–167
  "running through the bit" 168–169
  "scissoring" 167
  signs of problems 166
  "star gazing" 168
Bitting up 51–52
Boisjoli, Mario 16, 17
Bosal
  materials used for 114–115
  parts of 115
  quality 115–116
  use in competition 179
Bosal hackamore 109
Bosals
  sizes of 116–117
Bridle teeth 33
Bridling
  adjusting 70–71
  proper technique 51
California style bit 95
Canine teeth 30, 33
Cannons 38
Caps 32
Carma Corona 16, 17
Cathedral bits 24, 132
Cavesson 42. *See also* Noseband
Chain-type mouthpiece 74
Chambon 143
Chavez Company 116
Chavez, Dale 116
Cheeked snaffle 62
Cheeker 138
Cheeks 38
Chin strap 44
Collection 55, 161–162
Correction bit 77, 92
Crickets 79, 131
Curb bit 21
  action of curb strap on 39, 84–85, 96
  balance of 88–89
  defined 39
  and leverage 82–83
  mechanics of 80–82
  medium port 14
  ratios of 83–84
  shanks 85–86, 87
  signal 85, 86–87
Curb chain. *See* Curb strap
Curb strap 96

adjusting 26, 77, 96
in competitions 172–174
effect on curb bit 39
function of 84–85
D-ring snaffle 60
Darnall, Greg 62, 97, 151
De Gogue 143
Direct rein 48, 49
Dodge, Don 62, 112, 122, 129, 130, 131
Don Dodge snaffle 60, 61–62
Double twisted wire mouthpiece 74
Dr. Bristol 58, 74
Draw reins 26, 142–143
Dropped noseband 136–137
Dunning, Al 112, 114, 119, 123, 124
Easy stop 110–111
Egg-butt snaffle 59
Elevator bit 84
Endurance Riders Handbook *180*
Fiador 117, 122
Figure 8 noseband 137
Flash noseband 137
Floating 33–34
Foreman, Monte 97
French snaffle 74
Frenulum 23
Full-cheek snaffle 63
Gackle noseband 137
Gag bits 26
in competition 177
Duncan cheeks 101
gag snaffles 102
mechanics of 98–101
Pessoa 100
shanked gags 103
types of 105
use with martingales 101
German martingale 143
Gogues 26
Grazing bit 38
weight of 40–41
Ground driving 53–54
Ground work 51
Hackamore
adjusting 125
bosal 114–115
fiador 122
horse's sensitivity to 125
mecate 118–119
proper use 122–125
Half-breed bits 20, 24, 131, 132, 133
Half-cheek snaffle 63
Hayes, Gordon 98
Headstalls
parts of 42–44
Hooks 34
Incisors 28, 30
Indirect rein 49
Interdental spaces
and bit selection 20–21
injury to 18–20
width between 21
Irish martingale 141
Jawline
sensitivity of 26
Jerk line 141–142
use in competition 179–180
Kick Dee Bar 42, 48
Laminitis 167
Las Cruces mouthpiece 132
Leverage
defined 82–83
Leverage bit. *See* Curb bit
Lip guards 22
Lips
injury to 22
sensitivity of 21–22
Loomis, Bob 97
Loomis shanked snaffle 153
Low-port mouthpiece 74
Martingales
german 143
Irish 141
proper use 143
pulley martingale 141
running martingale 139–141
standing martingale 138–139
use with gag bit 101
use with snaffle bit 65
Mecate
materials used for 118–119
selecting 118
tying 119, 120–121
Mechanical hackamore 109–110
Molars 28–30
Mona Lisa mouthpiece 131–132, 133
Monkey mouth 34
Moore, Dave 159
Mouthpieces
cathedral 151
chain 74, 177
and competitions 175–177
design of 71
double twisted wire 71–72, 74
fitting 68–69
jointed 72–74
Las Cruces 132
materials used for 78–79
Mona Lisa 131–132
mullen 75
polo mouthpiece 176
port design 75–77
Salinas 76, 131–132
San Joaquin 131–132
selecting 69–70
single twisted wire 71–72
solid 74
sweetwater 75
tongue relief 75–77
types of 36–38
U.S. mouthpiece 76, 92
Mullen mouthpiece 75
Myler Bits 86, 94
National Cutting Horse Association 177
National Reined Cow Horse Association 58, 130, 175
National Reining Horse Association 179
National Snaffle Bit Association 58, 172, 175, 179
Navicular disease 167
Neck
effect on poll flexion 27
Neck rein 51
Nippers 28
Nose
sensitivity of 25–26
Noseband 42
cheeker 138
dropped noseband 136–137
figure 8 noseband 137
fitting 26, 134–136
flash noseband 137
function 134
gackle noseband 137
materials used for 136
proper use 137–138
O-ring snaffle 61
Ortega, Louis 119
Palate
and bit selection 24–25
sensitivity of 23–24
Parrot mouth 34

Paso Fino bit 174
Pelham bit 96, 146
Peruvian bit 172
Pessoa gag bit 100
Plow reining 49
Poll
  flexion 26–27
Polo draw rein 143
Polo mouthpiece 176
Port height 24
Premolars 28–30
Professional Rodeo Cowboys Association 179
Pulley martingale 141
Racing ring (Dexter) bit 169
Reins
  materials used for 45
  romal 45
  roping 45
  selecting 27
  single 45
  split 45
  types of 45
Retained teeth 32
Romal reins 45
Roof of the mouth. *See* Palate
Roping bit 86
Roping reins 45
Running martingale
  adjusting 139–140
  proper use 140, 171
Running reins. *See* Draw reins
Rutledge Roper bit 77, 176
Saare, Sharon *181*
Salinas mouthpiece 76, 131–132, 133
San Joaquin mouthpiece 131–132
Santa Barbara bit 78, 133
Sawtooth mouthpiece 74
Schwartzenberger, Steve 16, 42, 148, 152
Segunda mouthpiece 74
Selecting a bit. *See* Bit selection
Shanks 38, 85–86, 87
  length in competition 174–175
Side reins 52
Sidepulls 108–109
Signal 85, 86–87
Single reins 45
Slip-cheeked bit 86
Slip-mouth sidelining bit 169
Snaffle Bit Futurity 58
Snaffle mouth 34
Snaffles
  cheeked 62
  contact with corners of mouth 21
  D-ring 60
  defined 38–39, 56
  Don Dodge 60, 61–62
  egg-butt 59, 60
  French 74
  full-cheek 63
  half-cheek 63
  mechanics of 58–59
  O-ring 61
  O-ring smooth 12
  proper use 59, 64–65
  rings of 59–61
  use with martingale 65
  used for ground driving 53–54
Solid mouthpieces 74
Spade bits 12, 14, 20, 24, 96, 177
  dangers of 128
  history 126–128
  mechanics of 76, 128–130
  proper use 130
  weight of 40, 130
Split reins 45
Standing martingale 138–139
  adjusting 139, 171
  use in competition 179
  use with dropped noseband 139
  use with head tossing 168
Stone bruise 167
Straight bar mouthpiece 74
Sweetwater mouthpiece 75
Teeth
  and age of horse 24–25, 30–31
  bit seats 34
  and bit selection 25, 31
  bridle teeth 33
  canine teeth 30, 33
  caps 32
  floating 33–34
  hooks 34
  incisors 28, 30
  molars 28–30
  monkey mouth 34
  nippers 28
  numbers of 28–30
  parrot mouth 34
  premolars 28–30
  retained teeth 32
  snaffle mouth 34
  symptoms of problems with 35
  wolf teeth 30, 32–33
Thompson, Terry 157, 159
Tie-down. *See* Standing martingale
Tom Thumb bit 93, 153
Tongue relief 23
Tongue ties 169
Tongues
  and bit selection 22
  injury to 23
  movement 22–23
  sensitivity of 22
Training
  bitting up 51–52
  chewing on the bit 169
  collection 55, 161–162
  developing a soft mouth 148–152
  developing rider's balance 156–159
  developing soft hands 154–156, 162–163
  direct rein 48, 49
  "getting ahead of the bit" 167
  "getting behind the bit" 167
  getting the tongue over the bit 169
  ground driving 53–54
  ground work 51
  hand position 159–161
  head tossing 167–168
  indirect rein 49
  introducing the bit 48
  leg cues 54
  neck rein 51
  plow reining 49
  pressure and release 48–49
  pulling to one side 169
  resistance to bit 164–167
  "running through the bit" 168–169
  "scissoring" 167
  signs of bitting problems 166
  "star gazing" 168
  stirrup length 157
  weight cues 54
U.S. mouthpiece 76
W-mouthed bit 74
Walking Horse bit 83, 87
Western pelham 97
Weymouth bit 85
Wolf teeth 30, 32–33
  extracting 33